Governing as New

Governing as New Labour

Policy and Politics under Blair

Edited by

Steve Ludlam

and

Martin J. Smith

palgrave
macmillan

First published 2004 by
PALGRAVE MACMILLAN
Houndmills, Basingstoke, Hampshire RG21 6XS and
175 Fifth Avenue, New York, N.Y. 10010
Companies and representatives throughout the world

PALGRAVE MACMILLAN is the global academic imprint of the Palgrave Macmillan division of St. Martin's Press, LLC and of Palgrave Macmillan Ltd. Macmillan® is a registered trademark in the United States, United Kingdom and other countries. Palgrave is a registered trademark in the European Union and other countries.

ISBN 1–4039–0678–5 hardback
ISBN 1–4039–0474–X paperback

This book is printed on paper suitable for recycling and made from fully managed and sustained forest sources.

A catalogue record for this book is available from the British Library.

Library of Congress Cataloging-in-Publication Data
Governing as New Labour: policy and politics under Blair / edited by
      Steve Ludlam and Martin J. Smith
          p. cm.
      Includes bibliographical references and index.
      ISBN 1-4039-0678-5 (cloth)
          1. Labour Party (Great Britain) 2. Great Britain–Politics and
government–1997- I. Ludlam, Steve, 1951- II. Smith, Martin J.
(Martin John), 1961-
JN1129.L32G595 2003
324.24107–dc21   2003051443

10 9 8 7 6 5 4 3 2 1
13 12 11 10 09 08 07 06 05 04

Printed in China

Contents

List of Tables, Boxes and Figures

Tables

Boxes

Figures

Preface

In an earlier collection, *New Labour in Government*, also published by Palgrave, we set out to assemble a book that would, at the mid-point of New Labour's first term of office, help students of British politics to answer the questions of how far New Labour, in its thought and practice, was reflecting 'old' Labour agendas, Thatcherite agendas, or distinctly new social democratic agendas. Positive feedback has encouraged us to produce this new book, not as an update of the earlier one, but as an almost entirely new collection of specially-commissioned essays that survey the whole first term record, and consider how far the first half of the second term record suggests that New Labour has embarked, as its leaders insist, on the modernisation of social democracy in Britain. All the authors are actively engaged in research in the areas about which they write, and we hope readers will find the results of their labours useful.

In the course of assembling this book, several debts have been incurred. Steve Ludlam thanks the Economic and Social Research Council for the funding (R000223495) for the study of trade union campaigning that informs his chapter, which was conducted with Andrew J. Taylor and Paul Allender. Rajiv Prabhakar is grateful for financial assistance received from the Economic and Social Research Council under its post-doctoral fellowship scheme, as well as for funds awarded by the Charlottenburg Trust, and for comments on his chapter by the editors. Jim Buller thanks Keith Alderman for comments on an earlier draft of his chapter. As in their previous collaborations, the editors have greatly appreciated the support and encouragement of Steven Kennedy of Palgrave Macmillan, whose knowledge of and enthusiastic contribution to the study of politics would surely have earned him several honorary degrees by now had he not chosen a career in the suspect profession of publishing! Finally, it is a pleasure and a relief to acknowledge the work of Keith Povey, our copy-editor, whose extraordinary attention to detail rather undermines our designation as editors of this volume.

STEVE LUDLAM
MARTIN J. SMITH

Notes on the Contributors

Claire Annesley is Lecturer in European Politics in the Department of Government at Manchester University. Her research interests and publications are on the British and German welfare state, and she is currently completing a book entitled *Postindustrial Germany: Services, Industrial Transformation and Knowledge in Unified Germany.*

Jim Buller is Lecturer in Politics at the University of York. His research interests include the relationship between 'domestic' and 'external' policy, especially the Europeanisation of British Politics. His publications include *Post-war British Politics in Perspective* (co-author) (1999), *National Statecraft and European Integration: The Conservative Government and the European Union, 1979–97* (2000), and *The Europeanisation of National Politics* (co-editor) (forthcoming).

Ben Clift is Lecturer in French and Comparative Politics in the School of International Studies at Brunel University. His book entitled *French Socialism in a Global Era: The Political Economy of the New Social Democracy in France* is forthcoming from Continuum. He has written several articles on the French Socialists, and the comparative political economy of Social Democracy, including 'Social Democracy and Globalisation: The Cases of France and the UK' in *Government and Opposition*, Vol. 37, No. 4 (October 2002).

Matthew Flinders is Lecturer in Government at the University of Sheffield. His research interests include constitutional reform, governance and public policy. His publications include *Quangos, Accountability and Reform* (1998) and *The Politics of Accountability in the Modern State* (2000). He is currently completing a book (with Ian Bache), entitled *Themes and Issues in Multi-Level Governance* (2003) and conducting a research project entitled 'Constitutional Governance in Britain: Statecraft and Dynamics'.

Bob Franklin is Professor of Media Communications in the Department of Journalism Studies at the University of Sheffield, UK. He is co-editor of *Journalism Studies*. Recent books include *British Television Policy: A Reader* (2001), *The New Handbook of Children's Rights* (2001), *Social Policy, the Media and Misrepresentation* (1999), *Making the Local News: Local Journalism in Context* (1998), *Tough on Soundbites, Tough on the Causes of Soundbites: New Labour and News Management* (1998), *Newszak and News Media* (1997) and *Packaging Politics: Political Communication in Britain's Media Democracy* (1994).

x   *Notes on the Contributors*

Andrew Gamble is Professor of Politics and Director of the Political Economy Research Centre at the University of Sheffield. He is co-editor of *Developments in British Politics* (2002) and author of *Politics and Fate* (2000).

Steve Ludlam is Senior Lecturer in Politics at the University of Sheffield. His principal research interest is labour movements. He convenes the Political Studies Association's specialist Labour Movements Group. His publications include *New Labour in Government* (2001), with Martin Smith, and *Understanding Labour: Approaches to Labour Politics and History* (2003), with Steven Fielding and John Callaghan.

Charles Pattie is Professor of Geography at the University of Sheffield. He has published numerous books and papers on various aspects of electoral geography, and is currently working on a study of citizenship in the UK. He recently published *From Votes to Seats: The Operation of the UK Electoral System Since 1945* (2002) with Ron Johnston, Danny Dorling and David Rossiter.

Rajiv Prabhakar is Ludwig Lachmann Fellow at the Department of Philosophy, Scientific Method and Logic at the London School of Economics. He won the Political Studies Association's 2001 Walter Bagehot prize for best dissertation on government and public administration. He is author of *Stakeholding and New Labour* (2003). He is currently directing, with Professor Andrew Gamble, at Sheffield University, an Economic and Social Research Council (ESRC) project on asset-based welfare.

Nick Randall is Lecturer in British politics at the University of Newcastle. His research interests include the politics of the British Labour and Conservative Parties, the territorial politics of the UK and the issue of European integration in British Politics. His publications include 'New Labour and Northern Ireland', in David Coates and Peter Lawler (eds) *New Labour In Power* (2001), and 'Understanding Labour's Ideological Trajectory' in Steven Fielding, John Callaghan and Steve Ludlam (eds) *Understanding Labour* (2003).

David Richards is Senior Lecturer in Politics at the University of Liverpool. His research interests include British Politics and the reform of the Civil Service. His publications include *Changing Patterns of Governance in the United Kingdom* (2001), with Dave Marsh and Martin Smith.

Eric Shaw is Senior Lecturer in the Politics Department, University of Stirling. He has written extensively on the Labour Party. His works include *Discipline and Discord in the Labour Party* (1998), *The Labour Party Since*

1979: Conflict and Transformation (1994), and *The Labour Party since 1945* (1996).

Martin J. Smith is Professor of Politics and Head of Department at the University of Sheffield. His research interests are in British Politics and Public Policy. He has recently published *Governance and Public Policy in the United Kingdom* (2002) with Dave Richards.

List of Abbreviations

ABI	Association of British Insurers
AEEU	Amalgamated Engineering and Electrical Union
ASLEF	Associated Society of Locomotive Engineers and Firemen
BEPS	British Election Panel Study
BES	British Election Study
BSA	British Social Attitudes
BSE	Bovine Spongiform Encephalopathy
CBI	Confederation of British Industry
CLP	Constituency Labour Party
COI	Central Office of Information
CWU	Communication Workers Union
DFID	Department for International Development
DTI	Department of Trade and Industry
DTLR	Department for Transport, Local Government and the Regions
DWP	Department for Work and Pensions
EAZ	Education Action Zone
ECB	European Central Bank
EMU	European Monetary Union
ERM	European Exchange Rate Mechanism
ESRC	Economic and Social Research Council
EU	European Union
FBU	Fire Brigades Union
GDP	Gross Domestic Product
GLC	Greater London Council
GP	General Practitioner
IPPR	Institute for Public Policy Research
ICT	Information and Computer Technology
JPC	Joint Policy Committee
KWS	Keynesian Welfare State
LSE	London School of Economics and Political Science
MAFF	Ministry of Agriculture, Fisheries and Food
MORI	Market and Opinion Research International
MPC	Monetary Policy Committee
NACRO	National Association for the Care and Resettlement of Offenders
NAIRU	Non-Accelerating Inflation Rate of Unemployment

NEC	National Executive Committee
NGO	Non-Governmental Organisation
NHS	National Health Service
NMD	National Missile Defence
NPF	National Policy Forum
NVQ	National Vocational Qualification
PASOK	Pan-Hellenic Socialist Movement
PCS	Public and Commercial Services Union
PES	Party of European Socialists
PFI	Private Finance Initiative
PIU	Performance and Innovation Unit
PPP	Public–Private Partnership
PS	Partido Socialista (Portugal)
PS	Parti Socialiste (France)
PSA	Political Studies Association
PSX	Cabinet Committee on Economic Policy
PvdA	Partij van der Arbeid (Holland)
QMV	Qualified Majority Voting
RDA	Regional Development Agency
RMT	Nation Union of Rail Maritime
SAP	Socialdemokratiska Arbetarepartiet (Sweden)
SDP	Sozialdemokratische Partei Deutschlands (Germany)
SERPS	State Earnings-Related Pension Scheme
SME	Small/Medium Enterprise
SPÖ	Sozialdemokratische Partei Österreich
TIGMOO	This Great Movement of Ours
TGWU	Transport and General Workers Union
TUC	Trades Union Congress
TUCC	Trades Union Campaign Committee
TULO	National Trade Union Labour Party Liaison Organisation
WEU	Western Economic Union
WFTC	Working Families Tax Credit

1

Introduction: Second Term New Labour

STEVE LUDLAM

New Labour's second term, secured with another massive parliamentary majority that all but guarantees a third term, was always likely to be more interesting to students of Labour politics than its first. New Labour leaders had stressed repeatedly that it needed at least two terms to achieve key policy objectives, and the (fulfilled) promise in 1997 to implement the Conservatives' planned public spending cuts for two years, together with the general anxiety not to damage the 'big tent' electoral coalition that had delivered the 1997 landslide, suggested that the full picture of what New Labour represented politically, beyond an electoral rebranding by Labour's right wing, was unlikely to emerge until the second term was in the bag. In a speech delivered at the London School of Economics (LSE) in March 2002, intended to persuade invited academics that New Labour was intellectually coherent, Tony Blair himself offered a three-part periodisation of 'the New Labour project' that confirmed the centrality of the second term in office. The first phase (1994–7) had been 'becoming a modern social democratic party fit for government'. The second phase (1997–2001), Blair argued, 'was to use our 1997 victory to put in place the foundations that would allow us change the country in a way that lasts'. Blair's third phase – the task for Labour's unprecedented second full term – was thus 'about driving forward reforms, building lasting change – and a better society – on the foundations so carefully laid' (Blair, 2002a).

Blair's first phase was the period of New Labour's construction of the Millbank media and election machine. It brought the dramatic rejection of the party's old Clause Four commitment to common ownership, and of renationalization of privatised utilities. It saw Labour's turn towards a 'welfare for work' social policy approach, and most importantly its adoption of the macroeconomic approach of neo-liberalism, not least prioritising

1

monetary stability over full employment, fiscal conservatism and promises not to increase income tax rates. In his second phase, the first term of office, as our earlier collection made clear, New Labour was determined above all to prove its competence to manage the market economy and keep its electoral base intact. It would stick to its own 'golden rules' of fiscal behaviour and its commitment to maintaining the framework of Margaret Thatcher's anti-union laws (Ludlam and Smith, 2001). It would link rights to welfare benefits to responsibilities to enter the workforce, and demonstrate, through target-setting and 'naming and shaming', its drive to attend to 'standards not structures' of 'education, education, education'. An avalanche of policy reviews and task forces was unleashed, instructed that ideological thinking was out, and that 'what counts is what works'. Redistribution 'by stealth', through the windfall tax on privatised utilities and through indirect taxes, took the form mainly of 'targeted', means-tested tax credits and minimum income guarantees, of action zones and social exclusion initiatives. There was periodic anger, not least within the Labour movement, at the low rate of increases in universal benefits (above all, the basic state pension), and at over-spun spending announcements. Yet Gordon Brown's comprehensive spending reviews during the first term also began to announce dramatic future increases in health and education spending. Social democrats drawing up an audit of the first term acknowledged progress, but concluded that:

> The Third Way was a convenient fog and a second term would need a new clarity of message. Things did get better. They could get a lot better still but not unless Labour confronts the ghosts of the Tory past and announces itself as the party of the public weal, higher taxes included. Without a far bolder stand on where the boundary between public good and private possession is to be placed, those great promises to abolish child poverty or make health and education the best and transport tolerable are likely to stay just that – promises. (Toynbee and Walker, 2001, 240)

Labour's essential 2001 election messages were modest and reassuring, 'a lot done, a lot still to be done', and 'schools and hospitals first'. But during the course of the election campaign, Labour's manifesto, with its central emphasis on investment in and reform of the public services, and the way it was spun to place particular focus on a much extended role for the private sector in providing them, announced that the second term would indeed involve radical new departures in (at any rate, British) social democracy. In pursuing what he came to refer to as New Labour's 'core mission: to improve our public services', Blair's phase three was not going to be one of consolidation (Blair, 2003a). One aspect of this mission, the raising of new tax income to fund health and education reform, albeit through increased National Insurance payments rather than income taxes, was symbolised by the dramatically presented 2002 Budget. Here was New Labour proclaiming that it had won a second landslide promising to raise spending on the great universal public services, and it would tax a willing electorate to do it. It produced angry expressions of concern from the Confederation of British Industry (CBI), and damaged New Labour's relationships with business. However it was the other aspect, the insistence that money was for modernisation, and that radical reform of public services was a condition of funding, that was to provoke the most anger within the Labour Party, among socialists and social democrats, and to provide evidence of what a New Labour modernised social democracy might look like.

First Term Accommodations

In our earlier collection, reflecting current academic and general concerns, we asked contributors to consider New Labour's relationship to both its Thatcherite and its Labour inheritance (in the latter case including both its pre-Blair modernisation and so-called 'old' Labour). We noted that academic debate on New Labour had tended to follow the pattern of analysis of Labour's modernisation process under Neil Kinnock and John Smith. Some saw little more than accommodation to Thatcherism; others a revival of older social democratic strategies dislodged by the economic disorders of the 1970s; and others an attempt to build a post-Thatcher, modernised social democracy (Ludlam and Smith, 2001, ch. 13, 27–30). At that time a large volume of material had already been published on the New Labour phenomenon (Ludlam, 2000). Subsequent work has further refined such debates. A very important debate has been conducted in the *British Journal of Politics and International Relations* between Mark Wickham-Jones, Colin Hay and David Coates on how far Labour, and social democrats more generally, are constrained to accommodate the Thatcherite inheritance and the wider forces of neo-liberal globalisation, or are at liberty to pursue radical economic strategies (Wickham-Jones, 2000, 2002; Coates, 2001, 2002; Hay, 2002). Steve Fielding has contested the accommodationist argument in a historically-grounded study which insists that Labour's past is one of 'unremitting transformation and adaptation', and that New Labour's performance in office is recognisably, if cautiously, part of Labour's social democratic tradition (Fielding, 2003, 217). Stephen Driver and Luke Martell have extended their earlier argument that New Labour is a post-Thatcherite transcendence of old Labour in a study of the first term, concluding that Blairism may not rest on a theoretically coherent 'third way', nor constitute a radical alternative in practice, but is a modernising middle way and 'no worse for it for that' (Driver and Martell, 2002, 222).

More generally, our understanding of the complex circumstances that produced the New Labour phenomenon has been greatly deepened by a number of new studies. John Callaghan has analysed the retreat of European social democracy in the 1980s and 1990s, out of which New Labour emerged (Callaghan, 2000), and Noel Thompson has investigated the failure of British democratic socialists to provide an alternative political economy for Labour in those decades (Thompson, 2002). The meaning of New Labour's 'third way' posture in general has been subjected to rigorous criticism (Callinicos, 2001; White, 2001), as has New Labour foreign policy in particular (Little and Wickham-Jones, 2000). Focusing on the internal dynamics of the construction of New Labour, important new studies have appeared on the composition and attitudes of the party's members (Seyd and Whiteley, 2002); on the party's policy modernisation since the early 1980s (Heffernan, 2001), and on the dilemmas of municipal 'labourism' in the 1980 and 1990s (Allender, 2001). On the basis of the rich series of British Election Studies, the crucial direction of the electorate's attitudes and behaviour up to New Labour's first triumph has been unpacked and analysed (Heath *et al.*, 2001).

Becoming *New* New Labour

Before and during the first term, the frequent reference to a 'third way' in politics implied a coherent strategy that would guide New Labour in all its works. As a slogan it may have worked to reassure voters that New Labour was not just a middle way between Thatcherism and corporatist, Keynesian 'old' Labour, but all attempts to identify a 'third way' political philosophy failed, as did attempts to create an alternative, 'third way International' of centre-left parties. Increasingly, New Labour's leaders insisted, rather, that the 'third way' stood for 'a modernised social democracy' (Blair, 1998a, 1), or, more inclusively, 'modern liberal social democracy' (Mandelson, 2002, xxix). In this collection we have therefore, once again in so far as their subject matter permits, asked authors not just to comment on the first term record and the direction the second term is taking, but to consider how far the second term is revealing a distinctly New Labour project. Having undergone Gordon Brown's 'prudence for a purpose', what has New Labour's purpose turned out to be? This concern reflects academic and general interest in the extent to which New Labour is achieving what Peter Mandelson called its 'fundamental task' in his second-term essay, 'to create the conditions in which modern social democracy embeds itself in the fabric and social architecture of modern Britain' (Mandelson, 2002, xii).

Studying this process is far from straightforward. Social democracy, at least in its modern, post-1945 manifestation, has been neither a social movement – for example, of labour or of nationalism – nor a coherent ideology. It has been a political movement, or rather a set of political programmes in various states, whose purpose, quite distinct from the socialist programme of transcending capitalism, has been to achieve a gradual amelioration of social conditions within capitalism and through the institutions of liberal democracy (Gamble and Wright, 1999). It has thus been a programme for advanced industrial states in which a dividend from economic growth can be redistributed to the poor without disturbing capitalist property relations. Dependent as it is on the relative health and prosperity of a free market economy, and regular electoral success in a parliamentary system, social democracy has needed to revise its programme repeatedly as national economic and electoral contexts have changed. Hence judgements of any claim to be a modernising social democracy can never take the form merely of a comparison with the programmes of either other social democrats in other states, nor of earlier generations of social democrats. As David Lipsey remarked in a volume focused on New Labour's relationship with Crosland's 'revisionist' social democracy in the 1950s, 'revisionists revise' (Lipsey, 1999, 15). Or, as Peter Mandelson puts it about the second term, 'to succeed, New Labour has to become *new* New Labour' (2002, xiii). Indeed, Mandelson describes New Labour's adaptations in terms of a model of the 'dynamic of modernisation' that goes through stages of 'action, reaction, new action', a model that looks remarkably like that of the 'thesis, antithesis, synthesis' of the official Soviet 'dialectical materialism' he presumably picked up in his Young Communist League days (2002, xi/xii).

One difficulty for students of British politics considering the modernisation of social democracy is semantic, in that the use of the term 'social democrat' in British Labour politics is contentious. It is possible to find among *Guardian* columnists a revolutionary socialist such as Paul Foot who will call himself a social democrat, because that is what the original mass Marxist parties in Europe tended to call themselves. In the same columns, a social democrat such as Roy Hattersley will, rather, call himself a democratic socialist because social democrats, during his political career, were deserters from the Labour Party to the short-lived Social Democratic Party. In a real sense, however, in the Labour Party they are nearly 'all social democrats now': Labour's infiltrating revolutionary socialists were expelled in the 1980s; its democratic socialists, those who seek to transform capitalism into socialism by parliamentary means in line with the party's old formal objectives, are a more marginal presence than ever before.

A further, and more substantial difficulty is posed by the fact that the focus of social democratic thought and strategy on social policy and political economy means that, for the student, there is no obvious starting point for analysis in relation to many areas of politics. As Rhiannon Vickers has pointed out, for example, applying a 'third way' to foreign policy is complicated by the fact that 'it is difficult to delineate a clear left/right, capitalist/social democratic stance in foreign affairs' (Vickers, 2000, 38). Nor does Labour's historical record offer very much evidence of a distinctly social democratic view of constitutional reform or of how the executive arm of the state should be managed. The internal structures and relationships of a political party are even more obviously the result of particular historical circumstances, in Labour's case most famously of the founding role of its trade union affiliates.

And a particular difficulty for students of British social democracy, many of whom had seen Labour's modernisation from the 1980s onwards as a process of convergence with European social democracy, has emerged with the alliance of New Labour on key issues, not with the main European social democratic parties and governments, but with the most right-wing leaders in the European Union (EU) in Aznar's Spain and Berlusconi's Italy. These alliances with the right have covered both strategic economic and social policy, and the diplomatic manoeuvring in the United Nations (UN) and the North Atlantic Treaty Organization (NATO) that marked the US campaign to launch another war on Iraq. However, although foreign policy, or more precisely war policy, came quickly to dominate New Labour's second term, as the Bush Presidency reacted violently to the terrorist massacre of 11 September 2001 in New York, the most explicit agenda for 'modernising social democracy' was that pursued in the domestic policy arena, above all in pursuit of Blair's 'core mission' to reform the public services.

'Our Core Mission'

The greatest interest in the second term was always going to be in the development of economic and especially social policy, once New Labour's fiscal credibility had been demonstrated to business and Middle England voters, the welfare-to-work programme had driven social security costs down, and low unemployment had raised the tax base. In their chapter, Claire Annesley and Andrew Gamble outline critically New Labour's achievements in macroeconomic management and in the development of supply-side initiatives. They appraise the dilemmas, political and economic, surrounding New Labour's commitment to take Britain into the euro, and consider the risks to New Labour of economic uncertainty. On social policy, they argue that New Labour has succeeded in building a welfare consensus that includes tax-based universal public services (above all health and education), and a non-universalist benefits system based on developing human capital and getting people into work rather than simply providing maintenance.

This, they point out, is similar in some elements to welfare systems developed by the 'new' Democrats in the USA, but also in social democratic Sweden. In its implementation it also bears many imprints of the report of the Commission on Social Justice initiated by John Smith during his brief leadership of the party (Commission on Social Justice, 1994), and policy transfer from Labour-led Australia has also been noted (Pierson and Castles, 2002).

The task of rebuilding a welfare consensus among voters has not, however, ensured a consensus among New Labour's leaders. In this respect, the important strategic second term arguments inside the Labour Party have been about what form of social democracy New Labour should pursue, and on some points have involved serious divisions among senior Cabinet ministers. In spite of the immediate post-election claims in 2001 to have fought and won on a tax and spend platform, New Labour has remained anxious not to make itself electorally vulnerable to accusations of having returned to the alleged excesses of 'old' Labour's state-centred, so-called producer-friendly generosity towards the National Health Service (NHS) and education. Not only has this resulted in a dramatic and damaging fight with Labour's affiliated unions over the implications for low-paid workers of privatising the capital investment in and management of public services (see Chapter 5), but also in some of the most bitter disputes within the government and the parliamentary party. Frank Dobson, for example, a central Cabinet figure and Secretary of State of Health in the first term, accused the government of undermining social democratic universalism and promoting elitism by encouraging, on his account, the emergence of a two-tier NHS with the most successful hospitals gaining 'foundation hospital' status and increased funding that might be expected to accelerate the gap between such hospitals and the rest. The same charge was levelled in relation to the extension of the principle of selection in secondary schools, which was portrayed by Labour critics as implanting *de facto* grammar schools within the comprehensive sector. And the White Paper on higher education published in January 2003 was met with similar cries of elitism, because of the facility for the existing elite among universities to widen the gap with the rest at the expense of their students who would be charged top-up fees and, obviously, because of the fear that such fees would put off even more young working-class people from aspiring to go to university, and particularly to one of the 'top' universities. One dimension of the argument has revolved around the general accusation, frequently propounded by a former Labour deputy leader and leading 1980s moderniser, Roy Hattersley, that New Labour is committed to 'meritocracy' rather than equality, an argument that echoes the 1950s social democratic critique by Michael Young that coined the phrase (Young, 1958). Meritocracy, on this view, is a liberal form of elitism that justifies great inequality of outcomes in terms of individual ability and effort. Even if there were to be genuine equality of opportunity in some future utopia, there would remain, for social democrats such as Hattersley, unjustifiable inequalities arising from natural ability and aptitude that would require the redistribution of wealth.

More ink was spilled over how far a 'new localism', promoted in general terms by both Blair and Brown, should go in giving local communities more control of health and education services. If success is rewarded or punished by the gain or loss of resources, would such an approach simply reproduce existing class divisions within the 'universal' public sector, while the old central social democratic state looks on helplessly as differentiation is traded against equity, as some social democratic commentators feared (Walker, 2003)? How far should the allegedly resulting elitism be tolerated to keep the 'big tent' electoral coalition intact, by providing the kinds of advantages and choices in the use of public services that will prevent a middle-class flight into the private sector? Blair's emphasis was on choice, through competition, to satisfy the individualism of the voter, but especially of the middle classes, who might otherwise 'buy their way out of the public service'. That, he argued, would produce 'real two-tierism' and elitism. His commitment to excellence produced by competition, 'within a framework of national standards and systems of accountability', was designed to avoid such a flight of the middle classes. As ever, Blair's eye was never far from the electoral pre-conditions of the 'project', the preservation of New Labour's electoral coalition. His recurring theme after the 2001 election was that New Labour would not be held back from public service reform by the 'forces of conservatism', that it was 'at its best when at its boldest', that it had now to 'move further and faster if our ideals as a Party are to be fulfilled for this generation', and that, ominously, 'we must not waste this precious period of power' (Blair, 2002a, 2002b, 2003a).

Gordon Brown and his closest allies, on the other hand, began to warn that the introduction of some forms of competitive 'marketisation' might threaten the modernisation of social democracy. A bitter row was conducted over the independent status of 'foundation hospitals', settled by Blair at Brown's expense. In part, Brown's objections were about the implications for Treasury control of the 'money for modernisation' process if, for example, universities kept the income from charging ever-higher fees, and 'foundation hospitals' borrowed capital on their own accounts. But he also developed an argument, presented to the Cabinet in a 50-page memorandum, about the limits in principle of marketising public services, a theme he returned to in a major speech in early 2003 (Brown, 2003). Outlining 'a modern agenda for prosperity and social reform', Brown insisted that 'agreeing on where markets have an enhanced role and where market failure has to be addressed is, in my view, absolutely central to the next stage of our project'. Much of the speech was devoted to demonstrating the limits of marketisation in health policy and the centrality to Brown's vision of the 'core mission' of the belief that 'if we were to go down the road of introducing markets wholesale into British health care we would be paying a very heavy price in efficiency and be unable to deliver a Britain of opportunity and security for all' (Brown, 2003). While he shared with Blair the commitment to the 'new localism' and the commitment to the Private Finance Initiative (PFI) and private-sector management, he did not share Blair's degree of enthusiasm for quasi-market forces within health, and by implication education services, to secure equitable access to higher standards. The week after Brown's speech, Downing Street presented the Secretaries of State for both Health and Education at a press conference, where they affirmed their commitment to Blair's vision of choice and competition in their services.

In his chapter on public service reform, Rajiv Prabhakar focuses on the record and character of health and education policy. He calls for a disaggregated judgement in these areas that acknowledges both the retention of the central role of increased public spending, and the potential of the institutional diversity in the government's proposals to generate a voice for working-class service users alongside the long-recognised ability of middle-class users to optimise their access to, and influence over, service provision. This can be seen as one feature of an emerging 'asset-based egalitarianism', less dramatic but just as significant as budget-headlined 'baby bonds'. In its second-term public service reform, Prabhakar thus argues, New Labour has begun to implement the 'third way' approach to public service universalism that was less visible in the first term than the struggle to justify, first, the spending moratorium between 1997 and 1999, and then the spending promises announced towards the end of that first term in the first of Brown's Comprehensive Spending Reviews.

Horses for Courses

The search for a simple characterisation of New Labour is not easily resolved, either, by analysis of its record and direction in other policy areas. As Ben Clift makes clear in Chapter 3, New Labour's apparent early success in spreading the gospel of its 'third way' among European social democrats has not been sustained. Indeed, New Labour has frequently formed alliances with conservative governments in the EU to block social protocol initiatives to benefit workers, to press forward a neo-liberal economic reform agenda, and to lament the anti-capitalist nature of the European social model. New Labour's view of the constraints imposed on national governments by globalisation has not been shared enthusiastically by other social democratic parties in Europe. Attempts were being made in 2003 to relaunch the international 'third way' through the agency of a 'think tank' fronted by Peter Mandelson. But divisions over war against Iraq reinforced New Labour's alliance with conservative governments in Italy and Spain, making the task of selling New Labour's brand of modernising social democracy in Europe more difficult.

And the clash between New Labour's pursuit of traditional, Atlanticist foreign policy objectives and the early aspiration to build an 'ethical' foreign policy, in itself a very old Labour aspiration, is a telling example of the need to acknowledge the complexity of constraints surrounding any would-be reforming government in the UK. Jim Buller's analysis gives full attention to such constraints, detecting elements nevertheless of a distinctly New Labour agenda in, for example, overseas development policy, but warns that the government's internationalist aspirations may be perceived in practice as little more than the UK's traditional support for the USA, even – as the rows over the US/UK invasion of Iraq demonstrated – at the expense of Blair's often-declared intention to fully integrate the UK into the mainstream of EU politics. Nelson Mandela angrily remarked of Blair that 'He is the foreign minister of the United States. He is no longer the Prime Minister of Britain' (*Guardian*, 31 January 2003). Blair himself revived his earlier claims that foreign policy was part of the modernisation of social democracy in an attempt, ahead of an international 'third way' seminar, to portray the attack on Iraq as a policy that 'fits squarely with our vision of progressive politics' (Blair, 2003b). Further, as Buller points out, active foreign policy, whether pro-Bush or pro-European integration, has domestic political consequences that may contradict the purpose of inventing the 'third way' in the first place: cementing an unassailable electoral base. The composition of, and debate surrounding, the gigantic anti-war march in London in February 2003 reinforces this point.

The complexities of characterising New Labour politically are nowhere more apparent than in home policy. Surveying the record on civil liberties, immigration and asylum, and crime and criminal justice, in Chapter 11, Nick Randall identifies both old Labour libertarianism and New Labour communitarianism underlying policies, and both an administrative pragmatism and a brazen populism. The latter was pursued against the opposition of those bad-mouthed by Jack Straw (as Randall reminds us) as 'Hampstead liberals' and 'BMW-driving civil liberties lawyers from the suburbs'. It is a mixture of Thatcherite managerialism, social democratic welfarism, and New Labour diversification of policy processes, that produce what David Richards and Martin Smith describe in Chapter 7 as a 'hybrid state' characterised by contradictory developments. The most complex contradictions, arguably, are those that arise in the great public services from New Labour's simultaneous continuation of the Conservative managerial agenda, pluralism and devolution in the funding and delivery of services, and the pursuit of highly centralised targeting regimes serving ostensibly social democratic objectives. The hybridity, it seems, is the product above all of recognisably social democratic objectives, however contentiously circumscribed by electoral considerations, and however controversially implemented. Without these objectives and the urge to retain central control that they require, the managerialism and diversification elements in New Labour's management of the state machine would be virtually indistinguishable from the Thatcher/Major approach.

New Labour's constitutional reforms have, Matthew Flinders suggests in Chapter 8, lacked clear goals or principles, other than avoiding any strategic shift to a new constitutional settlement that would undermine the supremacy of central executive dominance. Blair's determination to avoid creating a new Upper Chamber with any independent legitimacy – a 'revising chamber not a rival' in his formula – is an obvious example that has dragged on into the second term. Serious public disputes between senior ministers marked the House of Commons 'free' vote in 2003 on how much of the reformed Upper House should be elected: Blair arguing for none, and Robin Cook, his Leader of the House, arguing for most. In Scotland and Wales, though, the reforms may have longer-term consequences of unintended radicalism, as the new institutions defied some key New Labour Westminster policies and went their own way in certain symbolic health, education and welfare policies. And the drive to elect executive mayors, though it was derailed by the election of Hartlepool's football mascot (a man in a monkey costume), did have visible effects as the London mayor began to exercise his limited authority, notably to introduce traffic congestion charging, a measure too radical for the government to endorse.

Voters, Spinners and Members

New Labour published regular accounts of its record in implementing its 1997 election promises. A rare but prominent abandonment of such a promise, and the most prominent non-story of constitutional reform, was the failure to hold a referendum on the Westminster electoral system, avoided by the classic device of holding a grand commission on the subject (under Lord Jenkins, the Liberal Democrat Lord and ex-Labour founder of the Social Democratic Party, and thus one of the most influential architects of Labour's organisational schism in the 1980s). The junking of this once-central element of the 'project' had predictable effects on relations with the

Liberal Democrats. Apart from the fact that the immediate need to cement a Lab–Lib alliance to keep the Tories out evaporated with Labour's landslide in 1997, the proximate cause of New Labour's hesitancy, which strengthened the defenders of first-past-the-post, was the outcome of the Scottish and Welsh elections in 1999 held under forms of proportional representation. In both cases Labour failed to win an outright majority and was forced into coalitions with the Liberal Democrats. The European Parliament elections in the same year, held for the first time under a regional list system of PR, produced large Labour losses too, though these were partly an expected swing back to the Tories after their catastrophic 1994 performance at the height of their mutual throat-slitting over European integration.

But arguably the key factor has nevertheless been the size of Labour's majority, which has rendered electoral reform unnecessary – for now – in so far as its purpose was to keep the Tories out of office for the foreseeable future. This is linked, crucially, to the growing realisation – spelt out clearly in Chapter 2 by Charles Pattie – that the disproportionality of the present electoral system has come to favour Labour more than at any time since 1945. As Pattie points out in his analysis of its second landslide victory, Labour's electoral domination is underpinned by the inability of the Tories to offer a viable electoral alternative. But the size of the 2001 majority also reflects, to a surprisingly large extent, the bias inherent in Labour's favour in the constituency-based first-past-the-post electoral system. And, as Pattie also points out, the sources of this bias are not going to change significantly before the next election, which virtually guarantees New Labour a third term with a healthy majority. Perhaps if, after a fourth, or even a fifth, victory, New Labour's majority begins to look vulnerable, the party may return to the abandoned project of electoral reform to keep the Tories out of office.

The record low turnout at the 2001 general election sparked an anguished debate about why such a large proportion of the electorate had apparently lost interest in the political process to the point of abstaining from voting, to the extent that while 10.7 million voted for Labour and 8.4 million for the Conservatives, 18.0 million did not vote for anyone (Electoral Commission, 2001, 225). If, into its second term, New Labour was finding that public trust in politicians was still deteriorating, the explanation lay in significant part in the continued perception that Labour's style of government was over-reliant on 'spin', as, Bob Franklin notes in Chapter 6, even Peter Mandelson confessed (Mandelson, 2002, xliv). Early second-term declarations that spin was dead, and the government was building a new relationship with the people, were soon undermined by the political mud-wrestling that followed a departmental special adviser's suggestion, on 11 September 2001, that this would be 'a good day to bury bad news'. Franklin assembles the evidence on New Labour's second term political communications and political marketing behaviour. He suggests that, in both its news management strategy and its use (and alleged abuse) of the government's colossal advertising budget, it has merely refined and extended the strategy pursued in the first term, a strategy inherited in most important respects from predecessor Tory governments. In so far as New Labour, in its second term, faces a much more hostile Tory press that can be expected to become more hostile if a euro referendum takes place, and a more critical Labour press, at least in the *Daily Mirror* in its anti-war phase, news management has become even more fraught.

The loss of trust also reflected the steady stream of accusations that New Labour's relationship with business donors to the Party showed signs of continuity with the perception of sleaze that had so damaged John Major's Tories. Chapter 5 suggests not only that Labour's alliance with business was faltering in the second term, but also that it was doing the party's image more harm than the union link New Labour had once been so eager to marginalise. Ironically, the media backlash over business donations, both in public opinion and among wary business leaders, left the party once again increasingly dependent on union subscriptions and donations that business cash was intended substantially to replace. Arguably more significantly, the precipitous decline in party activism and in party membership – more than halved since 1997 to 180,000 by 2003 – also appeared to be leaving New Labour ever more dependent on its union affiliates for the organisational structures necessary to conduct the targeted constituency campaigning at the heart of Labour's triumphant electoral strategy. This new dependency had certainly eased the strains in the union–Party link in the second part of New Labour's first term, as had affiliated unions' appreciation of their access to ministers and of the gains, however modest, from early minimum wage and employment relations legislation. The second-term emphasis on public service reform, however, with the insistence on the centrality of the PFI and wider use of private enterprise to deliver services, immediately plunged the historic Labour alliance into a new crisis that encompassed both government policy and union political funding, and the firefighters' dispute that embittered many union leaders as well as activists.

Alongside its distancing itself from organised labour, a central component of New Labour's claim to have completed the transformation of the Party into a viable electoral force was the reform of its internal policymaking processes, institutionalised in the *Partnership in Power* reforms adopted in 1998. One objective of these reforms was, explicitly, to avoid the public conflict at party conferences between activists, unions and parliamentary leadership. Apart from a couple of quickly-disowned decisions against the platform (on earnings-linking the basic state pension in 2000, and on the PFI in 2002), this objective has been achieved, to the extent that the commonest complaint about the televised conferences now is that they are excessively stage-managed and boring, and that increasing numbers of constituencies are not bothering to send a delegate. But the other objective of the reforms, always more problematic and contentious, was the attempt to empower ordinary members in the policy process at the expense of allegedly unrepresentative activists. How far the 'rolling' policy process, having rolled for two years through a multiplicity of policy forums, would in fact empower individual members rather than embed leadership control was always a disputed question. With the benefit of having followed the whole cycle in New Labour's first term, in Chapter 4 Eric Shaw analyses closely the dynamics of the process with this crucial question in mind, and reaches the conclusion that while consensus has largely been achieved, it may have been at too high a price in terms of effective participation. Shaw also analyses the other key feature of New Labour's party management package, and the one that did the most in the first term to open the party to charges of 'control freakery': the selection of party candidates. Focusing on the high-profile cases of the London mayoral and Welsh Assembly leadership selections, but also on efforts to manage election to the party's National Executive Committee strongly suggests, not surprisingly, that New Labour's internal reforms have had ideological as much as procedural objectives.

Benchmarks and Norms

Herbert Morrison, deputy Labour leader and grandfather of Peter Mandelson, once replied impatiently to the question 'What is socialism?' that it was 'What the Labour Government does'. Perhaps it is too soon to answer the question 'What is modernising social democracy?' with the reply that it is 'What the New Labour Government does'. But given the wide variety of social democratic programmes that history offers us, and the complexities revealed in the chapters that follow, it may turn out to be as concise an answer as can be offered. At one level, the dispute about whether New Labour is social democratic or not has nothing to do with comparison against some objective benchmark, but is simply a convenient linguistic weapon in the battles over the desirability of this or that policy preference. One prominent Labour lord with a better claim than most to be able to identify such a benchmark is Raymond Plant, the political philosopher. In his contribution to Leonard's *Crosland and New Labour* (1999), Plant boiled down the distinctiveness of social democratic politics to the desire to reduce relative poverty: to do more than merely reduce absolute poverty and misery. In so far as welfare policy was aimed at fiscal redistribution to the working poor but, with the drive to 'incentivise' work being so central, not so clearly at raising the relative value of benefits to those unable to make the move from welfare to work, then, in Plant's definition, New Labour's stance contrasted with Croslandite revisionism (Leonard, 1999, 32–3). Even if it succeeded in rebuilding the effectiveness and popularity of the great universal public services, and made good the promise to eradicate child poverty, New Labour might still fall short of 'modernising social democracy' if it failed to raise the relative wealth of the poor, seen from this perspective. The general widening of income inequalities under New Labour points to the same conclusion. But this perspective can, of course, be challenged in terms of the 'social exclusion' efforts outlined in Chapter 9, and as failing to recognise the policy consequences of changing social attitudes and the need for revisionists to revise. All that is certain is that writing about labour movements, which historically have pursued political strategies to challenge the social and economic power of the ruling classes, has always and inevitably been more or less partisan. This work is intended to be scholarly, and makes available to students of Labour politics and of the New Labour governments the insights of specialist writers, all of whom are actively engaged in research in the areas they cover here. But there are, of course, normative assumptions underlying all of this book's chapters. The editors have made no attempt to dictate any particular line on New Labour, and would certainly not have succeeded if such an attempt had been made. We hope it is both informative and stimulating, but will also, and above all, lead readers to engage fully their own critical faculties. In 2003, with New Labour facing real and potential crises generated by the war against Iraq (including the biggest rebel votes by a government's MPs for a century); over joining the euro; over economic performance; over reforming public services; and over relations with its union affiliates, students of modernising social democracy certainly need to be relentlessly critical, in the best sense of that adjective.

2

Re-electing New Labour

CHARLES PATTIE

Since the New Labour project was launched in 1994, it has proved a difficult concept to pin down definitively. For some, it is an example of so-called 'third way' politics (Giddens, 1998; Gould, 1998). For others, it represents spin rather than substance (Jones, 1999). But whatever else it might be, New Labour is about winning elections. And, compared to 'old' Labour, New Labour has been very successful electorally. While the pre-Blair Labour Party twice won large parliamentary majorities, in 1945 and 1966, it was unable either to maintain those majorities, or to win two successive full terms in office. The 146-seat Labour majority gained in the 1945 landslide was reduced to a bare majority of five in the 1950 election, and Labour was forced into the premature 1951 election. And the 1974–9 Labour Government was always bedevilled by its small (and eventually nonexistent) parliamentary majority. It was defeated comprehensively in 1979, ushering in almost twenty years in the electoral wilderness. After four successive election defeats between 1979 and 1992, Labour seemed finished as a potential party of government (King, 1993; Heath *et al.*, 1994). If the party could not win even in the relatively auspicious conditions of 1992, against a weakened Conservative Government which had presided over both the unpopular poll tax and a serious economic recession affecting its own core supporters, how could Labour ever hope to win again?

The gloomy prognosis for Labour at the start of the 1990s proved to be unfounded (Pattie, 2001). First elected in the 1997 landslide, the New Labour government went on to win re-election in 2001 with a barely changed majority and only a slight fall in its vote share from four years previously (see Table 2.1). Tony Blair is the first Labour leader to win two successive landslide Commons majorities. Labour has never been in such a commanding electoral position before. How did the party achieve this? In this chapter, we analyse New Labour's evolving relationship with the electorate.

TABLE 2.1   *The 1997 and 2001 British general elections*

	1997		2001	
	% votes	Seats	% votes	Seats
Labour	44.4	419	42.0	413
Conservative	31.5	165	32.7	166
Liberal Democrat	17.1	46	18.8	52
Nationalist	2.6	10	2.6	9
Independent	4.4	1	3.9	1
Percentage turnout	71.4		59.2	
Parliamentary majority[+]		177		165

Note: [+] Majority includes all UK parties.
Source: The Electoral Commission.

Creating a New Electoral Coalition?

Central to the New Labour project has been an attempt to build a new electoral coalition supporting the party (Pattie, 2001). Labour's traditional constituency was the manual working classes, the trade unions, public-sector employees, and the industrial heartland constituencies of central Scotland, South Wales, and the urban north of England (Butler and Stokes, 1974). However, during the last quarter of the twentieth century, that electoral coalition was severely eroded by two factors.

First, social change meant that the manual working class declined from a majority (58 per cent) of the labour force in 1964 to just over a third by 1997. The proportion of households that were council tenants fell from 32 per cent in 1979 to just 17 per cent by 1997. And trade union membership, the core of the traditional Labour coalition, collapsed from 13.3 million individuals in 1979 to just 7.8 million by 1997 (all figures from Heath *et al.*, 2001, 13–15). By the 1990s, the party's traditional support base was no longer large enough to deliver victory.

In addition, a second process – dealignment – had weakened voters' attachments to parties (Crewe and Särlvik, 1983). Increasingly, the electorate was likely to vote, not on the basis of class or party loyalty, but on the issues and (especially) on the perceived economic competence of parties (Franklin, 1985; Sanders, 1996). Parties could no longer rely on the automatic support of their voters.

On the crucial battleground of economic competence, Labour was haunted by the economic crisis and rising union unrest that dogged the 1974–9 Callaghan Government (Holmes, 1985). The 1979 Conservative Government weathered a deep recession to win the 1983 election on the back of a military victory in the Falklands and an economic recovery (Sanders *et al.*, 1987; Clarke *et al.*, 1990). In the 1980s especially, the Thatcher Governments appealed successfully to aspirational members of the skilled working class, particularly those in the affluent South East of the country, whose incomes were rising rapidly (the so-called 'Essex man' vote; see Johnston *et al.*, 1988). Not only was Labour's traditional electorate declining in size, therefore, but dealignment enabled the Conservatives to erode it further.

New Labour's response was bold. The strategy was twofold: to expand the party's social base to encompass 'Middle England' and to re-establish Labour's credibility as a safe party of government (Gould, 1998). In part, this was in the Party's own hands. From 1994, Blair moved the Party firmly away from its traditional ideological core. Clause 4 of the Party constitution (calling for public ownership) was jettisoned. The Party accepted the privatisations of the Thatcher and Major years, and pledged to work with the market. It distanced itself from the unions, its traditional backers, and developed links with the private sector. The Treasury team promised to stick to Conservative tax and spend targets for the first two years of a new Labour Government.

In large part, too, Labour was lucky in that, just as it was moving rightwards, the Conservative Government was busy imploding. The 'Black Wednesday' fiasco of September 1992, when the pound was pushed out of the exchange rate mechanism (ERM), destroyed the Conservatives' reputation for economic competence (Sanders, 1996). Repeated stories of sleaze and deep splits over Europe in the Conservative Government completed the job (Mortimore, 1995; Evans, 1998).

The combination of a Labour Party 'made safe' for centre-ground voters and a Conservative Government in deep disarray was almost irresistible. The electorate noticed. To take one example, the balance between taxation and government spending has been one of the key battlegrounds of politics in the post-war period, an issue made even more important by the Conservatives' tax-cutting rhetoric after 1979. While the Conservatives gained a reputation for cutting taxes and controlling public spending, Labour struggled with an image as a high-tax, high-spending party.

Changing the Party's reputation on tax and spending was a key component of the New Labour project. We can see whether it succeeded by examining answers to a question included in the British Election Study (BES) surveys since 1983. Respondents were asked where they would place themselves and the parties on an 11-point scale examining preferences for taxation and public spending: a score of 1 on the scale indicated a preference for raising public spending, even at the risk of also increasing taxation, while a score of 11 indicated a preference for tax cuts, even if that meant public spending cuts too. After 1992, Labour was successful in repositioning itself (see Figure 2.1).

FIGURE 2.1   *Average score, tax versus spending dimension*

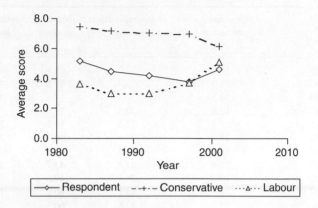

Source: British Election Studies, 1983–2001.

The gap between the average respondent's personal preference and their evaluation of Labour's position had narrowed; and Labour was perceived to have moved rightward on the issue. This was partly because, under Tony Blair, the party was felt to have moved away from tax-and-spend politics. But at the same time, public opinion has always been slightly more disposed towards high public spending than to low taxation – and, during the 1990s, public opinion became more radical on this dimension.

New Labour was also extending its appeal well beyond its declining working class support base. In the 1960s, around two-thirds of manual working-class voters supported Labour, while only around 16 per cent of professional voters did so (see Table 2.2). But from the 1970s onwards, the electorate became less divided along lines of class. We can see the extent of the decline in class voting by looking at trends in the Alford index since the early 1960s. The index is the difference between the percentage of manual workers who vote Labour and the percentage of Labour-voting non-manual workers: it varies from a theoretical maximum of 100 (a completely class-aligned electorate) to a minimum of 0 (no class alignment whatever). In the 1960s, it measured around 42, showing a strong class cleavage (Dalton, 1996), but thereafter it declined steadily. A change from expressive to instrumental voting weakened traditional class ties (Goldthorpe *et al.*, 1968). Growing numbers of manual workers, especially those in skilled manual occupations in the buoyant South East, could aspire to more middle-class lifestyles and so found themselves sharing interests with traditionally Conservative-voting groups (Dunleavy, 1979; Dunleavy and Husbands, 1985; Garrett, 1994; Hamnett, 1999). Labour therefore had to shift its

TABLE 2.2   *Percentage Labour vote by class*

	Professionals and managers (%)	Intermediate workers (%)	Manual workers (%)	Alford index
1964	16.0	27.7	65.6	42
1966	18.0	33.4	69.5	43
1970	24.3	32.7	57.1	33
1974 (Feb)	18.8	30.3	57.0	35
1974 (Oct)	18.5	32.6	58.2	32
1979	20.9	27.5	50.7	27
1983	13.1	19.4	42.6	25
1987	17.4	21.4	43.7	25
1992	19.0	26.1	49.6	27
1997	38.5	43.1	60.2	20
2001	32.7	43.8	60.3	22

Source: British Election Studies, 1964–2001.

appeal to more middle-class terrain, both to win back 'embourgoisified' working-class voters and to reach out to the increasingly numerous core middle class. The former was important in terms of reconsolidating the party's base; and the latter was vital if the party was to win enough votes to form a government.

The 'Middle England' vote was therefore a key target for Labour's reformers. The process of wooing them into the Labour fold began slowly under Neil Kinnock in the mid-1980s, then accelerated in the early 1990s. By then, a new recession, presided over by a Conservative Administration, was affecting many 'Middle England' voters badly, through rising service-sector unemployment and negative equity in the housing market as the housing boom of the late 1980s in the South East especially turned to a housing slump (Pattie *et al.*, 1995, 1997).

But it was only at the 1997 election that the realignment project came fully into effect: Labour's share of the manual working class vote, at 60 per cent, recovered to 1960s levels. But class dealignment continued, with the Alford index dropping to a new low of 22, because of the dramatic inroads New Labour had made into the intermediate workers vote (up from 26 per cent in 1992 to 43 per cent in 1997), and into the professional and managerial vote (doubling from 19 per cent in 1992 to over 38 per cent in 1997). New Labour became a 'catch-all' party, forging a new 'big tent' electoral coalition to win in 1997 (Katz and Mair, 1995; Evans *et al.*, 1999).

Building a winning coalition is one thing, but holding on to it is quite another. There was always a risk that the voters who had swung to the party so dramatically in 1997 could just as dramatically withdraw their support at the next election. Labour's coalition in 1997 was wide, therefore, but was it deep?

After four years in government, New Labour's electoral coalition held up remarkably well at the 2001 election. Labour's share of the vote was only slightly reduced, while the Conservatives' share hardly advanced. Ideologically, the median voter still felt closer to New Labour than to the Conservatives (see Figure 2.1). Indeed, after four years of Gordon Brown's 'prudent' economic management, voters placed New Labour slightly further to the right on the taxes versus spending scale, on average, than they placed themselves. New Labour had executed a classic Downsian manoeuvre and had colonised the centre-right of opinion (Downs, 1957).

New Labour in 2001 remained, to an important extent, a cross-class electoral force (see Table 2.2). Almost identical percentages of all manual and intermediate workers who voted supported Labour in 1997 and 2001. Although rates of support among the professional and managerial classes fell somewhat, from over 38 per cent in 1997 to under 33 per cent in 2001, a considerably larger proportion of voters in this class still voted Labour than at any election since at least 1964 (1997 excepted). The big tent remained inclusive.

Issues and Competence

How did New Labour achieve such a remarkable result in 2001? In part, the answer lies in perceptions of the party's performance in government. Four years in government, by and large, confirmed to Middle England that New Labour was a safe vote, and the economy grew relatively strongly compared to other major democracies. Unemployment fell from around 7 per cent in 1997 to 5 per cent in 2001. Inflation was very low, and incomes grew steadily. On the whole, voters felt better off at the end of New Labour's first term of government than they had at the start. The British Election Panel Study (BEPS) interviewed the same group of voters at several stages between 1997 and 2001, asking them how their standard of living had changed since the previous election (see Table 2.3). Immediately after the 1997 election, almost 33 per cent felt their standard of living had gone up, and about 38 per cent felt their living standards had declined. Not surprisingly, given this climate of relative economic gloom, the Conservatives lost the 1997 election. Immediately after the 2001 contest, in contrast, reflecting on four years of New Labour in power, more than 40 per cent of BEPS respondents felt their living standard had improved, while less than 16 per cent felt it had declined.

Most voters felt that New Labour had handled the economy well between 1997 and 2001. As part of the 2001 BES, respondents were asked to evaluate the Labour Administration's performance on a wide range of

TABLE 2.3   *Public perceptions of personal economic circumstances:
change in perceptions of living standards*

	1997 (%)	2001 (%)
Standard of living since the last election has:		
Improved	32.7	40.7
Declined	38.4	15.8
Improved because of government	21.4	28.6
Declined because of government	34.5	12.9

Source: British Election Panel Study 1997–2001.

TABLE 2.4   *Public perceptions of personal economic circumstances: New Labour
performance in government*

	Well (%)	Neither (%)	Badly (%)
How did New Labour handle:			
Inflation	66.8	21.3	11.9
The economy generally	61.2	26.2	12.6
Unemployment	60.1	24.1	15.8
Education	45.0	25.9	29.1
The European Union	37.7	37.0	25.3
Taxes	37.2	27.7	35.0
Making life better	34.5	36.2	29.3
Pensions	32.8	28.1	39.1
The NHS	30.3	22.7	47.1
Crime	28.2	31.3	40.5
Transport	18.1	23.8	58.1
Asylum seekers	17.1	22.4	60.5

Source: 2001 British Election Study.

different issues (see Table 2.4). Strikingly, the issues on which the government scored the highest were all economic: inflation, unemployment, and the general state of the economy were all pluses for New Labour. Just before the 2001 election, BES respondents were also asked which party would best handle the situation if Britain were to encounter economic difficulties: 56 per cent of those who expressed a view chose Labour.

All this represents a remarkable turnaround in public opinion. For most of the post-war period, Labour had been seen as a poor economic manager, while the Conservatives had enjoyed a reputation for economic competence (Sanders, 1996). But, as noted earlier, the 1992 ERM crisis destroyed that

TABLE 2.5   *Public perceptions of personal economic circumstances: economic evaluations and voting, 2001*

| | The general economic situation in the last 12 months has: | | |
	Got worse (%)	Stayed the same (%)	Got better (%)
Conservative	30.9	19.0	11.1
Labour	21.8	33.5	45.8
Liberal Democrat	14.4	13.3	16.4
Other	4.6	3.1	3.7
Abstained	28.4	31.1	23.1

Source: 2001 British Election Study.

Conservative reputation, and New Labour's handling of the economy between 1997 and 2001 was sufficiently surefooted (helped by a generally benign international economy and, ironically, by the legacy of the previous Tory administration) to lay the ghosts of Labour's economic past. New Labour – and Chancellor Gordon Brown in particular – had won public confidence on the crucial economic battleground.

The sense of relative economic well-being that pervaded the electorate in 2001 also found its expression in their votes. Just before the 2001 election, respondents to the BES survey were asked how they felt the national economy had fared over the previous year: just after the election, the same individuals were asked how they had voted (see Table 2.5). A relatively economically contented electorate voted to maintain the status quo – in this case a Labour Government (Fiorina, 1981; Lewis-Beck, 1990; Galbraith, 1992; Sanders, 1996). Whereas only 22 per cent of those who felt the economy had got worse voted for Labour, 46 per cent of those who felt it had improved did so.

Over the course of the 1997–2001 Parliament, Labour had come to be seen as the most competent party on a wide range of other issues too (see Table 2.4). On all but two issues (transport and asylum policy), the majority of voters felt the government had at least not made things any worse. Respondents to the 2001 BES were asked to rate which party would best handle the election issue they personally felt was most important. Of those who named a party as best for their issue, 62 per cent chose Labour. The Blair Administration seemed a safe pair of hands.

Popular or Tolerated?

On the face of things, then, New Labour in government had won over the electorate. Support for most previous governments has followed an electoral cycle (Miller and Mackie, 1973). Governments are popular at the start, lose support as the mid-term of the parliament approaches (usually as hard decisions have to be faced), but recover somewhat as the next election approaches. Not so New Labour. In opposition between 1992 and 1997, it seemed to have abolished the electoral cycle entirely. Monthly polling data showed Labour overtaking the Conservatives shortly after the 1992 ERM crisis. The party's poll ratings became even higher when Blair became party leader in 1994, and then stayed well above the Conservatives' rating for the rest of the parliament (Clarke *et al.*, 1998).

To some extent, the breakdown of the electoral cycle after 1992 was to be expected. The Conservative Government was in disarray, and New Labour avoided the presentational mistakes of previous Labour oppositions. The cycle's continued absence after the 1997 election was more of a surprise, however. New Labour was now in office, and governments must make hard decisions which risk alienating voters. What is more, the Conservatives had been the dominant electoral force of twentieth-century British politics, adapting rapidly to changing circumstances. Surely they would repeat the trick again, to recover quickly from their defeat and make a challenge for power once again? But the national opinion polls tell a quite different story. Once again, the electoral cycle seemed to have evaporated. The Conservatives stayed deep in the electoral doldrums, with little sign of a recovery. Labour, by contrast, polled well throughout the Parliament, better than almost any post-war government. From the polling evidence, the second term was never in doubt.

Even so, New Labour was not invulnerable. A number of factors gradually took some of the gloss off the new government. Once in office, the party's formidable news management operation came to be seen as an example of 'control freakery', over-concerned with policy presentation over substance. After the sleaze allegations of the Major years, New Labour had come into office promising to operate to higher standards of probity, but events such as the Eccleston and Hinduja affairs tarnished the party's image. In both cases, large donations were perceived to be linked to access to ministers and favourable policy decisions. And, perhaps most damaging of all for Labour's longer-term prospects, many voters felt the changes in public services they had hoped for under a Labour Government were very slow in coming. But in some areas, voters did see signs of delivery: during the 1997 election Mr Blair had declared New Labour's priorities to be 'education, education, education'. After considerable investment, particularly in the school system, a large plurality of voters (45 per cent) felt the government had handled education well by the time of the 2001 election (see Table 2.4).

Other public services fared less well. Pensions and the NHS, normally strong issues for Labour, were areas where the government's report card was marked 'must try harder'. Gordon Brown's efforts to raise pensioner incomes, though successful, were not widely noticed. But his apparently miserly headline increase in the state pension in 2000 of only 75p did attract criticism (Glennerster, 2001; Toynbee and Walker, 2001, 23–7). By 2001, more voters thought Labour had handled pensions policy badly than felt the party had handled it well. And almost half of all voters felt the government had handled the NHS badly. Crime, though not a traditional Labour strength, had been brought under the New Labour umbrella when, as Shadow Home Secretary, Blair had promised Labour would be 'tough on crime and tough on the causes of crime'. In office, New Labour was tough on crime, and crime rates fell. However, media panics over, for example, street crime and paedophilia, fuelled public concerns: by 2001, 40 per cent of voters disapproved of Labour's record on crime. Finally, the government's transport policy ran into difficulties. New Labour did not deliver its promised integrated transport network. And following a fatal crash at Hatfield in 2000, emergency track repairs severely disrupted rail services for over a year, creating chaos for many commuters. Not surprisingly, over 60 per cent of voters felt, in 2001, that Labour's record on transport was poor.

But neither of the two largest challenges to Labour during the 1997–2001 Parliament emerged from the traditional political battleground. A private member's bill to ban fox hunting served as a catalyst for a 'countryside rebellion'. Farming communities, battered by bovine spongiform encephalopathy (BSE), agricultural recession and (towards the end of the Parliament) foot and mouth disease, and feeling neglected by the government, formed the vociferous Countryside Alliance. However, the Alliance's electoral effects were very small: no Labour MPs were really under threat (Woods, 2002).

More threatening was the fuel crisis that erupted briefly in September 2000. British petrol prices were higher than those on much of the Continent, and the differential was widening, largely because of a 'fuel tax escalator' designed to push up the cost of fuel and hence encourage lower usage. Ironically, the tax escalator had been introduced by the previous Conservative Administration, but New Labour had let it run on, raising prices still further. A combination of small farmers and road hauliers argued that high fuel prices were pushing them out of business. During a week-long protest, they blockaded fuel depots, and organised mass rolling roadblocks on major highways. Petrol stations ran out of fuel as panic buying emptied the pumps and new supplies could not get through. Some months later, the fuel tax escalator was quietly dropped, but by then the damage was done. Labour's poll ratings dipped briefly, but dramatically. And while the party's standing very quickly recovered, New Labour no longer looked invulnerable.

Labour also lost some ground in mid-term elections (Crewe, 2001). In the 1998 and 1999 local elections, and in the 1999 elections for the new Scottish Parliament and Welsh Assembly, it still emerged as the largest

TABLE 2.6   *Perceptions of the party leaders, 2001*

| | Percentage seeing party leader as: | | |
	Tony Blair	William Hague	Charles Kennedy
Strong leader	77.4	28.9	56.3
Not strong leader	16.4	60.8	21.4
Keeping promises	42.8	29.5	46.2
Breaking promises	39.8	36.7	11.2
Caring	68.1	52.2	71.8
Not caring	21.7	30.5	7.2
Decisive	64.0	42.2	57.9
Not decisive	25.6	42.8	15.1
Sticks to principles	58.0	51.5	64.2
Doesn't stick to principles	30.9	29.2	8.0
Listens to reason	60.9	44.0	63.2
Doesn't listen to reason	25.6	34.1	9.1
Arrogant	44.1	41.0	10.6
Not arrogant	48.5	48.3	72.3

Source: 2001 British Election Study.

party, but its vote share fell substantially below its opinion poll ratings. And New Labour lost the 1999 European election (the party's first national election defeat since the 1992 election) and – narrowly – the 2000 election for the new London Assembly. Party strategists feared the polls might be exaggerating Labour support.

Compared to previous Conservative Administrations, New Labour's mid-term blues were slight. But there were signs support for the party was shallow. Two images encapsulated some of the public unease that built up around New Labour: the government's repeated attempts to 'spin' news stories; and its obsession with remaining 'on message'. Blair's reputation for trustworthiness fell throughout the 1997 Parliament. Immediately after the 1997 election, 74 per cent of British Election Panel Study respondents felt that he kept his promises, and 87 per cent felt he was decisive; but by 2001, less than 43 per cent and 64 per cent respectively, gave similar answers (see Table 2.6). Only 36 per cent of 2001 BES respondents felt New Labour had kept its promises, while 46 per cent felt it had broken them.

New Labour was elected in 1997 on a groundswell of voter optimism and goodwill. The Party's campaign song had promised 'Things can only get better'. By 2001, after four years in office, some things, voters felt, had improved; but others had not. The government had promised much, but delivered less. It was respected by the end of its first term in office, but it did not generate wide enthusiasm.

A Lucky Choice of Opponents?

Given its economic record, New Labour was never seriously at risk of losing in 2001. However, given the sense of public disappointment, Labour's majority could have been cut substantially. But in the event, it hardly changed. Why? Two factors in addition to the Party's record in office helped Labour to retain its majority: the state of the opposition; and the operation of the electoral system.

New Labour was remarkably lucky in its main opponent, the Conservative Party. During the 1970s and 1980s, as left and right fought over the Party's future, Labour had often been seen by voters as a Party divided, while the Conservatives were perceived as being united. But by the early 1990s, Labour had learned the painful lessons of poor party discipline, hence New Labour's obsession with being 'on message'. The Conservatives, on the other hand, exhausted by eighteen years continuously in office, faced by major issues (especially Europe) which split the Party, and – after the 1992 ERM crisis – increasingly panic-stricken by unremittingly poor opinion poll ratings, descended into internecine warfare. For the first time in a political generation, the Conservatives, and not Labour, were seen by 1997 as being relatively extreme and divided internally (Pattie, 2001).

The 1997 election was catastrophic for the Conservatives, its worst since the Great Reform Act of 1832. The 'big beasts' in the Conservative jungle were decimated. Some (like Michael Portillo and Malcolm Rifkind) lost their seats. Others (such as John Major and Michael Heseltine) retired from top-level politics. A leadership contest followed close on the heels of the defeat. William Hague, a young and relatively unknown candidate from the right of the party, defeated Kenneth Clarke, one of the last 'big beasts' still in the fray. But the change in leadership did not resolve the Party's problems. In truth, the new Party leader faced a difficult dilemma. After a defeat on the scale of 1997, it was imperative that the Conservatives both shored up their existing support (to prevent a further loss of votes in the future) and began to reach out to the median voter. But policies likely to appeal to core Conservative voters were unlikely to appeal to the median voter, and vice-versa. The new leadership never satisfactorily resolved the dilemma, and Hague was widely perceived as taking the Party further to the right as the Parliament progressed (though see Cowley and Quayle, 2002).

Mr Hague failed to make much impact on the public: both he and his party remained resolutely unpopular. If voters were equivocal about

New Labour after the initial post-1997 euphoria had worn off, they were positively scathing about the Conservatives. It is always hard to fight against a government that presides over economic success, but even among eventual Conservative voters, Labour's management of the economy between 1997 and 2001 was rated highly. The 2001 BES reveals that 44 per cent of 2001 Tories felt that Labour had handled the economy well; 63 per cent of Conservatives approved Labour's record on inflation; and 48 per cent approved the government's handling of unemployment. If many of one's own supporters think one's opponents handle such key issues well, then one is in trouble!

Perceptions of both the Conservative Party and its leader, already poor at the 1997 election, were almost uniformly dire by time of the 2001 contest. For example, 81 per cent BES respondents in 2001 thought the Conservatives were a divided party, compared to 25 per cent who felt the same about Labour. The Tories were rated as extreme by twice as many voters as had said the same of Labour (32 per cent versus 15 per cent). Only a third of voters in 2001 felt that the Conservatives were capable of strong government (compared to almost 80 per cent who rated New Labour a strong government). A substantial minority (41 per cent) of voters had felt New Labour was out of touch in 2001: but a very large majority (75 per cent) said the same of the Tories. And if few voters had felt in 2001 that New Labour kept its promises, even fewer (only one in five) felt the Conservatives did so. Most telling of all, only 17 per cent of respondents to the 2001 BES felt the Conservatives were the best party to handle the election issue they felt most important (40 per cent named Labour).

Nor did the Conservatives' leadership inspire confidence. William Hague was not a success with the public, polling consistently well behind Blair (see Table 2.6). Indeed, on some issues he was rated behind Charles Kennedy, the new leader of the Liberal Democrats by the time of the 2001 election. Hague was perceived as being: the weakest party leader; the leader least likely to keep his promises; the least caring leader; the least decisive; the least likely to stick to his principles (although the margin between Hague and the other party leaders on this issue was narrow); and the least likely to listen to reason. The 1997–2001 British Election Panel Study asked respondents to rate whether Blair or Hague would make a good prime minister (see Figure 2.2: the first 1997 comparison contrasts Blair with Major, as Hague had not yet been elected). Although Blair's standing fell during the course of the Parliament, a large majority always felt that he made a good prime minister (PM). But on no occasion did a majority of voters feel that Hague might make a good PM: he was not seen as prime ministerial material.

A well-worn aphorism has it that oppositions do not win elections, governments lose them. In part, this is true. It is always difficult for an

FIGURE 2.2   *A good prime minister?*

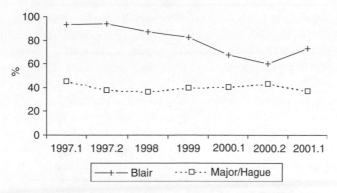

Source: British Election Panel Study 1997–2001.

opposition to make inroads against a successful administration. But equally, to stand any chance at all, an opposition must be seen by voters as a credible government in waiting. The Conservatives failed this test badly in 2001. Few voters could imagine the Conservatives forming a government in 2001. To a large extent, New Labour, whatever the disappointments engendered by its first term, was the only credible government available to voters.

A Helping Hand from the Electoral System

A combination of a strong economy and a moribund opposition made New Labour virtually unassailable in 2001. As a result, the contest itself was an anticlimax. Turnout slumped to only 59 per cent, as many electors decided it was not worth the effort of voting when the result was assured. But even so, the sheer scale of both of the New Labour landslides, in 1997 and 2001, is remarkable. First-past-the-post elections normally give the winning party a larger share of the seats than its vote share would seem to entitle it on grounds of strict proportionality. However, since the late 1980s, the electoral system has become biased increasingly towards Labour: the Party has won many more seats than it is entitled in terms of its vote share (Johnston *et al.*, 2001, 2002).

One way of illustrating this is to consider how many seats the winning party obtained compared to its share of the vote. Remarkably, all election winners since 1979 have obtained roughly the same national vote share (around 43 per cent), though the number of government MPs elected has fluctuated markedly (see Table 2.7). Between 1979 and 1992, the

TABLE 2.7   *Electoral bias since 1979*

Election	Winning party		Electoral bias
	% vote	Seats	
Conservative governments			
1979	43.9	339	26
1983	42.4	397	−5
1997	43.3	376	−6
1992	42.8	336	38
New Labour governments			
1997	44.4	419	82
2001	42.0	413	141

Source: Johnston *et al.*, 2002.

Conservatives went from a maximum of 397 MPs in 1983 to a minimum of 336 in 1992. In 1997 and 2001, New Labour, also with around 43 per cent of the vote, won many more seats: 419 and 413, respectively. Labour has tended to do better when it has won recent elections than have the Conservatives.

Not only is the winner's advantage from first-past-the-post highly variable, therefore, but it seems also to depend on which party wins the election. However, we cannot evaluate electoral bias just by looking at the vote shares and seats won. In part this is because to do so places undue emphasis on the winners. But an election system can be biased towards a party even if that party loses an election. For example, it might gain more seats than expected, but not enough to win power. And the exact size of the winner's advantage depends on a variety of other factors, including the level of support for the other parties. We need a standard yardstick to compare bias in one election with bias in another. One measure of electoral bias calculates the results of the election if a nationally uniform swing had produced equal votes for the two largest parties. The difference in the number of seats that would be won by the two biggest parties is therefore a measure of bias. If there is no electoral bias, two parties winning the same vote share should win the same number of seats. But the greater the electoral bias, the more seats one party will win relative to the other, *even if their vote shares are identical*. Here, the bias is calculated by calculating the number of seats Labour and the Conservatives would win with equal vote shares (assuming nothing else changed), then subtracting the Conservative total from the Labour total. A negative score therefore indicates a net bias towards the Conservatives, and a positive score a bias towards Labour. Applying this measure to recent British election results produces some dramatic results (see Johnston *et al.*, 2001, 2002). Between 1950 and 1964, the electoral system was biased towards the Conservatives, though the size of that bias declined quickly after 1959. Between 1966 and 1987, the bias was slight. But after 1987, the electoral system became progressively more biased towards Labour (see Table 2.7). In 1997, had Labour and the Conservatives tied on vote share, Labour would still have won the election, with 82 seats more than its nearest rival. By 2001, the pro-Labour bias had increased even further, to 141 seats. With the electoral system working so much in its favour, New Labour looks very hard to beat.

Labour's helping hand from the electoral system was not the outcome of political chicanery. Rather, it was a consequence of three sets of factors, two of which were largely out of Labour's control (Johnston *et al.*, 2001). As the population changes over time, some constituencies grow while others contract. In general, this helps Labour, as its seats tend to have smaller electorates than seats won by the Conservatives, which means that it takes fewer votes to elect a Labour candidate than a Tory. In part, this is a consequence of migration from Labour-voting inner cities to more Conservative suburbs. In part, also, it comes about because constituencies in Scotland and Wales (where Labour dominates Westminster elections) tend to be considerably smaller than their English counterparts. Together, these factors were worth 24 seats for Labour in 2001 (at equal vote shares with the Conservatives). But constituency size is not something the government can control: it is set by the independent Parliamentary Boundary Commissions in their Periodic Reviews (Rossiter *et al.*, 1999). Scottish over-representation in Westminster is being reduced in the latest Boundary Review (a consequence of devolution), but this is neither likely to take effect before the next general election, nor will it substantially reduce the pro-Labour electoral bias.

A second set of factors also influence how many votes are needed to win a seat: abstention and third-party performance. Ironically, the more voters who abstain in a seat, other things being equal, the fewer votes are required to win that seat. Turnout in both the 1997 and (especially) 2001 elections was very low. It was particularly low in Labour's inner-city strongholds, thus reducing the number of votes needed to elect a Labour MP. In 2001, the geography of abstention helped Labour substantially: had the two main parties won an equal share of the vote, the pattern of non-voting would have been worth an extra 39 seats to Labour. Third-party performance also played a part. The Liberal Democrats were mainly in competition with the Conservatives (only a few seats were a Labour–Liberal Democrat contests). Where the Liberal Democrats came second, more Liberal Democrat votes meant that it took fewer votes to elect the winner. As most winners in these circumstances were Conservatives, third-party votes meant Labour would have lost 25 seats to the Tories at equal vote shares in 2001. But where the Liberal Democrats won seats, they mainly did so at the expense of the

Conservatives, thus improving Labour's relative returns. And the 2001 election was the best post-war result for the Liberal Democrats or their Liberal predecessors: the party won 52 seats. Third-party victories were worth an extra 37 seats for Labour. Together, abstentions and third-party performance were worth 51 extra seats to Labour in 2001.

But the largest factor explaining why Labour did so well out of the electoral system in 1997 and (especially) in 2001 was the efficiency of its electoral geography. A party wants to avoid two different scenarios. First, it needs to minimise the number of seats it wins by landslide majorities. Under first-past-the-post, every vote over the minimum needed to win a seat is wasted, as it does not contribute to electing further MPs. Equally, a party would ideally avoid losing a seat narrowly: once again, votes cast in such a seat are wasted as they do not elect an MP. In 1997 and 2001, Labour's vote was better distributed than that of the Conservatives, winning fewer seats with large majorities, and losing fewer by narrow margins. It concentrated its constituency campaigning in the most marginal constituencies, largely ignoring seats where it was bound to win, or where it had no real chance. And this paid off (Denver *et al.*, 1998; Johnston *et al.*, 1998). In both elections, Labour amassed votes where it really mattered, in the marginals: majorities went down in safe seats, and fewer votes were wasted on seats the Party was bound to lose. Overall, there was a small swing away from Labour between 1997 and 2001. But in the key marginals Labour had to retain, the swing was in fact towards Labour (Curtice and Steed, 2001, 317; Norris, 2001; Johnston *et al.*, 2002). In 1997, the efficiency of the geography of the Labour vote (itself in part a function of Labour's campaign efforts) was worth 48 extra seats to the party. By 2001, the advantage accrued had jumped to 72 seats: Labour not only got more votes than its rivals, but it also managed to get them where they would matter most.

Conclusions

New Labour started the twenty-first century on a high. In the 1960s, a previous Labour leader, Harold Wilson, claimed that his Party had supplanted the Conservatives as 'the natural party of government'. In retrospect, given Labour's record between 1970 and 1997, this claim was not just premature, it was also absurd. But almost forty years later, the claim now looks much more reasonable. Labour has dominated the British electoral landscape since 1992, when it overtook the Conservatives in the polls. And New Labour has now won two landslide elections in succession, something no previous Labour Government had been able to achieve. In part, this success was helped by the construction of a new electoral coalition. In part, also, Labour's success has been a function of economic success during the first New Labour Parliament. Voters support governments that make them better off – a test New Labour passed easily in its first term.

Even so, New Labour's electoral dominance is a mixed blessing. As it entered its second successive term in office, New Labour was respected, but not widely liked. And record numbers of electors felt their vote did not count – whether because the result of the 2001 election was a foregone conclusion, or because of a deeper sense of malaise with electoral democracy. Economic stormclouds began to gather in 2001 in the aftermath of the collapse of the dot.com financial bubble and the events of 11 September 2001. New Labour will have to work hard, both to retain its hard-won reputation for economic competence, and to live up to the generous public spending targets laid out for the second term (and premised on what now seem overoptimistic assumptions about economic growth). The electorate gave New Labour the benefit of the doubt on public services after its first term in office, but they may not be so forgiving if things are not perceived as having improved substantially by the end of the Party's second term. Blair's personal ratings, after falling in the approach to war in Iraq, subsequently recovered. How far discontent over the war damages the Party's campaign base among its activists may be revealed in the mid-term elections.

Ironically, Labour might still survive if it fails in its attempts to revive the public services, and its activists, thanks to the Conservatives' continued disarray under Iain Duncan Smith. Given the minimal increase in the Conservatives' vote share between 1997 and 2001, the size of Labour's majority, and the substantial pro-Labour bias now operating in the electoral system, the opposition still has an electoral Everest to climb before they are back in contention. The Conservatives must re-establish their reputation as a potential party of government if they are to challenge Labour seriously. At their 2002 Annual Conference, they tried once more to begin the process under their new leader. But it will be an uphill struggle, and the prospects for the Tories are not promising; one of New Labour's greatest assets is the state of its opponents.

Overall, then, New Labour is in a strong electoral position to form a third successive majority government at the next election in 2005 or 2006. Echoing Wilson's claims, Blair has expressed his hope that the centre-left will dominate British politics in the twenty-first century in the same way as the centre-right had dominated the twentieth century. It is still early days, but that project has got off to a good start.

3

New Labour's Second Term and European Social Democracy

BEN CLIFT

Introduction

New Labour's electoral resurgence coincided with upturns in the electoral fortunes of many social democratic parties across Europe. At the start of 2001, social democratic parties were in government, either in coalition or on their own, in fifteen out of the seventeen Western European democracies. Commentators saw this as evidence of a sea change in European politics analogous to that of the all-pervasive neo-liberal new right twenty years earlier. The obituaries written for social democracy in the 1980s and 1990s by Dahrendorf (1988, 140, 172) and Gray (1998, 89), were, it seemed, premature.

The holding of governmental office also made the interrelationships between social democrats highly significant in a context where co-operation at the European level was increasingly important. The period of social democratic success saw institutionalised co-operation in a range of social and economic policies, including the European Employment Initiative, begun in 1997 at the Luxembourg jobs summit, and the common social policy agenda agreed at the 2000 Lisbon European Council. As we shall see, however, highly significant social democratic policy differences endure.

More recently, repeated electoral setbacks have undermined talk of a new social democratic dawn. Although the Swedish and German social democrats won electoral victories in 2002, elsewhere social democracy's electoral stock was falling. In France, Jospin's cataclysmic first round elimination from the 2002 presidential election cast a shadow over his successful premiership, and sent the French left into disarray. In Holland in 2002 the social democrats were ousted from a purple coalition largely because of the populist Right List, led by Pym Fortyn. There were major setbacks in the social democratic heartlands, such as Denmark and Austria. In Norway, in 2001, the Labour Party suffered its worst defeat since 1927. New Labour was thus in the unusual position of being one of the most (electorally) successful parties within a heterogeneous European social democratic party family. This chapter explores its evolving relationship with that political tradition. Given their centrality to social democracy, employment policy, welfare policy and labour market policy will be considered, in an attempt to establish the similarities and differences between New Labour and its European counterparts. The chapter considers the extent to which these similarities and differences are conditioned by ideological, institutional and electoral factors that affect national social democratic preferences – factors, it will be suggested here, that present severe obstacles to New Labour reinventing European social democracy in its own image.

European Social Democracy

The Labour Party has always differed in critical respects from continental social democracy. The explanation can be traced partly to the Party's origins within the trade union movement. The resultant incremental reformist mindset of a British Labour Movement 'incurious as to theory' (Tawney, 1961, 1) meant that Marxism was less influential on Labour than on its sister parties. Before exploring how this historically peculiar relationship between European social democracy and Labour has evolved recently, we must briefly outline what is understood by European social democracy. S. Padgett and W. Paterson identify the principle elements of social democracy: 'inspired by socialist ideals but heavily conditioned by its political environment and incorporating liberal values. The social democratic project may be defined as the attempt to reconcile socialism with liberal politics and capitalist society' (Padgett and Paterson, 1991, 1).

Attempting further precision can be problematic. For example, J. Gray's unhelpful, means-based definition – 'the combination of deficit-financed full employment, a comprehensive welfare state and egalitarian tax policies' – overstates the centrality of deficit financing to social democracy (Gray, 1998, 88). Furthermore it discounts prematurely social democracy's capacity for renewal, failing to grasp its *variety*. In order to take this variety into account, it makes sense to focus on social democratic *ends* at least as much as *means*. An ends-orientated definition is more amenable to cross-national comparison, and thus more useful for our purposes. P. Hirst identifies three core elements of social democracy: 'minimizing the cost of capitalism for individuals, either through growth and employment enhancing policies, and/or, through welfare state provision for the contingencies of unemployment, ill-health and old age'; attempting to 'tackle and reduce major and unjustifiable inequalities in power and wealth'; and seeking to accomplish these objectives 'within the limits set by parliamentary democracy on the one hand, and private property and the market economy on the other' (Hirst, 1999, 87).

Although it is a convenient organising concept, 'continental social democracy' encompasses a complex reality. Each socialist or social democratic party developed within a specific capitalist society, wedded to nation-states in various stages of democratic development, and conditioned by world wars and the scourge of Fascism. This national setting provides a set of laboratory conditions in which social democracy sought to deliver egalitarian commitments through full employment and extensive welfare states. Factors such as the nature of competition within the national party system, the financial relationship with the unions, the socio-economic structure of society, and the relative openness and competitiveness of the economy, all influence heavily the nature of each national social democratic project.

A clear example of this is how the strategic demands of different party systems affect ideological positioning. Of all the West European parties of the left, only the Portuguese socialist party; PASOK (the Greek socialists); and New Labour can hope to govern without coalition partners. New Labour's self-classification as 'centre or centre-left' shows similarities with the Dutch experience, where Wim Kok presided until 2002 over a 'purple' coalition government incorporating centrists and (neo-)liberals. A similar configuration (with centre-right liberals) has existed in Belgium since 1999. However, such centrist self-definition would be unthinkable in France or Sweden, where the imperatives of party competition and coalition government demand self-classification as left-wing. Inevitably, parties are also affected by competition with coalition partners, be they Greens (as in Germany and France), former Communists (as in Italy between 1996 and 2001, and Sweden), or Communists (as in France between 1997 and 2002).

(Whatever Happened to) The Third Way?

> Rarely in the history of world politics has a term gone from obscurity to meaninglessness without any intervening period of coherence. (Robert Reich, *New Statesman*, 1 May 1999)

Five years after the phrase 'the third way' was coined, events have gone full circle, and the term has returned to obscurity, since it almost never passes the lips of the New Labour elite in their second term. At the 2002 Labour

Conference only former US president, Bill Clinton used the term. Nevertheless, it was in relation to the 'third way' that Blair and others sought to elaborate their core values, and in Blair's case sought to convert his European counterparts after 1997. It is therefore worth exploring briefly before comparing the ideological positioning of other European social democrats.

According to Tony Blair, the third way stands for a 'modernised' social democracy and social justice, but 'flexible, innovative and forward-looking in the means to achieve them' (1998c, 1). It moves, he argues, 'decisively beyond' Old Left and New Right, aiming to reconcile 'a neo-liberal emphasis on economic efficiency and dynamism with a traditional left concern for equity and social cohesion' (White, 1998, 17). New Labour has employed the third way to distance itself from the traditional institutional features of social democracy, such as 'neo-corporatist' centralized wage bargaining, and high marginal rates of taxation.

Blair talks of 'the enabling state' (1998c, 4), which, he argues 'has a vital role in promoting competitive markets, encouraging long-term research and investment, and helping to equip citizens with the skills and aspirations they need in the modern economy' (Blair, 1998c, 10). The theoretical underpinning of such state intervention to combat the above market failures and 'externalities' is the 'public goods' theory of the state. This recognises that markets do sometimes fail, but nevertheless it is on markets that we must rely – or, as Blair puts it, 'competition where possible, regulation where necessary' (1998c, 1). State strategy is limited to tackling certain well-defined externalities. This predominantly supply-side outlook emphasises 'human capital' so that education and training are the key 'public goods' to be delivered.

The commitment to education and training is seen as a manifestation of economic egalitarianism, which also boosts productivity and economic growth. However, this assumption of the marriage of economic efficiency and equality is problematic. Giddens commitment to egalitarianism recognises that broadening of 'opportunity' is not enough, and that 'it is no good pretending that equality, pluralism and economic dynamism are always compatible' (Giddens, 1998, 100). The emphasis on *equality of access* to 'life chances' recalls Stuart White's 'Asset Based Egalitarianism'. Since more egalitarian market outcomes can only be secured if endowments of assets are more equal, the government's role is securing a more egalitarian redistribution of such assets (White, 1998). The implications of such asset-based egalitarianism are radical, since 'while asset-based egalitarianism may reduce the need for "old-fashioned" redistribution, it will by no means eliminate it. Redistribution of earnings must remain a central component of social democratic strategy' (White, 1998, 3). Yet how far New Labour accepts the need for greater economic equality (that is, of outcome) – with concomitant policy implications in areas such as redistribution and taxation – is questionable. Critics point to a far from convincing first term redistributive record 'the pursuit of greater equality by active redistribution of income is rejected in principle ... redistribution implies a zero-sum trade-off between the interests of rich and poor which New Labour considers misguided' (Glyn and Wood, 2001, 221).

New Labour's second term has witnessed very significant commitments to boost public spending, channelled primarily towards health and education. Spending targets are set to align more closely with continental European levels, sending the overall level of public spending once again to over 40 per cent of gross domestic product (GDP) (see Chapters 9 and 10). Whereas the first term lacked explicit commitments to redistribution (Vandenbroucke, 1998; Ludlam, 2000), New Labour's 'bolder' second term, with Brown's augmented counter-cyclical fiscal activism, has seen Blair reclaim the terminology of 'redistribution of power, wealth and opportunity to the many not the few' (Blair, 2002b). However, the targeting of health and education, the neglect of social security spending (Glyn and Wood, 2001), and the failure to reduce income inequalities (Goodman, 2001) continue to raise real questions about the redistributive credentials of a New Labour that continues to proclaim the centrality of globalisation.

Differing Social Democratic Values

D. Sassoon argues that, 'the unifying force of globalization' has affected most parties of the West European left in similar ways (Sassoon, 1998). Nevertheless, while similar pressures are currently felt by European Left parties, their responses are more varied. While the Dutch PvdA and the Finnish social democrats broadly share New Labour's outlook (Sassoon, 1996, 741–2), G. Bonoli (2003) notes that even parties whose outlook (in terms of the role of the state and waning egalitarianism) resembles New Labour's, such as the Dutch PvdA and the Portuguese PS, choose to eschew third way terminology. Furthermore, the distinction between New Labour's outlook and that of social democrats in Sweden, France and Germany is significant (notwithstanding the German party's brief dalliance with third way/Neue Mitte terminology). The Swedish SAP retains a strong egalitarian commitment: 'not an equality only of equal opportunity and chance, but also an equality in the form of a fair redistribution of wealth' (Persson, 2001). The commitment to equality remains central to the French PS (Jospin, 2002a, 2002b). Despite Labour's recent rehabilitation of 'redistribution', significant differences are clearly identifiable over the scale, scope and targets of redistribution (as testified by minimum welfare standards – see later).

There remain areas of ideological divergence, notably surrounding the analysis of global capitalism. A. Finlayson observes that Giddens 'is not convinced that capitalism has structural tendencies towards exclusion and oppression. Indeed, he does not understand contemporary society through the prism of analysis of capitalism as such' (1999, 276). The extent to which New Labour shares this benign view of the capitalist economy distinguishes them sharply from many European social democrats. The critical analysis of the inequities and inefficiencies of global capitalism which underpins French socialism (see Jospin, 1999, 2002a, 2002b) is echoed in the Swedish SAP's programme. The SAP offers sharp criticism of Anglo-Saxon capitalism, the power it affords to institutional investors, and the latter's lack of democratic accountability and imposition of damaging short-termism on economic organisation (Socialdemokratiska Arbetarepartiet, 2001). This contrasts markedly with New Labour. Similarly, the class-based analysis that runs through SAP texts, and the French PS world view, is anathema to New Labour (Clift, 2001). The German SPD's 2002 manifesto echoed Jospinian discourse regarding global capitalism, arguing 'We want to shape globalization through political means' to ensure the protection of 'solidarity', 'a strong and a cohesive social state' and the 'principles of a welfare state and of a cohesive society' (Sozialdemokratische Partei Deutschlands, 2002).

This is all a far cry from Blair's occasional hyperglobalism (Clift, 2002), which places New Labour on the opposite side of the debate over the strategic options open to social democratic governments in the global economy from the PS, the SAP, and the SPD. A significant degree of voluntarism, these parties argue, remains possible, despite constraining global forces. The Belgian social democrats' discourse on globalisation has been shaped by Frank Vandenbroucke, now a 'purple coalition' government minister. Vandenbroucke previously combined a critique of New Labour's analysis of globalisation with an optimistic take on the ability of social democratic governments to deliver 'egalitarian employment policies' in a global economy (Vandenbroucke, 1998).

We may conceptualise the ideological tension between New Labour and European social democracy as turning on the implications of globalisation for social democratic egalitarianism (and, in turn, redistribution), and for the role of state in the economy. To what extent do these emergent differences feed through into different policies? We shall examine the implications of ideological differences for macroeconomic policy, welfare policy and employment policy. In the process, we shall unearth divergent conceptions of the European social model, the labour market institutions and the appropriate minimum standards needed to underpin it.

Macroeconomic Policy

As Annesley and Gamble note in Chapter 9, Labour's macroeconomic policy approach is a pragmatic combination of monetarist ideas (particularly setting targets for inflation) and New Keynesian ideas, particularly that policy activism can improve economic performance. Ed Balls' characterisation of New Labour as 'post-monetarist' is perhaps questionable, since its macroeconomic analysis, in accepting the absence of a medium-to-long-run trade-off between unemployment and inflation, goes further than many other European social democrats would be prepared to do (Balls, 1998, 117). New Labour's macroeconomic stance nevertheless allows considerable scope for activism. Balls insists, contrary to monetarist thinking, that there is no 'natural' rate of unemployment unaffected by macroeconomic policy, and insists on 'the discretionary ability for macroeconomic policy to respond flexibly to different economic shocks – constrained of course, by the need to meet the inflation target over time' (Balls, 1998, 120).

New Labour's first term established a rules-based macroeconomic policy framework consistent with this outlook, characterised by Bank of England independence and stability, and fiscal 'golden rules'. New Labour's macroeconomic paradigm differs in some significant ways from social democratic macroeconomic frameworks in euro-member states. In monetary policy terms, the Independent Bank of England's symmetrical target for maximum and minimum rates of inflation alleviates the possible deflationary pressure of the European Central Bank's focus only on an inflation ceiling (Clift, 2002). In fiscal policy terms, non-membership of the euro offers considerable leeway in establishing public expenditure and deficit levels according to New Labour's priorities. After the first-term strictures of Conservative spending limits lapsed, Brown's Comprehensive Spending Reviews targeted rises in public expenditure. In the second term, the 2002 Spending Commitments were broadly counter-cyclical, consistent with commitments to stabilise public-sector investment at a high level.

Such fiscal activism among social democratic euro-member governments is tightly constrained by the Growth and Stability Pact. Paradoxically, more 'Keynesian' inclined social democratic governments, such as Jospin's in France, were hamstrung by the economic architecture of the euro to be more orthodox. However, the commitment to 'sound' public finances, deemed by all to be a necessary condition of economic credibility with deregulated financial markets, is common to social democrats within and outside the euro. Thus C. Green-Pedersen *et al.* (2001, 309) identify commonalities in the Dutch and Danish 'models', combining 'robust macroeconomic policy' (fixed exchange rates, sound public finances, deficit reduction – indeed even budget surplus), and low inflation. Similarly, the Swedish Social

Democrats remain committed to 'healthy finances ... public finances must maintain a surplus running equivalent to 2% of the GNP a year' (Socialdemokratiska Arbetarepartiet, 2002).

The Portuguese Socialists entered the euro successfully after four years of tight fiscal discipline. But subsequent sharp public spending increases led to a 4.1 per cent of GDP budget deficit in 2001, in clear breach of the Pact's 3 per cent limit. This triggered a severe warning from EU monetary affairs Commissioner, Pedro Solbes, and resulted in a rapid fiscal retreat, including 'structural reforms' of labour legislation and social security (*Financial Times*, 16 October 2002, 23 January 2003; Costo-lobo and Magalhaes, 2003). More dramatically, the German government breached the 3 per cent limit and in January 2003 was ordered by the Commission to reduce its deficit. France too was issued with a formal warning and instructed to make annual deficit reductions, prompting a new political crisis as the French Government responded that it would defy the Commission rather than exacerbate economic conditions by inappropriate deflation (*Financial Times*, 22 January 2003).

In February 2001, and again in February 2002, the European Commission criticised Gordon Brown, whose public investment commitments on transport, health and education were set to generate budget deficits in excess of 1 per cent of GDP until 2006–7, as profligate. Brown consistently defended his plans for investment and spending as 'prudent and cautious and fiscally sound' (*Financial Times*, 13 February 2001). With the increased fiscal activism of New Labour's second term, Brown attacked the 'over-narrow' and 'mechanistic' interpretation of the Growth and Stability Pact for taking insufficient account of the economic cycle, needs for public investment, and levels of national debt.

That the ultra-prudent Brown has been targeted demonstrates the constrictions of the ultra-orthodox Pact. More recently, Brown has found allies for his bid to reshape the Pact. Commission President, Romano Prodi, Italy's former social democratic prime minister, described the Pact's inflexible and excessively strict rules as 'stupid' in October 2002, and EU Trade Commissioner, Pascal Lamy (previously an influential member of the French Socialist Party elite), noted approvingly the UK's 'more sophisticated' and 'more intelligent' rules on public finances (*Financial Times*, 18 October 2002). Many argue that the EU has to acquire institutions ensuring a monetary and fiscal policy mix without a deflationary bias, and some look to the British model in rewriting the Pact (Lamy and Pisani-Ferry, 2002, 109–16).

Brown's bid to revise the economic architecture is thus comparable to the French socialists' more ambitious plans to establish an 'economic government' (Jospin, 2002a, 17). However, significant macroeconomic disagreements endure, notably over tax harmonisation. The Party of European

Socialists' Busquin working group called for harmonisation of tax policy at the European level, and Jospin reiterated these calls at the Nice Summit in December 2000. Jospin's ambition was a 'levelling up' to end 'unfair' tax competition, as part of a wider strategy to entrench a fiscally active and welfare-protected European social model. New Labour rejected this, and, ahead of the 1999 Cologne Summit, aligned with the right-wing Spanish Government in the Council of Ministers, perceiving harmonisation of corporate taxes as a threat to competitiveness (Aust, 2003). Jospin's reaffirmation in 2001 of his aspirations for tax harmonisation (Jospin, 2002a, 17, 24) was met by thinly veiled disdain from New Labour, illustrating differences (discussed below) over the future shape of the European social model, and the role and scope of taxation within it.

Macroeconomic Policy and Employment: Keynesians and Supply-siders

French socialist successes between 1997 and 2001 meant that full employment re-entered their discourse, and led them to emphasise an active, interventionist role for the social democratic state in reducing unemployment (Pisani-Ferry, 2000a). In this they are similar to the Swedish SAP (Socialdemokratizka Arbetareparti, 2001, 2002) and, while their recent employment record is less creditable, to the German SPD (Sozialdemokratische Partei Deutschlands, 2002). New Labour is now committed unambiguously to full employment (Brown, 1999), but differs over the means to achieve it, notably in the role of the private sector, of macroeconomic policy, and of labour market deregulation in promoting employment.

For New Labour, employment creation is a supply-side issue (Balls 1998, 113; Brown, 1999). Macroeconomic policy should provide a stable framework because, as J. Westergaard notes (1999, 430), New Labour assumes that 'supply side measures more or less on their own will prove enough to provide full work opportunities for all able to take them up'. This supply-side focus is shared by some other European social democrats, notably the Austrian SPO.

Some Keynesian economists criticise New Labour's stance, arguing that insufficient attention is paid to the roles that fiscal and monetary policy play in managing demand (Grieve Smith, 2001, 19–22). P. Arestis and M. Sawyer note the neo-classical aspects of New Labour's political economy, 'Say's Law holds, namely that the level of effective demand does not play an independent role in the (long-run) determination of the level of economic activity and adjusts to underpin the supply-side determined level of economic activity' (Arestis and Sawyer, 2001, 259). The relationship between inflation and unemployment, and the Non-Accelerating Inflation Rate of Unemployment (NAIRU) can be understood in different ways (Corry and Holtham, 1995, 15). New Labour's conceptualisation of the NAIRU is primarily as a labour market phenomenon, and 'this focus on the NAIRU has led to a range of policies to increase "employability", but with very few policies to increase the level and distribution of productive capacity or to ensure high levels of demand' (Arestis and Sawyer, 2001, 268). This view contrasts with the way the NAIRU was approached by the Jospin Government, for example, whose analytical framework envisaged more scope for active macro-policy (Pisani-Ferry, 2000a, 2000b, 21; Muet, 2000).

In Germany, O. Lafontaine was a convinced Keynesian who strongly prioritised demand-side macroeconomic activism at both national and supranational (EU) level (Lafontaine, 1998, 79). In the wake of his departure, the Blair/Schroeder joint statement signalled a shift in the economic analysis underpinning German social democracy (Arestis and Sawyer, 2001, 255). B. Hombach, closely associated with the German 'third way' flirtation, prioritised 'a supply-side economics of the left' (2000, 104–21), dismissively observing, 'most people have long since turned away from the idea of Keynesian panaceas that will work overnight' (2000, 103).

However, the German social democrats have subsequently rediscovered the distinctly Keynesian flavour to their analysis of the role of macroeconomic policy in achieving full employment, and attach analytical significance to demand-side measures as a necessary corollary of a supply-side agenda. The 2002 manifesto pledged to continue the 1998–2002 macroeconomic approach to employment, characterised as 'a prudent combination of supply and demand policy, which will put more money into workers' pockets', and 'consolidate Germany's economic strength with public investment in infrastructure' (Sozialdemokratizche Partei Deutschlands, 2002).

This difference of approach to macroeconomic policy was demonstrated eloquently in the elaboration of a European Employment Pact. Jospin was committed to ambitious 'Euro-Keynesian' co-ordinated action, combining interest rate cuts with large-scale public investment in infrastructural programmes to boost demand and reduce unemployment. The centrepiece was a multi-billion-pound development loan raised on Europe's financial markets. Schroeder, too, endorsed this 'European jobs pact' (Dyson, 1999, 203–4). Subsequently, the Social Democratic Party in the European Parliament elaborated a European Employment Pact, setting out how macroeconomic polices could deliver full employment within the EMU (PES, 1999). New Labour joined the right-wing Spanish Government in intergovernmental negotiations, prioritising flexibility, liberalisation and 'modernisation' of the welfare systems. As a result, the macroeconomic dimensions of a European employment strategy were not even mentioned in the Council of Ministers' deliberations (Aust, 2003). Unlike those of the French, German and Finnish Governments, the Blair Government's papers submitted in preparation for the 2001 Stockholm EU Summit did not mention macroeconomic policy at all (*Financial Times*, 22 February 2001).

Employment-centred Social Policy

In contrast to macroeconomic divergences in social policy reform, Blair has identified a European consensus on 'a social policy which seeks to encourage more and better jobs for all' (Blair, 2002a). The 2002 Barcelona European Council illustrated commonality in the social policy agenda among European social democrats (and others), furnishing EU-wide accords prioritising fiscal reform to reduce the burden on low-wage earners, and tax benefit systems reform to make work pay and remove disincentives to work.

Yet the common commitment to what R. Haveman terms 'employment-centred social policy' (Haveman, 1997) should not be conceived as a convergence on New Labour's approach. Indeed, the Portuguese socialists began to offer social security exemptions and state aid to hiring firms and business start-ups in 1995, pre-dating both New Labour's victory and talk of a third way (Costo-lobo and Magalhaes, 2003). The Swedish model has long been an 'active' welfare model, encouraging labour-force participation through retraining at least since the 1950s (Ryner, 2000, 341). Current tax system reforms in Sweden 'provide incentives to work ... [and] continue to improve conditions primarily for wage earners and small business ... directed at low and medium income earners' (Socialdemokratiska Arbetarepartiet, 2002).

The aim of 'employment-centred social policy' is 'to get social policy and labour markets working in tandem', protecting the poorest and creating jobs without undermining incentives to work. This fiscal approach has both supply- and demand-side dimensions, both reducing the 'cost' of (especially non-qualified) work for employers through financial incentives and social security contribution reductions, and 'in-work benefits', subsidies and tax cuts lightening the load on lower salaries, making work pay (Haveman, 1997, 35–9).

This approach is the inspiration behind New Labour's Working Family Tax Credit. Green-Pedersen *et al.* (2001, 309) identify 'employment-friendly and efficient tax and social policy' as a core feature of the Dutch and Danish 'models'. This has also been the rationale behind fiscal reform in Belgium, both 'making work pay' and bringing the older unemployed back into the labour market (Hoop, 2003). Similarly, Schroeder introduced state subsidies for low-earning workers, and the long-term unemployed and

welfare recipients receive financial incentives to take low-paid employment. The 2002 manifesto pledged to expand such social policy measures
(Sozialdemokratische Partei Deutschlands, 2002).

Employer hiring incentives form part of the French 35-hour week and the
Prime pour l'emploi (PPE). The French socialists progressively exempted
(lower) salaries from the *taxe professionnelle*, and introduced the PPE, a
benefit of on average of 144 euros, designed both to 'aid return to work' and
to 'make work pay', and which benefited an estimated 8.1 million households in 2001 (Ministère des Finances, 2001, 9, 24–5). Yet despite such
social policy similarities, profound differences remain regarding the future
shape of the European Social Model.

New Labour and the European Social Model

Two distinctive characteristics of recent New Labour thinking have been
critical suspicion about this European Social Model (and the social and
labour market institutions underpinning it) and an increasingly ebullient
advocacy of the Anglo-Saxon model. The problem, as D. Soskice has noted,
is that 'models' of capitalism are an *ensemble*, 'institutionally interlocked'
in local contexts from which their transplantation is seldom successful
(Soskice, 1997, 220). Deregulated and flexible labour markets are, New
Labour argues, necessary conditions of international competitiveness. Thus
New Labour is prepared to 'commit' to the European social model only
under certain exacting conditions. Most notably, it needs to 'modernise',
and the conceptions of minimum welfare standards and labour market
regulation need to change quite markedly along more Anglo-Saxon lines in
order to tackle disincentives to work and reduce the strain on firms.

Blair posits a dichotomy between 'moving people off benefit into work'
and 'heavy-handed regulation', identifying the former as 'the British
approach and increasingly the European one' (Blair, 2002c). Dovetailing
with this analysis are assumptions about the kind of welfare state compatible with globalisation. New Labour insists on 'minimum standards for pay
and conditions at work' (Blair, 1998c, 11), and Blair proudly defends his
Government's record guaranteeing 'fair rights at work' and 'a national minimum wage' (Blair, 2002b). However, this reveals New Labour's conception
of the 'ceilings' 'imposed' by the demands of international competitiveness.
The levels of regulation, minimum wage and social transfers involved are
very considerably lower than in many other European welfare states,
notably France, Germany and the Scandinavian countries.

The degree to which Blair's conception of the appropriate shape of the
European Social Model in a global age differs from his European social

democratic counterparts is demonstrated by his allegiances forged in preparation for European Council meetings. Blair has identified Conservative Spanish Prime Minister Aznar as a kindred spirit, sharing his understanding of the appropriate direction and pace of economic and labour market reform. The two worked closely together ahead of the crucial 2000 Lisbon European Council, where Blair criticised sharply the labour market and employment policies of France and Germany, and which established a ten-year agenda for liberalising economic reform across Europe (*Financial Times*, 18, 20 March, 2000).

At the 2002 Barcelona European Council, Blair and Aznar welcomed Berlusconi into their alliance against social democratic governments in France and Germany. A joint Blair/Berlusconi statement identified the 'overriding objective' of creating more flexible labour markets, and reviewing 'existing labour market regulation at both EU and national level to ensure that it takes account of both the business need for flexibility and the employee's need for job security and employability'. The assumption underpinning the statement that essential minimum labour standards had been achieved across the EU was criticised as being 'astonishingly complacent' by the Trades Union Congress (TUC) (*Financial Times*, 1 March 2002). The axis, cemented together by a common vision of liberalising reform of the European employment protection laws and Europe's social model, was described as 'bloody stupid' by TUC chief, John Monks (*Guardian*, 18 March 2002).

After the Barcelona European Council, a draft EU directive under Maastricht's social chapter – advocated by French, Belgian and German ministries in particular – sought to deliver enhanced employment rights to agency workers and staff made redundant by big corporations. The three-way alliance between the UK, Spain and Italy sought to block these proposals. This initiative giving temporary and agency staff the right, after a six-week qualifying period, to the same pay as permanent employees doing the same work was characterised by the EU labour and social affairs commissioner, as a 'basic minimum of protection across the EU', rejecting the notion that 'employers can benefit from the flexibility of staff and at the same time pay them less' (*Guardian*, 21 March 2002). Clearly, New Labour's conception of what constitutes 'basic minimum protection' is less encompassing.

New Labour's second term has seen an attempt to shift the balance between individual workers' rights and labour market flexibility underpinning the European social model decisively in favour of the latter. The New Labour Government have been very sympathetic to the UK business lobby's trenchant opposition to *any* further European directives, be they about consultation, workers rights, or justification of lay-offs. Industry Minister,

Patricia Hewitt, sought to extend the qualification period (before agency workers enjoyed social protection) from six weeks to at least eighteen months.

However, what New Labour interprets as heavy-handed regulation is, to many other social democrats, a core feature of the employment protection of the European Social Model. Indeed, John Monks noted in his angry reaction to the Blair/Berlusconi joint statement, that Blair is further to the right on labour market issues than most Christian Democrats in Europe (*Guardian*, 15 March 2002). Blair's approach contrasts starkly with Jospin's, whose instrumental role in establishing European employment strategy, and the National Action Plans for employment, was part of a wider agenda. This involved aspirations for binding commitments to create twelve million jobs in Europe in five years, and EU-level regulation of employment policy, including mandatory commission approval of industrial redundancies and closures (Clift, 2003).

The Swedish model also remains predicated on a regulated labour market, and flexiblising reforms have taken place within clear limits. The Swedish SAP's 2002 manifesto committed the party to improve the security of those in casual employment, and increase the say of employees over planning working time. 'Labour law,' they argue, 'must be developed and not dismantled. In the case of redundancies, the rules must be objective and leave no room for willfulness' (Socialdemokratiska Arbetarepartiet, 2002).

Similarly, the German SPD's 2002 manifesto, which sought to enhance co-determination and protection against wrongful dismissal, criticised CSU candidate Stoiber's deregulation plans as attacks on 'fundamental workers rights' and the core principles of the German social model (Sozialdemokratische Partei Deutschlands, 2002). Despite the superficial commonality of approach in the Blair/Schroeder third way/Neue Mitte statement, Schroeder's first term was not characterised by a marked deregulation of the labour market (*Financial Times*, 8 March 2001). The SPD are less than convinced that flexibility is a necessary condition of international competitiveness in the new global economy. Indeed, Schroeder stated in July 2001, 'we don't want an American-style labour market because we believe a higher level of (job) security and certainty is a right' (*Financial Times*, 13 July 2001).

Thus, while there is a common logic underpinning 'employment-centred social policy' reforms, all seeking to make social policy operate more effectively as a springboard to employment, and to ensure that the taxation system and labour market work 'in tandem', these commonalities of rationale must be situated in very widely differing labour markets, ensuring widely divergent minimum standards, and regulated to very different degrees. Identifying a common direction (towards a more flexible labour market), fails to specify the widely divergent starting points (from much more regulated labour markets than the British pattern), which will probably lead to very different outcomes. Each move to greater flexibility must be placed in a national context, in terms of both levels of labour market regulation and degrees of ideological commitment to further flexibility (see Hay, 2002).

Welfare and Social Minima

At the 2000 Lisbon Summit, Blair emphasised reforming welfare systems 'so they become springboards for employment rather than safety nets' (*Financial Times*, 20 March 2000). However, this is regarded as a false dichotomy by other European social democrats, who may want welfare systems to become 'springboards', but not to cease to be 'safety nets'. They may concur with the Lisbon presidency conclusions that 'the best safeguard against social exclusion is a job', but not that it is or can be a sufficient safeguard on its own. New Labour's conception of the (relatively low) minimum standards necessitated by the global economy is not shared by other social democrats, whose experience is not consistent with New Labour's analysis.

Sweden's 'active' welfare reform, promoting labour force participation, as noted by Annesley and Gamble in Chapter 9, shares some characteristics with New Labour's welfare to work agenda. Persson, like Blair, emphasises the need for 'active and dynamic welfare states', and for European countries to 'step up efforts to reform their welfare systems to promote labour force participation while safeguarding and enshrining the concept of solidarity in our social model' (*Financial Times*, 14 January 2002). However, the meaning of 'solidarity' in a Swedish context is fleshed out if one examines the Swedish social democrats' recent electoral manifesto and campaign.

The Swedish social democrats' successful 2002 re-election campaign began with a commitment to a £1 billion boost in welfare spending, in preference to the tax cuts advocated by the Conservative Moderate opposition, presented explicitly as a reaffirmation of the 'Swedish Model' (*Financial Times*, 20 August 2002). The manifesto pledged new resources to 'increase security and justice ... We want to see a Sweden with full employment where income gaps shrink ... Welfare policies must cover everyone, must be financed in a spirit of solidarity via taxation and be distributed according to people's needs' (Socialdemokratiska Arbetarepartiet, 2002). Given Sweden's 90 per cent unionisation levels, and unemployment benefit replacement rates at 80 per cent of previous income (Vartiainen, 1998, 23), the concept of 'solidarity' here has a very different meaning, and the idea of appropriate levels of social minima are correspondingly more generous.

New Labour's understanding of the implications of the global economic context for welfare provision is not borne out by the evidence. Claims that globalisation of trade and finance 'rule out' social democracy by driving all societies and economies towards a residual, minimalist, liberal model of labour market governance and social protection are without empirical foundation in cross-national quantitative analysis of government expenditure and deficit levels. D. Swank's analysis finds no evidence that increased capital mobility is 'systematically associated ... with retrenchment in social welfare provision'. Thus 'internationalization has not resulted in large, systematic rollbacks of social welfare effort' (Swank, 2002, 89).

C. Pierson, too, highlights the *success* of advanced welfare states in maintaining income and protecting the most vulnerable from a shift to indirect taxes. But for all the talk of retrenchment, government spending, funded in large part by corporations, still creeps up. Welfare states remain crucial sources of income and well-being for millions, and the principal mechanism for redistributing wealth and opportunities (Pierson, 2001, 86–9). Welfare state retrenchment in the UK since the late 1970s is the exception, and not the rule. E. Huber and J. Stephens argue that, 'not only have the cuts in entitlements and service in all but a few cases [notably the UK and New Zealand] been modest, the achievements of the welfare state in terms of income equalization and poverty reduction have largely been preserved' (Huber and Stephens, 2001, 306).

Indeed, the different types of welfare regime remain *very* distinctive and clearly discernable, not least because overall tax revenues and levels of public spending have seen little or no decline in the last twenty-five years (Swank, 2002). A. Glyn notes that, as a result of different welfare state trajectories, 'differences between the most and least egalitarian OECD countries have been and remain huge ... unexciting sounding differences in Gini coefficients measuring income inequality mask really enormous differences in distributive patterns' (2001b, 6).

Employment Policy: Public-Sector Job Creation and Working Week Reductions

Many social democrats continue to insist upon the role of public sector job creation in tackling unemployment. New Labour's active labour market policy is distinctive in the degree of emphasis on the private sector, both in the provision of training, and as the site of all employment creation associated with the New Deal. Furthermore, there is a conspicuous lack of 'state involvement in employment creation in areas where high unemployment and low skills are concentrated' (Huber and Stephens, 2001, 308).

In Denmark, the Netherlands and Sweden expansion of permanent public-sector employment for low-skilled groups became a means by which social democrats sought to achieve full employment in the absence of private-sector employment growth (Iversen, 2001, 259–61). The French socialists also favoured the state's role as employer. Their *Plan Aubry* pledged to create 350,000 public-sector jobs, matched by 350,000 new private-sector posts. By March 2001, 274,900 public-sector jobs had been created, and a further 25,000 *emplois-jeunes* were created in 2001 (see Clift, 2002, 2003). In Germany, the 'JUMP' youth employment and training programme involves a more preponderant role for the state, particularly in East Germany, in creating 100,000 jobs for young people after they have completed their initial training (Sozialdemokratische Partei Deutschlands, 2002).

Another continental approach to interventionist employment policy is a state-orchestrated reduction of the working week. Jospin Government's implementation of the 35-hour working week proved to be successful (Clift, 2003). German Social Democrats have emulated the initiative, and even the Belgian 'purple coalition' Government, using employer incentives copied from the French, pledged a 38-hour week by 2003 (Hoop, 2003). In contrast, New Labour has been so unwilling to enforce even the 48-hour week working time directive that, in April 2002, the trade union Amicus enlisted the European Commission's support in investigating inadequate enforcement, with the possibility of a European Court of Justice hearing.

Conclusion

New Labour's calls for a reshaping of the European social model along more flexible, and less generous lines is difficult to reconcile with regulated continental labour markets securing higher minimum standards. Furthermore, many European social democrats are unconvinced of the need for such radical reform, not least because the empirical basis of such an approach is very dubious. The simplistic assumptions about higher unemployment associated with more regulated labour markets are exposed as myths by recent research, which offers little evidence of continental labour market institutions increasing aggregate unemployment levels (see for example, Nickell *et al.*, 2001). Similarly, arguments that generous welfare states are incompatible with the new global economy are confounded by the evidence (Huber and Stephens, 2001; Swank, 2002).

Thus deeply embedded national specificities, preventing the import of foreign labour and social market models, are not the only explanation for tepid responses to Blair's call for liberalising reform of the European social model. At the intellectual level, there is also a rejection of some New Labour assumptions, a less thorough-going commitment to deregulation, and an attachment to higher levels of regulation and social transfers than

New Labour chooses to recognise as viable. There appear to be emergent differences at the level of ends between New Labour and other European social democratic parties, notably the absence of firm egalitarian commitments within New Labour, and their acceptance of lower levels of employment security.

European social democratic parties are, however, more similar now than at any time in the twentieth century. In some policy areas, the degree of similarity is remarkable, such as calls for 'employment-centred social policy'. All social democratic parties also accept (more or less grudgingly) the discipline of the new economic orthodoxy enshrined in the euro's economic architecture, and pursue a stability-centred policy aimed at securing 'sound' public finances. Similarly, New Labour's desire to reform the Growth and Stability Pact to generate more 'room to manoeuvre' and a less deflationary policy mix also reflects a wider European social democratic agenda.

Yet the importance of the national context to each formation engenders enduring and significant differences between these 'sister' parties, in terms of both national institutional settings and intellectual aspirations. As a result, there is little to suggest the European Social Model is evolving in a manner that New Labour would like, even if the rhetoric might hint otherwise. Underlying these differences are different conceptions of the implications of globalisation for social democratic commitments to egalitarianism and the role of the state in securing full employment. For example, despite commonalities in macroeconomic policy, some European social democrats place more emphasis on the potential role for Keynesian demand-side macroeconomic policies, at both the national and European levels. New Labour's scepticism towards 'Euro-Keynesianism', macroeconomic co-ordination, tax harmonisation and demand activism is at odds with French and German conceptions of a European jobs pact to promote growth and employment. Furthermore, New Labour's active labour market policies differ from its continental counterparts in eschewing public-sector job creation, or any preponderant role for the state.

The erratic electoral fortunes of European social democrats has led in some cases to periods of post-defeat ideological flux, and to a sharpened need for post-success programmatic clarification in others. New Labour's second landslide marks them out as a success story, but the policy paradigm, and the analysis of capitalism that underpins it, are by no means as universally admired as New Labour's electoral record. Other successful parties, such as the Swedes and Germans, have combined (more equivocal) electoral success with more generous social and labour market policies. This presents significant obstacles to New Labour's desire to reinvent European social democracy, and the European Social Model in its own image.

4

The Control Freaks? New Labour and the Party

ERIC SHAW

Introduction

Throughout the 1970s and 1980s Labour was plagued by severe internal dissension culminating in the breakaway of part of the right and the formation of the Social Democratic Party in 1981, and in a veritable civil war into which the rest of the party plunged. Left and right were split over a host of issues – policy, strategy and organisation – and the tight control that the leadership had once exercised crumbled. These divisions were exploited remorselessly by a largely hostile media, and the public was left with an enduring impression of a party perennially at war with itself. Party management was, in fact, tightened greatly under Neil Kinnock, its leader from 1983 to 1992, and by the 1990s the party was presenting a much more united and disciplined face to the electorate (Shaw, 1994). But would the strife that had engulfed the previous Labour Government recur if the Party again held office?

This problem troubled Tony Blair and his fellow 'modernisers' gravely after Blair's election to the leadership in 1994. They were determined to introduce changes in the Party's organisational structure to ensure that any future Labour Government would not be as embarrassed by internal strife as its predecessors had been in the 1960s and 1970s. This was part of a wider project to convince the public that New Labour was veritably a new party, free of all such voter-alienating features of old Labour. Policy was revamped on a range of key issues. Symbolically, in 1995, Clause 4 of the constitution, which had committed Labour to the extension of public ownership, was replaced by a new anodyne formula. And a series of wide-ranging reforms were introduced in the Party's institutional arrangements.

Peter Mandelson, Blair's senior adviser, avowed that 'the fact that the party is running itself in radically different ways now' constituted 'the most

52

fundamental evidence for the existence of a "literally new Labour party"'. The new structures would ensure that 'the party's mass, grass-roots membership, rather than unrepresentative groups of activists, has the greatest say in the agreement of policies and the election of its leaders' by devolving more power to the constituency rank and file (Mandelson, 2002, 216, 215). The Party would be equipped with a new policy machinery, giving members unprecedented opportunities 'to get involved in the party processes and debates, widening their rights to engage in policy development through a more deliberative and extended procedure, without detracting from the sovereign powers of annual conference' (Labour Party NEC, 1997). Yet New Labour attracted heavy criticism of its allegedly heavy-handed management of the party's internal life. Thus, P. Mair has claimed that dissent is stifled systematically by 'marginalising representative procedures inside the party, introducing plebiscitarian techniques, going over the heads of the party conference and the activist layer in favour of widespread membership ballots'; as well as by seeking to influence the selection of candidates to the European Parliament and the new elected bodies in Wales, Scotland and London (Mair, 2000, 177).

All political parties which lay claim to being democratic have to strike a series of balances: between participation and accountability, on the one hand, and firm and effective leadership on the other; between the need to preserve internal order and cohesion, on the one hand, and safeguard the rights of minorities and the freedom to dissent, on the other. How have these balances been struck by New Labour? The conventional view is that the emergence of the 'electoral-professional party, defined by the professionalisation of all party operations' will lead to a looser and more lenient management of the mass membership (Panebianco, 1988). To what extent does the New Labour case substantiate this?

Because of the limits of space, this chapter will focus on two issues. First, we review the workings of the new policy-making system laid down in the 1997 document *Partnership in Power* (Labour Party NEC, 1997), and consider how far it has opened out the Party to broader membership involvement. Second, we appraise the role played by the leadership in internal Party elections, concentrating on two highly publicised episodes, the selection of the Party leader in Wales, and the London mayoral candidate.

Partnership in Power in Action

P. Seyd (2001) has described the introduction of Labour's new policy-making system. Here we shall summarise briefly its main elements. Before the changes, the National Executive Committee (NEC) formulated policy statements and managed policy-making between the annual conferences to which it, the unions and local parties submitted motions. Now, at the hub lies the twice-yearly National Policy Forum (NPF), charged with oversee- ing the development of a comprehensive policy programme, the basis of the manifesto. To ensure that the decisions reached by the Forum reflect 'the priorities and views of the party of a whole' its membership (175 in total, 72 to be women) is designed to represent all 'stakeholders'. Party policy is reviewed systematically via a rolling programme, with each major policy statement taking two years to formulate. Standing Policy Commissions, each covering a major area of policy, carry out the detailed elaboration of policy. With nine members, three each from the government, the NEC and the NPF itself, they prepare reports for the NPF. The Joint Policy Committee (JPC) exercises the strategic oversight previously the preserve of the elected NEC. Chaired by the prime minister, the JPC includes equal numbers from the government and non-government members of the NEC.

Policy-making is divided into two stages. In the first year, drafts approved by the NPF are circulated for comment throughout the party and affiliated organisations, and to a wide range of voluntary organisations outside the Party. The first stage aims to set 'the agenda for the second year, identifying key issues and priorities and reflecting on currents of opinions inside and outside the party' (Labour Party, 1997). The second allows for more detailed discussion, consultation and refinement of policy. The NPF and JPC redraft the reports and submit them to the Party's Annual Conference. As the sovereign policy and decision-making body of the Party, Conference ratification finally makes the NPF policy statements official.

According to Robin Cook, NPF chairman until 2002, Labour 'is setting the pace with our way of making policy through the NPF and local policy forums. Parties on the European left are looking with great interest at our model. They have noted that the policy forums encourage participation, high-quality dis- cussion and robust policy' (Cook, 2001b). Has this claim been borne out? For purposes of exposition – drawing upon Easton's systems analysis – we visu- alise Labour's policy process as a micro-political system, a series of stages, or screening devices, into which inputs in the form of wants and demands are fed, and out of which an output, or decision of some sort, materialises.

From Wants to Demands

Easton distinguishes between 'wants' and 'demands' (Easton, 1965, 70–1). The former are the raw materials of the political process and, as we use the term, represent the desires, preferences and aspirations of the various Party stakeholders, while the latter are those wants that formally enter the policy-making process. To succeed, a want must navigate a series of 'gateways', operated by 'gatekeepers', which constitute 'structural points in the system ... regulating the flow along the demand channels' (Easton, 1965, 88).

New Labour claims that the new machinery considerably multiplies opportunities for membership participation in policy development. Most notably:

- All-member local policy forums are convened to discuss policy, and summaries of their conclusions dispatched to the Policy Commissions.
- All party units have the right to present submissions and propose amendments to the seven standing Policy Commissions.
- Many party members belong to affiliated organisations such as the Socialist Health Association and the Socialist Education Association – as well as bodies not formally affiliated, such as the Campaign for State Education – and these too can tender recommendations.

How effective are these mechanisms? To what extent have members been able to place their wants effectively on to the policy agenda as demands and have them debated seriously? Here we must investigate the role performed by the 'gatekeepers', who sift through the mass of 'raw material' and decide what will be processed, organise and monitor local policy forums, write summaries and convey them to head office, and scrutinise and compile reports from constituency and other submissions to Policy Commissions. For the most part, these gatekeepers are Party officials accountable to Labour's general secretary and (*de facto*) ultimately to the Party leadership in the government. The extent to which wants are converted into demands is largely a function of the political weight, organisational significance and expertise of the bodies submitting evidence. For example, constituency party wants are far less likely to make progress, particularly if they are at odds with existing policy, than those articulated by large affiliated unions. Furthermore, wants and demands enter into a framework of discourse that is largely shaped by existing government policy. Rank-and-file representatives who query this discourse are at a major and systematic disadvantage, as they lack independent access to information and expertise, and so are ill-equipped to resist recommendations hammered out by an immensely-sophisticated government machine.

Demand Progression

How does the leadership handle well-supported demands that contradict the established policy framework? Here, New Labour's 'gatekeeping' processes merit careful inspection. The NEC is empowered to devise the regulations, standing orders and operating procedures which determine how Party institutions operate. In defining the circumstances in which 'alternative proposals' could be considered, the following rules now operate:

- To qualify as amendments to be tabled at the NPF (and possibly become minority reports to the Conference), resolutions must enlist the support of at least eight of its 175 members.
- An amendment could be ruled out of order on the grounds that it would be discussed more appropriately in the context of a report other than the one to which it referred, or if it concerned an issue which had already been addressed in the rolling policy process.
- Amendments could also be refused on the grounds that they were inconsistent with existing or planned Labour Government legislation.
- For an amendment to be accepted for submission to the Conference as a 'minority position' it requires the support of 25 per cent of the NPF membership or 35 delegates (whichever was the greater), and backing from at least three of the seven groups represented on the forum: constituency parties, trade unions, regions, MPs, European MPs, councillors, socialist societies, the government, and the NEC.

These provisions equipped party 'gatekeepers' with many managerial tools to control the flow of demands, smothering or deflecting, if they so chose, items that might cause embarrassment if allowed to intrude on to the Conference agenda. Initially, the 'gatekeepers' set about their task with such alacrity that at the 1999 Conference no amendment qualified as a 'minority position', leaving delegates with the option of either accepting the official reports or rejecting them *in toto*, a drastic step few would wish to take because it would unravel years of work and generate considerable negative publicity. Subsequently, as protests over 'control freakery' mounted, some modest easing took place. Thus the following year, thirty-seven NPF resolutions (winnowed from hundreds initially submitted) were granted the status of 'amendments' and fully debated. These included controversial ones opposing the government's stance on performance-related pay for teachers, the part-privatisation of the London Underground, and freedom of information; and calling for the phasing out of the upper National Insurance earnings limit, and the renationalisation of the rail network. But none of these cleared the steep hurdles necessary to proceed further, and were either rejected or remitted to workshops and thereby effectively lost to sight. Seven amendments reached the 2000 Conference, but none raised issues that threatened embarrassment to the government (*Tribune*, 30 June 2000; *Guardian*, 7 July 2000; *Independent*, 6 July 2000). With the important exception of issues raised by the unions (see below), the bulk of matters that could be deemed as challenging government policy were stifled or sidetracked in the NPF process. In short, to a substantial degree, the new policy machinery has domesticated Labour's policy agenda.

But here we must qualify our account. So far, we have only considered the role of constituency representatives. But what of the unions? The fundamental distinction between the two is that the latter are *institutions in their own right*, with constitutional prerogatives which they have *the capacity* to operationalise. As wielders, still, of a considerable number of NPF and Conference votes they can affect outcomes in a way that eludes individual constituency delegates. They have their own (albeit modest) research staffs, press officers and progress-chasers. But, above all, they are major players in the political arena, possessing power resources independent of their constitutional position within the Party, with direct channels of communication to the government and able, with relative ease, to co-ordinate their activities. At every stage of the NPF process, John Edmonds, leader of the General and Municipal Workers Union (GMB), commented, 'a very robust trade union network regularly concerted its tactics and worked in a resolute fashion to ensure that outcomes amounted to something we could tolerate' (John Edmonds, Speech at Labour Reform Conference on 'Parties and Democracy', London, 1999; author's notes). Thus the unions have the ability to ensure that their wants will be registered automatically as demands and that these will then progress through the various demand channels. When unions are engaged, real negotiations over tangible matters of importance then occur. And if a satisfactory outcome cannot be achieved, the unions can bring the matter to the Conference for further debate. Critical union objections, as the left-wing former NEC member, Liz Davies, recorded, tended to disconcert Millbank far more than those emanating from constituency representatives, though – she adds immediately – such objections were muted, and 'rarely translated into votes or any follow-up action' (Davies, 2000, 174–5).

From Demands to Outputs

In the past, the preliminary conference agenda was generated by the activity of constituency parties and, more formidably, by the unions in the run-up to the annual event. Under the new system, the bulk of its agenda is pre-set and consists of NPF reports. However, there are two exceptions: Contemporary Issue Motions (CIMs), and emergency resolutions. The former entitles all constituency parties and affiliated organisations to submit one resolution on a topic not 'substantively addressed' in the reports to Conference. Only four CIMs may be placed on the Conference timetable.

Emergency resolutions can be submitted if they cover a matter of real urgency which has surfaced in the immediate run-up to the Conference. In practical terms, such motions, if they raise matters of real significance and are critical of the leadership, will only figure on the agenda if backed by the majority of the larger unions.

In fact, affiliated unions much prefer to iron out their disagreements with the government behind closed doors. Union leaders will only push them on to the Conference agenda if they feel that negotiations have reached an impasse. There have been only two examples of this in recent years: the issues of pensions in 2000 and the Private Finance Initiative (PFI) in 2002. In the former case, unions called for the restoration of the link between rises in the basic state pension and real wages (abolished by Mrs Thatcher); in the second, they demanded an independent investigation into the use of PFI for financing public capital projects. The PFI involves consortia of private companies building and owning new hospitals and schools, and running their non-core services, which are then rented or purchased by public authorities. The unions contend that PFI will be far more costly in the long run, that its 'efficiency savings' will largely be at the cost of wages and working conditions, and that it amounts to 'creeping privatisation' (Shaw, 2003).

Critical motions were passed in both cases, the only two instances of leadership defeats since Blair's election in 1994, representing rare instances of issues of a fundamental character being aired thoroughly in lively Conference debates. In both cases, the government shrugged off the defeats. Thus, over the pensions issue, Gordon Brown insisted that it was 'for the country to judge ... not for a few composite motions to decide the policy of this government and this country. It is for the whole community, and I'm listening to the whole community' (*Guardian*, 28 September 2000). The government responded in precisely the same way to its 2002 defeat over PFI.

The new policy machinery has armed Labour's leaders with a firm grip over the whole policy-making process. No proposal that is at odds with leadership wishes on a significant matter of policy normally has any prospect of navigating its various gateways. The Conference has virtually been divested of its policy-making power, and the effect on policy of the odd critical motion is, as we have seen, negligible. Notwithstanding, New Labour devotes unprecedented energy to Conference management. Why is this? The principal reason is to preserve and enhance the Conference's prime function as a showcase to the nation. The accent on meticulous management reflects the 'communications imperative', the relentless struggle to 'influence and control popular perceptions of key political events and issues through the mass media' (Blumler, 1990, 103). This means seizing every opportunity to project key messages, placing the best spin possible on significant stories, exploiting those precious minutes on the TV news bulletins that the conference season makes available, and trying to keep damaging items away from the public. To achieve this, tight control over the Conference is deemed to be essential. This we shall now explore briefly.

According to *Partnership in Power*, while 'in the past, policy statements have been presented to Conference on an-all-or-nothing basis, under the rolling programme Conference would for the first time be able to have separate votes on key sections and proposals in the policy statement'. However, any attempt to invoke this right by referring back sections of NPF reports have been blocked on procedural grounds. The bulk of Conference business is now transacted with little dissent, and the high-spots are the big set-piece occasions, the oratorical displays of the prime minister, the chancellor and (to a lesser extent) other ministers. All this reflects the extent to which the function of the Conference has been transformed. Its prime purpose is to act as the leadership's window to the electorate, providing a series of photo-opportunities, soundbites and spectacles designed to attract and impress a television audience. Thus the timetabling is so organised as to ensure maximum television coverage for speeches by the prime minister and other senior leaders.

According to *Partnership in Power*, the Conference Arrangements Committee 'would be expected to make a substantial amount of time' available for debates. In fact, debates are now dominated by the platform to a quite unprecedented degree. The leadership has four bites of the cherry. A minister introduces the debate in a major set-piece speech, the mover and seconder of the NPF report then speak and, finally, the NEC has the right to wind-up the debate. As the leadership dominates both the NEC and the NPF, all four speak with the same voice. In the past, rules confined the right to speak from the platform (and therefore to speak at much greater length) to members of the NEC. In 1991 it was extended to frontbenchers and, since 1997, to a new category best defined as government cheerleaders. Further, much of the Conference's scarce time is now taken up by question-and-answer sessions and policy seminars, thus restricting the time left for genuine policy debate.

Some 'unofficial predetermination of speakers' called from the floor at the Party Conference has always happened (Minkin, 1978, 220), but now it appears to be much more methodical. A 'Delegate Support Office' and a regional network of officials vet requests from delegates to speak. A list of preferred speakers is then compiled, and at each conference session the chair is provided with guidance notes setting down their names, a plan locating them in the auditorium, and additional means of recognising them. As a result, speakers from the floor are – in sharp contrast to the past – more likely to lavish congratulations on the government than to criticise it. During the 2002 PFI debate, not only did all Constituency Labour Party (CLP) delegates back the government line, but they were almost invariably armed with examples of how a specific PFI project had benefited their area. Similarly, in the equally heated debate on Iraq, pro-government speakers outnumbered critics by thirteen to four. The endless succession of laudatory speeches from constituency delegates 'eventually became so blatant [that] delegate anger boiled over: hecklers demanded the chair pick some anti-war voices' (Jonathan Freedland, *Guardian*, 1 October 2002).

In the past the majority of constituency delegates (then commanding only about 10 per cent of the vote compared to the present 50 per cent) generally backed left-wing resolutions. This has now changed – and quite striking so. Almost two-thirds of constituency delegates (64 per cent to 36 per cent) voted in 2000 *against* a restoration of the earnings link, while the unions voted very heavily (85 per cent to 15 per cent) in favour (*Guardian*, 27 September 2000, 28 September 2000). Similarly in the 2002 PFI debate, 58 per cent of CLPs opted for the government line, while the unions voted 92 per cent to 8 per cent for the resolution. Unfortunately, we have no data on membership attitudes, though polls indicate that 63 per cent of Labour members say they support the demand for a full review of existing PFI schemes before new contracts are awarded (ICM poll, *Guardian*, 27 September 2002). Why CLP delegates have become so supportive of the leadership is unclear, since no systematic research has been conducted on this topic. Such factors as loyalty to the government, reluctance to rock the boat in public, and genuine backing for Labour's policies undoubtedly play a part. But the leadership also commits far more effort to managing and cajoling delegates than in the past. Before the main Conference, regional conferences are used to brief delegates; on the first day of the main Conference further regional briefing sessions are held; and throughout the week delegates are advised – and lobbied – by regional liaison officers. According to Mick Rix, general secretary of the train drivers' union, ASLEF, 'large numbers of delegates [at the 2002 party conference] were hand-picked by regional parties' (*Tribune*, 27 September 2002). Party officials also ensured that supportive pro-PFI composites would figure on the agenda by persuading eight constituency parties to submit emergency resolutions with near identical wording welcoming 'additional' private investment (*Guardian*, 26 September 2002).

To what extent did the deliberations of the new policy system of policy formation in fact influence the content of the 2001 manifesto – the only document that, formally, can constitutionally bind a Labour Government? A definitive answer is not possible without more systematic research.

However, some provisional generalisations are possible:

- The more specific the item, the more it corresponds to the basic thrust of government policy, and the greater the support it can command among the unions and the rank and file (in that order), the more likely is its eventual inclusion in the manifesto (for example, making the Low Pay Commission permanent).
- Since the leadership has the power of the drafter and the agenda-setter, it fixes the basic parameters of political acceptability. Wants and demands that are deemed unacceptable will be suppressed or deflected via the numerous gateways operated by official gatekeepers.
- There is little to prevent the government from more or less ignoring the whole policy process if it wishes to push through policies that might arouse resistance. Examples include the promotion of specialist and 'faith' schools, and the rapid intensification of private involvement in the delivery of public services.

Seyd concludes: 'After four years of the new policy-making structures, involving hundreds of local policy forums, a vast number of submissions to the policy commissions from local parties and trade unions and numerous meetings of the NPF and policy commissions, the dominance of the party leadership has become even greater' (Seyd, 2001, 101).

However, it does not follow that the new arrangements serve no purpose. Two, in particular, can be identified. First, they aimed to improve communication between 'the Party in power and the Party on the ground'. Party leaders were well aware that previous Labour Administrations had neglected their relationship with the rank and file: 'If the party and the government were to drift apart, as happened to us in the 1970s,' Charles Clarke commented, 'that is obviously a recipe for political disaster for the Labour Party' (*Guardian*, 15 November 2001). Thus a range of devices have been instituted to ensure, 'a continuous dialogue and exchange' between Party and government. The NPF, its policy commissions and *ad hoc* meetings with ministers afford opportunities for NPF members to communicate their concerns to the government representatives. Similarly, at the Conference, new mechanisms, such as question-and-answer sessions addressed by ministers, policy seminars and workshops, are used to facilitate feedback. These are both listening devices through which Party managers could tap into the wider Party mood, and openings for ministers to defend their policies. The object is to embed norms of receptivity and mutual understanding institutionally and therefore bolster allegiance to the Party and the government.

Second, no voluntary organisation could survive for long unless it rested on the consent of its members. The belief that a structure of political authority is properly and fairly constructed, and that therefore all have an obligation to accept its decisions, is vital if a party is to survive the disappointments and conflicts that are a normal part of political life. It forms the basis of what Easton calls 'diffuse support', arguing that, in every system, 'part of the readiness to tolerate outputs that are perceived to run contrary to one's wants and demands, flows from a general or diffuse attachment' to the organisation. This provides 'a reserve of support that enables a system to weather the many storms when outputs cannot be balanced off against inputs of demands' (Easton, 1965, 272, 273). The most effective way to build up and sustain diffuse support is the sense that all 'stakeholders', from the top leadership to the constituency foot soldiers, are engaged in a common enterprise. This, in turn, presupposes institutional devices which give – or appear to give – ample opportunities for the rank and file to articulate its wishes and demands. It is this crucial function that the system erected by *Partnership in Power* was meant to fulfil.

It is difficult without more research to determine the effectiveness of the new arrangements. On the one hand, the government has enjoyed – compared to its predecessors in the 1960s and 1970s – a comfortable ride. The Blair Government has lost only two votes at the Conference. Criticism generally is uttered in much more modulated tones, and fierce denunciations liberally laced with accusations of betrayal have virtually disappeared from Conference platforms. But, on the other hand, if critics appear not to be using 'voice' as much as in the past, they are queuing up to 'exit'. In 2000, a report by senior officials disclosed that more than 200 of the 641 constituencies had not picked delegates to attend the Conference. Furthermore, the Party is experiencing increasing difficulty in persuading members to stand in elections for the NPF, with a growing number of candidates elected unopposed, and positions unfilled (*Guardian*, 14 April 2000). Similarly, the proportion of the membership participating in elections to the NEC is sliding, from over 40 per cent in 1997 to 25 per cent in 2000 (*The Times*, 25 May 2000). And most notable of all, party membership has plummeted from 405,000 just before the 1997 election to around 270,000 in 2002 (*Guardian*, 30 October 2002). Anecdotal evidence suggests that the decline in activism is even greater, with attendance at meetings at an all-time low, branches and constituency parties meeting more sporadically, and few members involving themselves in campaigning.

Control Freaks?

In her valedictory pronouncement shortly before she died, Labour's *grande dame*, Barbara Castle expressed her dismay at the 'growing intolerance inside the Labour Party towards people who do not always take the "on-message" view'. She added:

> I do not think the party can hold together unless people have the right to disagree. You cannot keep together a labour movement, which has been built by people who want to change society for the better, if everyone is ordered to hold exactly the same view. People in the Labour Party want the right to have the freedom to express their views. The move towards the intolerance of diversity within the Labour Party is a tragedy. (*The Times*, 4 July 2000)

The most celebrated instances of New Labour 'control freakery', according to critics, were the efforts to impose the leadership's will on the selection of the Party leader in Wales, and the mayoral candidate in London (for a fuller discussion, see Shaw, 2002). No problem had arisen in Scotland where Donald Dewar was elected unopposed, but the leadership confronted an unexpected dilemma in Wales when Ron Davies, the Welsh Secretary and leader of the Party in Wales resigned in unusual circumstances. Rhodri Morgan MP, recently defeated by Davies for the Wales leadership, immediately threw his hat in the ring. For reasons that never became entirely clear, Tony Blair was determined to block Morgan's election, and government briefers immediately went into action attacking him as 'off-message' and a 'loose cannon'. Alun Michael MP, a junior minister in the Home Office regarded as a 'safe pair of hands', was persuaded to stand. As the mechanism for electing the leader, the Party opted for an electoral college, divided equally between members, candidates for the Welsh Assembly and MPs for Welsh constituencies, and affiliated organisations. In his own election in 1994, Blair had insisted that, in the electoral college, affiliated unions must poll their members individually. The same method would have elected Morgan, for not only did he win two out of every three votes among the 25,000 individual party members but also in every union that balloted their members. All this had been anticipated by the leadership, so an agreement had allegedly been struck with senior Welsh officials in three powerful unions to cast the votes of their organisations as a block for Michael, without consulting their individual members. These votes proved to be decisive, as Michael narrowly beat Morgan by 53 per cent to 47 per cent. In fact, Michael did not savour his triumph for long. His standing, already fragile because of the row over his election, was further weakened by Labour's very poor showing in the Assembly elections of 1999 that left Michael, as first minister, presiding over a fragile minority administration, which eventually collapsed. Michael resigned – to be replaced without opposition by Morgan.

The row over Ken Livingstone dwarfed all others as sustained and at times, desperate, attempts were made to prevent him from becoming Labour's candidate for London mayor. Despite the modest powers given to the post, Downing Street feared that the former leader of the Greater London Council (GLC) would use his formidable communication skills to embarrass the government and reactivate a dormant Labour left. As a senior insider bluntly put it, 'If you think we toiled for 18 years to create New Labour to allow Livingstone to take one of our main prizes, you must need your head examining' (*Channel 4 News*, 10 November 1998). Finding a credible alternative candidate was not easy, and the leadership toyed with the names of a number of candidates before landing on the hapless Secretary of State for Health, Frank Dobson. All the evidence suggested that, in a selection process involving a free election, he had scant chance of winning the Labour nomination. But Number 10 was determined to block Livingstone: 'It cannot be allowed to happen, it must not happen, it will not happen' a prime-ministerial aide confided to the BBC political correspondent Nick Jones (Jones, 2002b, 96).

An NEC working group agreed that the Labour candidate should be selected solely by a poll of London Party members. However, an alternative method, drafted by Margaret McDonagh, the Party's General Secretary, and the Downing Street Political Unit, was presented to the NEC, in which affiliated organisations were specifically required *not* to ballot their members. The NEC was then told flatly that the choice was 'being with Tony or against him', and the working group's recommendations were rejected in favour of McDonagh's alternative. Blair loyalists were delighted: 'we want to see Ken's blood on the carpet. This is the way to do it' (*Independent*, 13 November 1999).

Some still urged that Livingstone be blocked by being excluded from Labour's panel for mayoral candidates, but Blair reluctantly agreed to include him, partly through anxiety about bad publicity, and partly because he was assured by Margaret McDonagh that the electoral college would guarantee Dobson's victory (*Guardian*, 13 November 1999; *Observer*, 14 November 1999). The college was composed of three equal components: a representatives' section (MPs, MEPs and Greater London Authority candidates); a members' section; and an affiliated organisations' section. This gave each of the seventy-five MPs, MEPs and Greater London Authority candidates (in the main, hostile to Livingstone) a vote equal to that of about 1,000 party members. All seventy-five were given identifiable numbered ballot papers, and those known to be waverers or inclined towards Livingstone were reminded of the benefits that would accrue, or forfeited, depending on how they voted.

The bulk of affiliated organisations (generally more to the left than in Wales) opted to poll their members, and virtually all mustered big majorities for Livingstone. The crucial votes that swung the race were from two affiliated organisations that refused to ballot members: the AEEU, whose national leadership was then very close to the prime minister, and the South London Co-operative Party. Together they cast a decisive 8 per cent of the total electoral college vote for Dobson. In breach of the rules mandating neutrality in election contests, the Millbank machine threw its whole weight behind the generously-financed former health secretary, as London members were deluged by telephone and post, urging them to back him. In another violation of the rules, a full list of Labour's London membership was supplied surreptitiously to the Dobson camp, and which Millbank then delayed handing over to Livingstone and Glenda Jackson until January 1999, giving Dobson a three-month advantage. Throughout the whole period, both the Millbank and Downing Street press machines worked flat out to discredit Livingstone, supplying a whole dossier – prepared by Millbank – spelling out his acts of disloyalty (*Guardian*, 16 February 2000).

The outcome was a narrow victory for Dobson over Livingstone, by 51.5 per cent to 48.5 per cent after the votes for the third candidate, Glenda Jackson, had been redistributed. Livingstone then decided to stand as an independent (at the cost of expulsion from the Party). Livingstone was relentlessly and bitingly attacked by his former party, which probably did him little, if any, harm. In the event, he secured 40.5 per cent of the vote, with the Tory runner-up, Steven Norris, gaining 25.7 per cent, and Dobson gaining a mere 13.8 per cent, just ahead of the Liberal Democrat with 11.2 per cent. In the second ballot, Livingstone triumphed easily with 58 per cent against Norris's 42 per cent. Although an uneasy working relationship between the government and the new mayor was established, Blair was adamant in refusing to allow Livingstone back into the Labour Party.

These episodes were the most highly publicised, but not the only instances of leadership attempts to influence internal Party elections. According to the rules, Party officials are required to adopt a neutral stance in NEC elections, but in 1998 a concerted effort was made to hold at bay a coalition of left and centre-left, loosely organised in the Grassroots Alliance. A Blairite MP with close contacts with both the leadership and party headquarters, worked behind the scenes to organise a rival, loyalist slate called 'Members First'. The slate was bankrolled by grants totalling £100,000 donated by a recently ennobled Labour lord and a major trade union, which appeared to have contributed the bulk of the money. A private marketing firm which was reportedly run by a friend of the same Labour lord, was employed to canvass support for the Blairite slate (*Guardian*, 11 September 1998, 16 September 1998). However, the campaign backfired when Grassroots representatives won four of the six NEC seats representing constituency parties. In subsequent years, Millbank sought to influence election outcomes by encouraging high-profile figures whose loyalty it felt it could rely on to stand for the constituency section. These included Lord Sawyer, the party's former general secretary, and the actors Michael Cashman and Tony Robinson, all of whom were elected while left-wing representation dropped to (and has remained at) three (*Independent*, 12 June 1999).

A party official admitted that Millbank had launched 'an orchestrated campaign involving MPs to win support for an [loyalist] unofficial slate. The aim is to prevent the Left using the elections to fire a shot across Tony Blair's bows' (*Independent*, 12 June 1999). There is some evidence indicating that Labour's head office is still seeking to influence election outcomes, though in a more cautious and discrete manner. Methods used include requesting officials to secure nominations for preferred candidates to the constituency sections of the NEC, Conference Arrangements Committee and the NPF, and efforts to mobilise support for them (*Tribune*, 27 September 2002). *Tribune* added that a leaked email sent to all regional directors by Alicia Chater, head of general secretary, David Triesman's, office, included the phrase: 'you will all have your own NPF candidates'.

Perhaps the most extraordinary aspect of the leadership's so-called 'control freakery', exemplified by its bids to block the Morgan and Livingstone candidatures, and to influence elections to the constituency section of the NEC, is that it already enjoyed an effectively immovable grip on the Party. Neither Morgan as Wales' first minister, nor Livingstone as London mayor, nor, indeed, a handful of dissenters on the NEC, represented any serious threat to the New Labour regime. In the aftermath of the government's defeat over earnings-related pensions at the 2000 Conference, the then leader of Unison, Rodney Bickerstaffe, expressed his puzzlement over the New Labour steamroller: 'Why do they want to control everything? Are they saying delegates can never ever tell the leadership what we think? We weren't instructing the Chancellor to do anything. All we wanted to do was to show that we believed in something' (Jones, 2002b, 36). The pattern, it could be added, is replicated in government: in Blair's disinclination to allow serious debate in Cabinet, in the close scrutiny that Downing Street staff exert over departments and – from Brown – the Treasury tentacles that have extended to the major spending ministries. This trend towards more astringent central control contradicts the expectations of scholars, who have been predicting *looser* party organisation, in which strongly institutionalised 'mass bureaucratic parties' will be transmuted into electoral-professional parties typified by weaker institutional ties, decentralised structures and more diffuse patterns of authority (Panebianco, 1988, 232). Party organisation, it is argued, is dispensable, a large membership a hindrance, and party machines obsolescent. The party of the future seems to be moving in the direction of a feeble apparatus staffed by officials whose 'main job is to co-ordinate the contribution of professionals coming from outside the political realm to win elections'. The party structure is 'ever-weakening' and parties themselves 'by-passed' by power-holders relishing their direct contact with voters through the new information technology (Mancini, 1999, 242–3).

The New Labour Party does not, as should now be apparent, bear this out: the drift is towards a more powerful central apparatus, greater organisational centralisation, more concentrated patterns of authority, and tauter discipline. Indeed, the very factor, 'electoral professionalisation', that commentators have adduced as being the cause of organisational relaxation within parties is, we would contend, directly and indirectly (in the British context at least) responsible for its tightening. The systematic application of modern communications methods *required* a higher level of central co-ordination, the orchestrated and disciplined transmission of key campaign themes and arguments, and 'on-message' exponents of the party's line. All this, in turn, presupposed a single, all-powerful command structure. 'Only a unitary system of command,' Gould wrote, 'could give Labour the clarity and flexibility it needed to adapt and change at the pace required by modern politics' (Gould, 1998, 240–1).

This insistence on discipline was reinforced greatly by a crucial characteristic of Britain's media culture: its obsession with 'splits'. According to Michael White, political editor of the *Guardian*, it is almost 'impossible to have a civilised and reasonable debate about, let us say, the merits of the Euro within a political party ... because people like us cry "split". The reason we cry split is because it is one way of getting things into print in an adversarial media culture' (Select Committee on Public Administration, 1998, 19). Unity, loyalty and self-discipline come to be seen as virtues *indispensable* to a party's success. If disagreement over policy is aired publicly, coverage will almost invariably be dominated by talk of voter-alienating 'wrangles' and 'squabbling'. Labour is especially vulnerable here, given the debilitating conflicts that rent the party in the 1970s and early 1980s. Blair expressed forcefully his determination not to permit a 'return to the factionalism, navelgazing or feuding of the Seventies [for] this ill discipline allowed us to be painted as extremist, out of touch and divided. It helped keep us out of power for 18 years' (*Independent*, 20 November 1998). Writing in 2002, Peter Mandelson recalled 'the fears that existed ... prior to the 1997 election': fears of a revival of pressure from activists demanding economically damaging rises in public spending, of a revival of trade union militancy, of the re-emergence of ideological warfare, factionalism and a destablising left–right split (Mandelson, 2002, xxv). Hence the vital need, in Blair's words, to transform Labour into 'a modern, disciplined party with a strong centre' (quoted in the *Independent*, 20 November 1998).

Conclusion

This chapter has explored two internal processes within the contemporary Labour Party: policy-making and internal elections. In examining the first, we traced the operations of the system – drawing on Easton's analysis – from the registering of inputs (or 'wants' and 'demands') via their navigation through the policy machinery and their materialisation as outputs, or official policy commitments. Although, in theory, the new system claimed to allow a large measure of rank-and-file participation, opening-up policy-making to a much wide range of groups and views than in the past, in practice it was firmly controlled. Multiple filtering points within the new system enabled the leadership to deflect serious misgivings over government policy into relatively innocuous channels and, at the Conference itself, a range of agenda-managing and procedural stratagems inhibited the expression of 'voice'. However, the NPF system has functioned in this way because it has been underpinned by a structural transformation of Party organisation manifested in a much more solidly implanted centripetal pattern of power. Thus previously constitutionally autonomous centres of power – the front bench and the NEC – have effectively been welded together under the direction of the Party leader. As part of this process, the NEC has effectively lost its autonomous policy-forming role. Equally, although individual members have been given more rights, units at constituency and local level have been by-passed progressively, and divested of functions.

However, the reforms *have* accomplished a second principle aim. This was to facilitate consensus within the Party, in particular to prevent a repetition of the discord between the government and the extra-parliamentary organs that had dogged the Party in the past, by creating institutional incentives for the reconciliation of disagreements through compromise and mutual accommodation. In stark contrast to the 1974–9 experience, Party–government relations have been largely free of acrimony.

This chapter also analysed the conduct of internal party elections – to the top post in the Labour Party in Wales (and, hence, the new Welsh Assembly), the Labour candidature for the mayoralty in London, and the constituency section of the NEC. The action of Party leaders – notably Tony Blair himself – has here attracted considerable criticism for what came to be known as 'control freakery' and, in so far as this referred to major and sustained central intervention and intolerance of internal dissent, we found evidence to substantiate it. Heavy-handed discipline, critics feared, would squeeze the life out of the party, and evidence began to accumulate of falling membership and declining levels of activism. By the autumn of 2001, the leadership had appeared to take note. The *Guardian* reported that Blair had 'sanctioned a drive to reverse the tide of "control freakery" within the Labour party as part of a concerted effort to end the mood of "disaffection and cynicism" within the ranks'. The new general secretary, David Triesman, would – the party was promised – reverse the centralising style of his predecessor ('Labour drive to reverse "control freak" tendency', *Guardian*,

15 November 2001). Furthermore, Party managers acknowledged problems with the NPF process: it had, Charles Clarke, the party chairman from 2001 to 2003 conceded, lacked feedback and exchange, while Triesman pledged measures to stimulate membership involvement (*Guardian*, 29 January 2002). However, the 2002 Party Conference appeared to indicate a reluctance on the party of Party managers to relax the reins. By mid-2003 the Party had another new chairman, Ian McCartney, who, with a reputation for closeness to the branches and unions, was reported to be planning yet another attempt to involve members in the policy-making procedures. Only time will tell whether reform can revive a shrinking and increasingly lethargic party.

5

New Labour, 'Vested Interests' and the Union Link

STEVE LUDLAM

Introduction

At the beginning of the twenty-first century, the British 'Labour alliance', the century-old organised link between the Labour Party and its trade union affiliates, presented the political world with a puzzle. On the one hand, it was unique among the potentially governing parties of Western Europe. Of the 6.8 million trade unionists affiliated to the Trades Union Congress (TUC) in 2000, 5 million belonged to unions affiliated to the Labour Party. Nowhere else in Europe did trade unions participate in democratic politics in this way, affiliating mass memberships to a party in which they enjoyed entrenched constitutional rights. Yet, on the other hand, New Labour did nothing to revive institutionalised tripartite co-operation, destroyed by the Tories, that characterised union–government relationships across the European Union (Dorey, 2002, 67–70).

Indeed, to the despair of most union leaders, New Labour apparently acted as the ringleader of governments hostile to EU legislation designed to improve worker protection and representation. Time and again, unions were infuriated by their perception that the government was determined above all to satisfy the demands of British business, whose dominance in policy-making during the Thatcher/Major years 'Labour has been keen to affirm' (Gamble, 2002, 304). Bill Morris, veteran leader of the Transport and General Workers Union (TGWU) and a tough Labour loyalist, lamented after the 2001 election victory that, 'this is the most pro-business government I can remember' (*Financial Times*, 29 June 2001). The widespread expectation that the union–Party link would fracture after a New Labour election victory in 1997 had, however, proved to be premature. Indeed, in the run-up to the 2001 election, the link had apparently ceased to be contentious. Yet New Labour's second term was launched amid repeated public rows between unions and the Party, and renewed speculation about the link's future. What this chapter seeks to do is to explain both the improvement in relations between 1997 and 2001, the deterioration since 2001, and to add to the speculation about the future.

The Link in the Rise of New Labour

Historical analysis suggests that the form of union–Party linkages shifts periodically under the pressures of changing political economy and electoral strategy (Ludlam, Bodah and Coates, 2002). On both counts, the British link could be expected to weaken from the 1980s. Labour's embrace of neo-liberal political economy implied prioritising monetary stability over full employment, a strong preference for 'flexible' labour markets, and a refusal to repeal Tory anti-union legislation. Well before Tony Blair became leader, Neil Kinnock's policy review had ended the convention that the affiliated unions determined the party's industrial relations policy (Hughes and Wintour, 1990, 144–52; Bassett, 1991, 308). Second, driven by social change and electoral defeat, Labour needed to abandon its original class basis and become a 'catch-all' party with cross-class appeal (see Shaw, 1994). In such a party, New Labour's advocates argued, membership should be individual, free of union block votes (Mandelson and Liddle, 1996, 226). During the Party's review of the union link in 1992/3, Blair had advocated this position, unsuccessfully (Rentoul, 1995, 309). New Labour's electoral strategy after 1994 emphasised rejection of an 'old' Labour inextricably bound up with the union link (Gould, 1998, 257–8). Before the 1996 TUC, Blair's shadow employment minister briefed journalists, off the record, that New Labour might hold a party plebiscite on ending the link within weeks of an election victory (Anderson and Mann, 1997, 324). Blair had summed up the cultural revolution that had taken place when he told the annual conference of the Transport and General Workers Union in July 1995 (Blair, 1996, 133):

> I want to be quite blunt with you about the modern relationship between today's Labour Party and the trade unions. There was a time when a large trade union would pass a policy and then it was assumed Labour would follow suit. Demands were made. Labour responded and negotiated. Those days are over. Gone. They are not coming back.

By contrast, Labour's links with business appeared ever closer. The 'prawn cocktail offensive' launched by John Smith as Neil Kinnock's shadow chancellor was accompanied in the early 1990s by an increasing profile for business organisations at Labour's conferences and promotional events. From 1993, a Labour Industry Forum channelled business donations; later a 'high value donors' unit solicited donations from individual business figures. Following the Party's abandonment in 1995 of its old 'Clause 4' commitment to common ownership of the economy, Gordon Brown delivered keynote speeches to Labour's Finance and Industry Group presenting his 'economic credo for government', outlining New Labour's commitment to a competitive market order, and to guaranteeing monetary and fiscal stability through strict targets for inflation and public debt. New Labour would 'not attempt to substitute our judgement for the commercial judgement of investors and managers' (cited in Routledge, 1998, 224). It would greatly extend, into school and hospital building, New Labour's commitment to public–private partnership through a reformed Private Finance Initiative (PFI) programme (Osler, 2002). Blair told the 1995 annual conference of the Confederation of British Industry (CBI):

> There is a new era opening up in relations between today's Labour Party and the business community. With assistance from the regional CBIs and Chambers of Commerce, I and my colleagues are currently visiting every centre of commerce and industry throughout Britain, meeting thousands of businesspeople in every part of the country. The dialogue will continue up to and after the election. (Blair, 1996, 107)

The Link in the First Term

In his unrivalled study of the union link, *The Contentious Alliance*, Lewis Minkin listed the factors which suggested that, despite Labour's 'modernisation' in the 1980s, the link would not be severed (Minkin, 1992, 647–9). Analysis of these factors in the middle of New Labour's first term suggested a significant, if gradual, weakening of the link (Ludlam, 2001). The Party no longer looked to the unions for insights into working-class life: market research had taken over. Nor was the link seen as legitimising Labour's claim to be the 'people's party'. On the contrary, it was seen as the main obstacle to re-branding Labour as a 'big tent' party attracting the 'new middle class'. The unions still provided political 'ballast' against party radicals, but this seemed less important as the 1998 *Partnership in Power* reforms to the Party's constitution entrenched Party leaders' control. Although its share of Party funding fell from 90 per cent in 1994 to 40 per cent by 1998, union funding, and especially election donations, remained vital. Further, millionaires might give money, but they would not deliver campaigning muscle as affiliated unions had in Labour's triumphant 1997 'key seats' campaign.

Only two of Minkin's factor's binding the unions to the party apparently remained effective. Labour leaders had largely lost affection for 'This Great

Movement of Ours' (TIGMOO); nor could unions assume that these leaders would honour what was left of the convention of Party solidarity with unions in struggle. However, unions were recovering access to the government policy machine, even if New Labour refused to return to tripartite public policy-making, and union access contrasted starkly with that of business. Of the 3,103 appointments to the first 259 government taskforces established after 1997, just 2 per cent were trade union representatives, compared to 35 per cent who were business representatives (Barker *et al.*, 2000, 26–7). Yet, despite the *Partnership in Power* reforms, affiliated unions retained significant policy-making access inside the party. And in terms of Minkin's 'shared historical projects', which aligned unions with Labour, unions could still look forward to a 'supply-side New Labourism', with the unions providing training and even welfare services, as well as becoming advocates of the new rights delivered by the Employment Relations Act (1999) and the long-awaited National Minimum Wage.

Journalistic predictions of the imminence of Party–union divorce thus appeared precipitate. But the hostility of the party's 'ultra-modernisers', and the plurality of alternative political avenues for representing the union interest, such as the devolved institutions in Scotland, Wales and London, the institutions of the EU, and the British courts under the new Human Rights Act, nevertheless suggested that the link in its federal form might not last long into the twenty-first century.

A Happy Hundredth Birthday

In the second half of New Labour's first term, however, the link strengthened significantly, and was described by insiders as having 'matured'. Chancellor Brown told the engineers' union, celebrating the Party's centenary, 'We've enjoyed working closely with our trade union colleagues ... Our relations have never been better' (*AEEU Union News*, February 2000). Several developments explained the improved atmosphere. First, unions' resources and bargaining experience gave them considerable clout in the Party's new 'rolling' policy-making process, despite reduced formal voting power. In 2000, key unions inflicted Blair's first-ever Party Conference defeat, making an earnings-linked basic state pension Party policy (this was immediately disowned by Brown). Unions also saw off the Party's consultation document, *21st Century Party: Members – the Key to our Future*, described by a national officer of the normally ultra-loyal AEEU as 'little more than a thinly veiled attempt to abolish the ward party and end the trade union link' (*Tribune*, 21 April 2000). The trade union groups in the Parliamentary Labour Party (over 350 MPs in all) also became more effective at representing union concerns. And it is impossible to exaggerate how important increased direct access to ministers has been. As the TUC general secretary, John Monks, put it, 'There is constant dialogue...There is no alternative for the unions. The achievements in recent years are a sea change from what happened under the Conservatives' (*Unions Today*, March 2001). And in 2000, Blair agreed to regular quarterly meetings with senior union leaders.

Important public policy frustrations also eased. By the end of 2000, unions had taken up £12.5 million of government Union Learning Fund grants. The government gave union 'lifelong learning' representatives time off work to fulfil their functions. Unions also took up grants from the £5 m Union Partnership Fund, and the TUC launched its Partnership Institute. The TUC and several individual unions became providers of private 'stakeholder' pensions, lending legitimacy to New Labour's pensions policy. This was 'supply-side New Labourism' in practice. Crucially, armed with the Employment Relations Act (1999), unions saw recognition deals settled in 2000 at twice the 1999 rate (*Labour Research*, February 2001). The Low Pay Commission was made permanent in 2000, and during 2000 both Brown and Blair began to proclaim full employment, rather than 'full employability' or 'full employment opportunity', as New Labour's objective. With little publicity, several troubled industries received government subsidies: not the manufacturing strategy that some unions wanted, but they did save some jobs. And anger over the public spending cuts of the 1997–9 period, fulfilling the election pledge to stick to Tory plans, gave way to satisfaction at health and education announcements in the 2000 Comprehensive Spending Review. As the 2001 election campaign approached, unions acknowledged a long list of achievements for working people. Unison's *What's the Labour Government Ever Done for Us?* ran to almost fifty pages of policy gains, and the TGWU published a list of nearly 400 such items.

There remained sharp policy disagreements, however, notably over EU social dimension issues. In the courts, unions challenged the government's implementation of directives. Only the UK insisted on opt-outs from the working time directive, and there was widespread anger over the non-introduction of the information and consultation rights directive, especially when multinationals announced mass sackings to the press before telling their workers. The *Financial Times* reported that, with the CBI determined to 'fight tooth and nail' against this directive, 'The government backs the CBI's view and has secured allies among a group of countries ... that would be enough to block the measure' (7 July 2000). Bill Morris wrote bitterly, 'as our government panders to big business and uses every trick in the book to block regulation that would have ensured Rover workers are consulted, we face the grim reality: it is too cheap and too easy to sack British workers' (*TGWU Record*, April 2000). Tension was exacerbated when Blair 'negotiated an effective opt-out from employment measures contained in the controversial [EU] charter of human rights' (*Financial Times*, 28 November 2000). Key union leaders saw themselves as fighting for the EU social partnership model against the government and the CBI. Bill Morris complained, 'The political agenda is that the Labour Government is struggling hard to pacify business leaders by watering down employment rights' (*Tribune*, 17 March 2001).

Nevertheless, factors binding party leaders to the union link strengthened in the second half of the first term. In 1999, they became reliant dramatically on the 'political ballast' role of the unions, as key unions cast block votes without balloting their members for Blair's candidates to lead Wales and London. Less dramatically, key unions protected Labour's leaders in the party's new policy machinery. After the summer National Policy Forum (NPF) in 2000, the Graphical, Paper and Media Union (GPMU) leader wrote bitterly that other unions had abandoned TUC policy on employment rights to help out the Party leadership (*GPMU Direct*, June 2000; *Tribune*, 1 August 2000). In September 2000, during the fuel blockade, TUC leaders worked closely with ministers to overcome the protests, in retrospect a key moment in the rehabilitation of the union–Party link.

The Union Cure for the Mid-Term Blues

However, the main reason for the relaxation of tension was Labour's need for financial and logistical support to fight elections. In 1999, Labour fought four campaigns – in Scotland, Wales, Europe, and local authorities – losing seats and money in the process. Seven large unions made special donations totalling £6 million to help out (*Labour Research*, January 2001). As the 2001 election approached, dependence on union money remained entrenched. For the campaign period after 16 February 2001 when reporting to the new Electoral Commission became obligatory, unions donated £6,080,790: 55 per cent of Labour's total campaign expenditure of £11,140,019. And the Commission's figures underestimate union cash donations. The giant Amalgamated Engineering and Electrical Union (AEEU), for example, donated just under £1.3 million in cash during the reporting period, but calculated that it gave £2.1 million in all.

Union campaigning was even more important in 2001 than in the past. First, the decline of activism among individual Party members, revealed in the 1999 campaigns, created greater dependence on the affiliated unions' officer corps and activist base. Second, union resources had become vital in

Labour's 'key seats' strategy. In 1997, affiliated unions seconded full-time officers to each of Labour's 93 key seats, of which 92 were won. In 2001, the party prioritised all of the 146 seats Labour gained in 1997, and unions again focused resources on these key seats, albeit under some paradoxical constraints from new election law (Ludlam, Taylor and Allender, 2002). Third, the unions had direct access to much of the 'heartland vote' in working-class communities, where turnout fell alarmingly in 1999.

The Economic and Social Research Council (ESRC)/Sheffield University study of union campaigning in 2001 revealed that affiliated unions delivered (see *www.shef.ac.uk/~pol/unionsinelections*). They mailed their members millions of items of pro-Labour election material. The eight largest affiliates mailed their 4.5 million members, about 10 per cent of the electorate (not counting family members), far more campaign materials than all the parties put together mailed out. The relationship between union membership and voting Labour is not one of simple causation, of course, but the efforts unions make to link union consciousness to voting Labour must have some impact, and the empirical evidence suggests that it is positive. MORI polling data and the 2001 British Election Study show that union members were up to 10 per cent more likely to turn out and vote than were voters in general, and that Labour's union vote remained 10 per cent stronger than its non-union vote. For the second successive election, an absolute majority of trade unionists voted for Labour in 2001.

The electoral significance of local campaigning is now well-established (Denver and Hands, 1997, 47–50, 267–303; Seyd and Whiteley, 2002, 111–36). Affiliated unions made crucial contributions at this level too. Under the umbrella of the National Trade Union and Labour Party Liaison Organisation (TULO), they co-ordinated the Party's transport provision, set up phone banks, co-ordinated key speaker tours, led the drive to register postal voters, and provided Labour's national postal vote processing centre. Regional TULO Committees appointed special campaign co-ordinators, and mobilised officials and squads of activists. Nationally, TULO appointed Trade Union Constituency Co-ordinators (TUCCs) in all of Labour's 146 key seats and in 26 other constituencies. Most unions also supported campaigning in other seats where they had political links, and TULO focused special efforts to register postal votes for 52 seats (50 of them key seats).

Several points emerged from the Sheffield study. First, University of Plymouth data collected for the Electoral Commission on Postal Voting showed that, compared with seats not prioritised by TULO, the average number of postal votes cast was 36 per cent higher in TULO's 52 specially-targeted seats, 30 per cent higher in the 146 key seats, and 11 per cent higher in the 26 other TULO seats. Second, in the 146 and the 52 seats, turnout in

2001 was significantly higher than the UK average, and the average for Labour-held seats (and also higher in the 26 other TULO seats). Third, while Labour's overall vote share fell by 2.5 per cent, in the 146 and 52 groups of seats there was almost no loss of vote share. Of course, the key seat effect reflects the greater effort of the Party as a whole, but differential effects in the specially-targeted 52 seats and in the other 26 TULO seats suggest that a real 'union effect' was present. This effect can also be explored by comparing the Sheffield study's survey of union constituency co-ordinators with the survey of Labour agents conducted in the ESRC/Lancaster University 2001 Constituency Campaigning study (see *www.lancs.ac.uk/staff/macallis/results*). Labour agents' responses show that unions did target resources effectively in the key seats. And comparison with the Sheffield survey suggests that unions mobilised between 30 per cent and 40 per cent of constituency campaign workers during the election campaign. Before the election, Party strategists warned that a 5 per cent fall in turnout would cost 60 seats. In the event, turnout overall fell 12 per cent, but Labour only lost a handful of seats. Targeted union campaigning in 2001 was a vital part of achieving Labour's second landslide.

The 'contentious alliance', then, had revived by the end of the first term, and the 'union issue' had ceased to register as a negative factor in Labour's focus groups and private polling. Party strategists needed the unions both as campaigning forces and as a voice among 'heartland' voters. They also needed key unions to revive their old 'praetorian guard' role inside the Party. Most unions had overcome initial suspicion of the new Party policy-making process, and union leaders listed many legislative measures that they believed could not have been achieved as external lobbyists to the Blair government. From a historical perspective, the union–Party linkage may have weakened, but that process had apparently halted. In a pre-election interview, John Monks insisted, 'We are coming back in from the cold. Much of the suspicion and anger inside the unions during the early years of the Labour government has gone' (*Financial Times*, 7 May 2001). The divorce papers drawn up by leaders of the New Labour 'project' in the mid-1990s appeared to have been withdrawn.

The Link in the Second Term: 'The Shortest Honeymoon on Record'

But after the 2001 general election, after what John Monks called 'the shortest honeymoon on record' (*Tribune*, 7 September 2001), the link suddenly became more fraught than at any time since the beginning of the New Labour era in 1994, and arguably, before that, since 1981, when the Party's civil war was at its height. There were several causes of the deterioration, said to have been exacerbated by the departure from Downing Street of experienced union liaison staff.

The immediate cause was the emphasis in the Labour manifesto, and especially in the 'spin' that accompanied its launch, on the role of the private sector in the future of the great public services. Labour's strategists were, it later transpired, looking for a dynamic image for a second term, for a *new* New Labour as some put it. News of the TUC Executive Committee's anger was quickly leaked. Several annual union conferences during the election campaign witnessed bitter outbursts as it became clear that Blair was utterly committed not only to the PFI funding device, but also to the alleged rigours of private sector management of public services through forms of Public–Private Partnership (PPP). The increasingly outspoken GMB general secretary, John Edmonds, summed up the post-election mood among many union leaders, writing that:

> Trade unions kept very quiet during Labour's first term. We all knew that after two decades of Thatcher and Major, Labour needed at least ten years in power.... In one meeting Tony Blair ... set out the beguiling prospect of a first term of consolidation followed by a second term of radical reform ... Unfortunately that hope was shattered during the second week of the election campaign. The press were told that the key change in Labour's programme was an increased role for private sector companies. What our hospitals needed, according to Downing Street, was the management expertise of the private sector and the commercial discipline of private entrepreneurs ... Some supporters suggested it was all a mistake, but no denial came. (*Socialist Campaign Group News*, 1 September 2001)

The autumn 2001 conference season did not witness the anticipated public rows, because the events of 11 September led to the abandonment of the TUC Conference and the curtailment of the Party Conference. The TUC led a national public service rally in December 2001, protesting against PFI. And at the Welsh Party Conference in the spring of 2002, Blair portrayed unions as 'wreckers', allied with the 'forces of conservatism' and obstructing public service 'modernisation'. John Monks, a close Blair ally, lamented, 'I think it is bizarre. It is erratic and it is not worthy of the Government to indulge in juvenile terminology about a subject which is very serious' (*Tribune*, 8 February 2002). Ministers routinely referred to the unions pejoratively as 'vested interests'. The row over 'two-tier' pay and conditions in privatised public service workforces was to take two years to settle (see below). The GMB and Unison ran mass advertising campaigns attacking the government, and PCS, the biggest civil service union, announced a campaign to bring farmed-out services back into the state sector. Bill Morris told his members that the government's legislative plans for the public services left it 'difficult to find the line between Labour and the Tories' (*TGWU Record*, December 2002).

Second, conflict worsened over EU policy. Unions were delighted when the 'blocking minority' against the information and consultation directive collapsed, but not when the government boasted that it had negotiated provisions leaving 99.2 per cent of British businesses exempt. There was more anger at UK attempts to weaken new rights for temporary and agency workers, and when Blair produced a paper with the right-wing Italian prime minister, Silvio Berlusconi calling for more flexible labour markets, softer regulation of business, and using the private sector to increase public service effectiveness, ultra-loyal AEEU leader, Sir Ken Jackson, warned that such coalitions should not be 'at the expense of working people' (*Financial Times*, 7 May 2002). John Monks called Blair 'bloody stupid' (*Financial Times*, 28 June 2002).

Third, tension grew over the pace and scope of Labour's review of the Employment Relations Act, promised in the 2001 manifesto. The CBI warned New Labour publicly against further concessions. In a pre-CBI conference interview, the director-general, Digby Jones warned Blair, 'You have got to make a decision. Are you pro-business, or are you going to be with the unions? Now, make your choice ... I think since the election, the unions have got their tails up. I am looking for more action from the Government to show that the unions are not getting it all their own way' (*The Times*, 2 November 2001). When the review was published, the immediate union response was furious. The TUC's key demands had been to remove the small firms' exemption from union recognition provisions, scrap the 'threshold' rule in recognition ballots, and make sacking strikers illegal again (TUC, 2002); none of the three demands were met. New TUC general secretary Brendan Barber warned that the government would 'be unwise to ignore the real anger in unions today' (TUC Press Release, 27 February 2003). The GMB's general secretary was more abrupt: 'The Government has capitulated to the demands of the CBI ... This Government needs to decide if they are the Party for British workers and therefore stand up for worker's rights or they are the Party for the fat cats' (GMB Press Release, 27 February 2003).

The Employment Bill introduced in late 2001 contained welcome provisions on maternity pay, and parental and adoption leave, and the proposed statutory rights for union 'learning reps', but no review of the 1999 Act. It also introduced significant limitations on access to employment tribunals, in response to a long-running campaign by the CBI. In July 2001 the CBI listed its lobbying achievements with the government. Statutory rights to part-time working for parents had been 'dropped after concerted CBI lobbying' and the replacement 'right to ask' gave employers the final say (*Labour Research*, November 2001).

As evidence of its influence, the CBI also cited the limited increase in the National Minimum Wage in 2001, and its persuading the government not to introduce a statutory requirement on employers to carry out equal pay audits, as the TUC and the Equal Opportunities Commission had demanded. It applauded when three businessmen were appointed to a new seven-strong Department of Trade and Industry (DTI) 'strategy board'. The TUC was furious: there was no union leader on the board, nor had unions been consulted. Bill Morris called the DTI the 'provisional wing' of the CBI, and told the *Financial Times*, 'I know of very few DTI policy decisions which are not being driven by the CBI ... The perception on the street is the CBI gets the favours and the Trades Union Congress doesn't even get the fairness' (5 February 2002). A few months later, an ex-CBI director-general was appointed to chair the Low Pay Commission. The government also stood by as employers reduced social costs by abolishing final salary pension schemes, and failed to implement a 1999 promise to legislate to permit charges of corporate manslaughter to be brought against companies.

But CBI–Labour relations deteriorated soon afterwards. The CBI took the view that in not consulting with it over the National Insurance increase in the 2002 spring Budget, New Labour had undermined an agreement to consult and avoid confrontation. CBI president, Sir John Egan, accused Brown of treating business as 'voteless cows to be milked' (*Financial Times*, 25 June 2002). On the eve of Brown's Mansion House speech in July 2002, the CBI said relations with Labour were at a low point, and later warned that the government faced the fiercest opposition yet from business. It is worth noting that the subject of this anger was not employment law or the power of the unions, but taxation and public spending, the subject of the CBI's 'most critical press release yet' on the tax burden, before the CBI annual conference, and a point returned to angrily in the director-general's annual review in December (*Financial Times*, 22 November and 30 December 2002).

In the run-up to the 2003 Budget, Brown was highlighting the closeness of his consultation with the CBI over the Budget details (*Financial Times*, 10 February 2003), but later in February 2003 the government announced a settlement of the 'two-tier workforce' issue in local government that left business furious. A deal between unions and the Treasury reached in March 2001 had been derailed by the post-election confrontations. In March 2002, Brown had declared that 'Labour is more pro-business, pro-wealth creation, pro-competition than ever before' (*Financial Times*, 28 March 2002). The previous day, the CBI and the Business Services Association (BSA), which represents PFI contractors, had welcomed a voluntary code of practice requiring 'broadly comparable' terms for new workers entering contracted-out services in local government. The parallel arrangements for NHS PFIs had earlier been denounced by the BSA as 'a political fix to buy off trade union opposition' (*Financial Times*, 19 March 2002). While business welcomed the proposed local government code, it split the unions, with the

GMB calling it a betrayal of promises made to unions at the 2001 Party Conference. Negotiations dragged on, and a second pledge to end the 'two-tier' workforce was made by Blair at the 2002 annual Party Conference, in the course of (failed) efforts to prevent an anti-PFI vote. In the run-up to Labour's spring conference in 2003, negotiations collapsed and union leaders warned of serious industrial action 'in weeks' if Blair did not make good his pledge (*Financial Times*, 10 January, 17 January 2003). The subsequent deal conceded the unions' main demand that new workers in PFI and PPP deals should be rewarded on a basis 'no less favourable' than local government employees. This reversed the previously expected 'broadly comparable' formula and left the CBI fuming that the government had 'capitulated' (*Financial Times*, 14 February 2003).

Return of the Funding Issue

The post-election conflicts further weakened factors binding Party leaders to the union link. The financial link became highly contentious again. In 2001, the Fire Brigades Union (FBU) conference voted in principle to support non-Labour candidates if they supported FBU policies. At its 2001 conference, the Communication Workers Union (CWU) voted to withhold £500,000 from the party, to spend on campaigning against government policy. The CWU general secretary commented that 'Trade unions are not withdrawing funds because they think it is a clever way of obtaining influence. It is because they are being screwed by the government in the same way that they were screwed by the Tories' (*Labour Research*, May 2002). Unison's 2001 national conference voted to review its Party funding arrangements, and in 2002 postponed a resolution of its position. The historically ultra-loyal GMB withheld £2 million from the Party to pay for an advertising campaign against privatisation. It also asked local election candidates in 2002 to express their position on privatisation of public services before it would consider requests for union support. The Nation Union of Rail, Maritime and Transport Workers (RMT) conference in 2002 cut national funding by £100,000, and ended its direct funding of the constituency parties of its parliamentary group of MPs. The Socialist Alliance launched a campaign to end unions' exclusive funding of Labour candidates, and had sufficient support in most important unions to ensure that debates took place. Union political fund ballots, due by law to begin in March 2003, would provide a further opportunity to debate the Labour link.

By mid-2002, the Party's financial crisis was described as the worst in its history, but union parsimony was only part of the story. Embarrassing stories about business donations were portrayed in the media as being linked to government policy decisions, in one case involving a £100,000 donation from a well-known pornographer. As a consequence, 'high value donations' collapsed in 2002. New Labour's business links were now causing more trouble than was the union link. And individual party membership fell to 180,000 in 2003, less than half the 1997 number. Affiliated unions donated £100,000 to allow pressing obligations to be met, but plans to guarantee a third of the Party's running costs over a Parliament, equivalent to £40 million over five years, were soon reported to have been shelved temporarily because of the firefighters' dispute and other policy discontents (*Tribune*, 31 January 2003).

Having previously rejected the option as being politically impossible, in 2002 Blair initiated a debate on the state funding of parties that was immediately interpreted as signalling the end of the union link. The Party chair said the only question was how far state funding went (*Tribune*, 19 July 2002). The Institute for Public Policy Research (IPPR) think-tank, closely linked to New Labour, produced state funding proposals that, its authors' protestations notwithstanding, were immediately interpreted as implying the abolition of the national, federal union link, because of a proposal to limit organisations' donations to a party to £5,000 a year. The report seemed unaware of the distinction between unions' mass subscription fees and unions' other donations, and its pre-emptive answer to the charge that it risked destroying the link amounted to the single assertion that, 'Even with a donation cap, we believe that this historical relationship can continue' (Cain and Taylor, 2002, 31). The rival think-tank Catalyst published a pamphlet by Keith Ewing, who had presented Labour's evidence to the Neill Committee hearings on party funding. Ewing's pamphlet addressed the union link directly, argued against any cap and defended mass subscription, but called for the procedures for determining the size of union affiliation fees to be democratised (Ewing, 2002).

There were several significant manifestations that the 'political ballast' factor was weakening. First, as noted above, key unions, especially in the public services, conducted high-profile anti-government protests. In spite of strenuous efforts to prevent it, union votes carried a motion demanding an independent review of the PFI programme (which Blair and Brown immediately dismissed). Second, in union election after union election, senior posts were won by candidates identified as being anti-New Labour, partly reflecting a context of tight labour market conditions and some renewed rank-and-file militancy. The general-secretaryships of CWU, RMT and PCS, and the deputy general-secretaryship in the TGWU were won by left candidates. And in 2002, Sir Ken Jackson, known as 'Blair's favourite union leader', dramatically lost the leadership of AMICUS-AEEU to a left-wing regional official. In 2003, Kevin Curran beat a more anti-New Labour candidate to become GMB general secretary. But then the sitting CWU deputy general secretary was ousted by an anti-New Labour challenger. And, crucially, Tony Woodley, the strongest leftwing candidate, won the TGWU general secretaryship.

Third, the new anti-New Labour leaders began to act in concert, recalling the left–right factionalism that remains the nightmare of party leaders. And figures on Labour's new left and its old right called on the unions to flex their muscles further. On the new left, Bob Crow and Mick Rix, leaders of RMT and ASLEF, issued a joint call for Labour to be reclaimed for Labour, arguing that, 'Trade unions are still potentially decisive in shaping Labour policy. The party is still our representation committee – if we choose to make it so ... If we have a government that is more Berlusconi than Bevin, it is only because we tolerate it' (*Guardian*, 1 May 2002). From the old right, ex-deputy Party leader, Roy Hattersley, in a *Guardian* column headed 'Only the unions can save Labour', insisted that 'Social justice depends on a return to social democracy ... Only the trade unions, working from inside the party, have the strength to bring it about ... The unions should pay their subscriptions, vote their full strength and save the party they created' (22 July 2002).

Fourth, in 2002, the public service unions launched mass strikes over pay in local government, attracting unexpected public sympathy, and pitting some of the most important affiliated union leaders against Labour's local and national government leaders. And in autumn 2002, the firefighters' pay strike produced a political crisis that saw the deputy prime minister, John Prescott, despatched to preside over talks and attack the FBU in Parliament. The government repeatedly warned that it would not allow new money for public services to be used to fund above-inflation pay rises unless linked to 'modernisation' and, in the fire service, to job cuts and station closures. One Labour minister (in the Scottish Executive) had to resign after calling the strikers 'Fascists'. Unlike in 1977, the TUC backed the firefighters. A deal between the FBU and the employers brokered by the TUC, based apparently on a pay deal acceptable to the government, and binding arbitration on disputed 'modernisation' issues, was then ripped up by Prescott, leading John Monks to attack the government's 'shoot from the hip approach' (TUC Press Release, 23 November 2002). The strike was further embittered by government announcements (later reversed) that it would send troops and police across picket lines to seize fire engines, by mutual recrimination over the implications of 'modernisation', and notably by Prescott's announcement that he would bring back 1940s legislation giving him power to decree firefighters' pay and conditions. The *Daily Mirror* dubbed Prescott, the one-time union militant, a union-busting 'working-class zero' as talks and strikes stretched into the winter (29 January 2003). Not until February 2003 did unions, employers and government representatives sit round a negotiating table for the first time. In the same month, a group of FBU candidates announced they would run against Labour in the Scottish Parliament elections.

In New Labour's second term, then, the factors binding the link identified in Minkin's (1992) *Contentious Alliance* appeared once again to be under severe pressure. Factors that strengthened briefly in the first term were again weakening, some rapidly. And research suggested that other vital aspects of the link at individual and local level were also measurably weakening. Studies of Labour's individual membership revealed striking changes during the 1990s, especially after the Party, in 1993, dropped its constitutional requirement that eligible members should be a member of a union. In 1990, two-thirds of Labour's members were union members, but by 1999, two-thirds were not, and the proportion who had joined after 1994 and were non-union was even higher (Seyd and Whiteley, 2002, 35, 41). And the other side of the coin of the unions' successful marshalling of resources in Labour's key seats in 2001 was a generally low level of organised union involvement with the Party at local level. Successive annual surveys of local union branch links, conducted by the Labour Research Department, revealed a low and declining level of local affiliation, and low and declining levels of participation in local party activity (*Labour Research*, October 2002).

New Century, New Alliances?

A fundamental fact of the link is that, in terms of the Party's own constitution, the unions cannot be forced out. But if Labour's parliamentarians legislated along the lines of the IPPR proposals for party funding, the existing federal link, based on the payment of mass subscriptions far beyond the IPPR's proposed £5,000 limit on donation per organisation, would simply become illegal. Few union leaders would welcome the prospect of extended internal debate over the reform of union constitutions necessary to put their political links on a new footing. Alternatively, some of the residual problems for New Labour's image associated with the union link could be tackled along the lines suggested by Ewing (2002): regulating the payment of union subscriptions is a way to prevent individual union leaderships varying the total amount to protest against party or party-in-government policy. It is certainly possible to envisage forms of progressive disengagement that might satisfy some unions. The parliamentary leadership might offer to meet regularly with union leaders to discuss policy; unions could continue to engage in the Party's rolling policy process, which was designed to incorporate contributions from outside bodies. Informal structures could also be established, in which Party strategists could seek the unions' financial and logistical support for particular campaigns, and of course for elections.

If the Party moved to a single category of individual membership, ending all organisational affiliations, as Blair advocated in the 1992/3 review, unions would still have the opportunity of organising and mobilising their members within the Party, as some already do at local level. Foreign models of union–Party links offer plenty of adaptable alternatives.

From the union point of view, there might be some advantages in redirecting their considerable political resources. In addition to EU policy-making, which attracts increasing union attention, unions have seized opportunities to advance members' rights through the European Court of Justice, and through invoking the Human Rights Act (1998), through the Scottish Parliament and Executive, the Welsh Assembly, and the Greater London Authority. These avenues circumvent the central legislative authority of Westminster that historically underpins the union–Labour link, and present the possibility of closer links with the other parties (or independent mayors) with power in the new institutions. Unions established new consultation mechanisms with the Scottish Executive, and negotiated the sort of deal for workers in 'PFI-ed' public services that New Labour, at the time, refused to introduce in England (*Labour Research*, December 2002). Through the formally non-partisan vehicle of the TUC, unions have developed more constructive relationships with the Liberal Democrats, whose leader became the first non-Labour leader to address a TUC Congress in 2002. Frustrated with the government position that requires workers to rely on private pensions but not making such saving obligatory, the TUC praised the Liberal Democrats' pensions policy for having 'grasped the nettle of compulsion' (TUC Press Release, 22 November 2002). Unison general secretary, Dave Prentis, warned, 'If we can no longer rely on Labour as allies in supporting public services, we will have to look elsewhere. We will go into uncharted territory and talk to the Liberal Democrats and others' (*Guardian*, 19 July 2001). Any foreseeable euro referendum campaign is likely to see the TUC itself in the 'yes' camp with a multitude of partners, while Labour's individual affiliates are likely to be found in both camps.

How far, and how fast, such alternatives might be pursued will also importantly be determined by the direction of New Labour policy in areas of the greatest significance to unions. Some non-industrial issues have the potential to generate schisms in the Labour movement. In the past these have tended to be foreign policy issues, and the war in Iraq was such an issue during 2002–03. But the key underlying question in New Labour's second term was what kind of social democracy would it pursue, and with what implications for core union activities? John Cruddas, a first-term Downing Street adviser on union relations, who won a parliamentary seat in 2001, openly attacked the direction of policy. Noting a government report that showed that white-collar workers were better off after being 'PFI-ed' into the private sector, but blue-collar workers were worse off, he commented that:

> At best, it tacitly supports the growing inequality. At worst, it is culpable in a strategy that actively intensifies the exploitation of big parts of the working class ... Why are elements in the Government so hostile to labour market regulation? And why is it that every single labour market initiative has to be fought line by line, almost street by street? Why are we now seeking to rewrite, or de-write, earlier commitments made to protect people at work? This ideological hostility is not simply the product of deference to corporate wealth and power. Its basis lies in the conception of the 'new economy' that underpins much Government language and action. (*Tribune*, 15 March 2002)

The judgement of one leading student of the politics of industrial relations offered the cautious conclusion that 'in the industrial relations field New Labour represents a continuation of the neo-liberalism of the Conservative government, but one required to make more concessions than its predecessor with trade unions and social-democratic policy preferences' (Crouch, 2001, 104). From this point of view, the second term has so far highlighted New Labour's commitments to radical, private-sector-led reform of the public services, to the so-called Anglo-Saxon model of capitalism and against the continental social market model in the EU, and to an industrial relations culture still constrained by Thatcher's legal constraints on trade unionism. There was tension in the link over all these features in the first term, but then they could be regarded as political devices to keep middle-class voters and organised business inside the 'big tent'. And they could be set against the benefits that the first term produced, notably signing the EU social protocol, the National Minimum Wage, and the Employment Relations Act. In the soured atmosphere of the second term, it was the limitations of these measures, and their derivation from 'old' Labour pledges, not New Labour values, that seemed to be more significant. Early union reactions to the government's review of the Employment Relations Act (1999), noted above, were extremely hostile.

'Real' New Labour now seems to have emerged, emboldened by Labour's second landslide. At the same time, the threat to the unions of the Tory alternative appears to be more distant. The terms of the union calculation about how much could be achieved inside the party are changing. The new reality, outgoing TUC general secretary, John Monks, advised, is that, 'We've got to start from the fact that this is not a trade union party. It was, but the relationship has altered because the sociology of Britain has altered' (*Guardian*, 9 December 2002). But, having made a strategic turn away from a collective bargaining strategy towards a legislative, rights-based strategy for advancing workers' and unions' interests, British unions now need to achieve more, not less, through their political campaigning. Affiliated unions could seriously contemplate the attractions of more independent and pluralist political activity even if, after a century of investment, dissolving the 'Labour alliance' would be a massive wrench. If the party leadership used state funding to end the federal union–Party link, some of Labour's affiliated unions might not put up fierce resistance. Other unions, though, would fight to reclaim Labour as a pro-labour party. The one safe prediction that can be made is that any non-consensual moves to end the link would be fought over bitterly.

In the mid-1980s, a social democrat in the Labour Party, if asked what single step would best transform Labour into a European social democratic party, would most probably have answered, 'Break the union link!' Most unions at that time were not prepared to abandon free collective bargaining for institutionalised corporatist collaboration; most opposed Britain's membership of the EEC; and, unusually, in the early 1980s key unions had rebelled against the Party's social democratic wing and supported the Labour left's radical 'alternative economic strategy'. Twenty years later, in New Labour's second term, a social democrat of that earlier era would undoubtedly regard the affiliated unions, long since converted to the European social market model, as the single most important force in the Labour Party, fighting to convert it into a European social democratic party rather than the force for pro-business neo-liberalism that its union critics accused it of having become.

6

A Damascene Conversion?
New Labour and
Media Relations

BOB FRANKLIN

Introduction

On 16 July 2002, for the first time since 1938, a British prime minister
addressed a Select Committee of the House of Commons. Tony Blair used
this exceptional parliamentary occasion to announce his 'Damascene conversion' and publicly to repent Labour's reliance on 'spin'. At a time when
'politics is under a relentless 24-hour media gaze,' he argued, 'there is often
so much focus on the issues of process and personality ... that there is a dan-
ger that people feel that's all we as politicians focus on'. Blair's new mission was to 'try to engage in the political debate in a different way', to
overcome 'what is perceived, often unfairly, as issues to do simply with
news management'. Labour's seduction by the temptations of 'spin'
reflected the party's eighteen wilderness years in opposition. 'When you are
in opposition ... there is a tendency to believe the announcement is the reality,' Blair argued, 'because ... you are not actually in a position to deliver
anything on the ground. I think for the first period of time in government
there was a tendency to believe that the same situation still applied. It does
not. For government the announcement is merely the intention: the reality is
what you have to go on to deliver on the ground' (Blair, 2002d). But not
everyone has subsequently been persuaded to the light: disbelievers abound.
Frank Field, for example, argued, 'you cannot separate spin from new
Labour. The electorate now do not believe what the government says. If
press releases were approved by St. Peter, they would still wonder if there
was some trick on the way' (*Control Freaks*, Channel 5 TV, 28 September
2002). Political correspondents also remain sceptical, if not agnostic,

suggesting that the government's commitment to openness and its rejection of news management does not signal the *end* of spin but merely the onset of a new *style* of spin: 'so "no spin is the new spin" has become this year's brittle joke' (White, 2002). In the words of one senior lobby correspondent, recent shifts in Labour's communication strategy represent little more than 'the latest twist in the game, a tactical ploy of no great merit' (Ashley, 2002, 16; see also Kavanagh, 2002, 17).

By 2002, Labour's reliance on spin had become a significant story in its own right, generating some of the most hostile press coverage about the government since 1997. The infamous Jo Moore email about 'burying bad news', the subsequent very public row between Jo Moore and Martin Sixsmith, respectively special adviser and head of information in the Department of Transport, combined with the protracted departure of their Cabinet Minister Stephen Byers, characterised in one *Daily Mirror* front page splash and photomontage as 'Spinocchio', had severely dented the public image and legendary reputation of the No. 10 and Millbank 'media machine' for managing news and promoting the government's policy agenda (*Daily Mirror*, 27 February 2002). Peter Mandelson, who had played a key role in devising and implementing Labour's media strategy was, by 2002, regretting that new Labour's image had become that of a government 'obsessed by spin' reflecting 'crude and clumsy handling of the media by overly controlling and politicised press officers', so that 'much of what the government is doing fails to make an impact because its words are dismissed as spin' (Mandelson, 2002, xliv–xlv). An editorial in *The Daily Telegraph* alleged that the word 'spin' had joined 'sleaze' and 'smear' as one of the 'increasing number of Ss' used to describe 'the downward spiral of the reputation of politics' (*The Daily Telegraph*, 7 June 2002).

Blair judged this growing public perception of a government predicated on spin and preoccupied with news management to be unhelpful and electorally damaging. It was necessary to spin the issue of spin: in the prime minster's own phrase, it had become necessary 'to try to engage in the public debate in a different way'. In the preferred phrase of Alastair Campbell, Director of Communications in No. 10, it was necessary for the media and the government to adopt 'a more grown up, a more honest dialogue, that encourages greater accessibility, accountability and interaction' (Campbell, 2002, 21). This chapter explores some of the predominant ways in which the Labour Government has tried to engage in, but more significantly to shape, the public debate since 1997. The first section examines the government's continuing efforts to set the news agenda through the use of a rigorous news management strategy, while the concluding section analyses new Labour's extensive and growing use of publicly-funded government advertising campaigns to promote key areas of government policy via the media.

There is a particular focus on government advertising in the run-up to the 2001 general election. The chapter concludes that there is little evidence to suggest any Damascene conversion or new Labour retreat from its reliance on 'spin'. Indeed, the suggestion here is that Labour is modifying, but entrenching, the robust and aggressive structures of news management that have prompted journalists and government information officers, as well as politicians from all political parties, to describe the senior politicians within the Labour Party and those special advisers who staff the communications organisations based at No. 10, as 'control freaks' (Jones, 2002b, esp. ch. 3). These developments, moreover, represent continuity rather than change. There is a clear line of descent connecting Bernard Ingham's 'politicising' and expansion of the office of prime minister's press secretary throughout the 1980s (Harris, 1990) with Alastair Campbell's development of the strategic communications unit designed to keep the government 'on message' and to shape news media coverage of the government (Seymour-Ure, 2000, 152).

The Three 'Rs': Rhetoric, Repetition and Rebuttal

The Labour Party entered government in 1997 with a systematic communication strategy, characterised by Romola Christopherson, a retired head of information in various Whitehall departments, as the three 'Rs'. The first 'R' she suggests is:

> rhetoric – getting the message and encapsulating the message in a marketing slogan – 'New Labour, New Britain', 'Peoples' Princess' – all those soundbites, getting that rhetoric absolutely clear and right and accessible. That's the first 'R'. Second 'R' is repetition, repetition, repetition, repetition. When you're bored with repeating it, it probably means that people are beginning to pick it up. The final 'R' is rebuttal, which is don't let any attack on you go without walloping back at it. (cited in *Control Freaks*, Channel 5 TV, 28 September 2002)

Implementing this strategy since 1997 has involved the increasing centralisation of communications at No. 10, a more assertive relationship with journalists and broadcasters, and the politicising of the Government Information and Communications Service (GICS) (Franklin, 1998; Oborne, 1999; Barnett and Gaber, 2001). A senior officer in the GICS outlined this threefold strategy along with what he considered to be its shortcomings:

> New Labour perfected a machine which could do several things. One, it kept on top of the media circus. Secondly, it was terribly strongly controlled. I remember Peter Mandelson saying privately, 'The trouble with ministers in this government is that they expected to be told what to say by the centre rather than to work it out for themselves.' But they

were very, very tightly controlled. They assumed a very aggressive stance towards the
media, particularly with individual journalists, which is a very dangerous thing to do, and I
believe that Charlie Whelan, Peter Mandelson, Jo Moore and Stephen Byers all reaped that
whirlwind. They came in with a very strong idea about how to win, and how to win was how
to get the message across. But they ran up against a civil service culture whose main aim in
life is to ... reach people to make them aware, warn them, advise them. But what the civil
service machine is not there to do is to persuade people that this policy is right. (Interview
with the author, 22 July 2002)

Telling Ministers What to Say:
The Central Control of Communications

Establishing the centralised control of communications at No. 10 under the
direction of Alastair Campbell has been the key ambition for Labour's
media strategy: control has been strict but highly effective (Franklin, 2003).
The Mountfield report on government communications suggested that 'all
major interviews and media appearances, both print and broadcast, should
be agreed with the No. 10 Press Office before any commitments are entered
into. The policy content of all major speeches, press releases and new policy
initiatives should be cleared in good time with the No. 10 private office' and,
finally, 'the timing and form of announcements should be cleared with the
No. 10 Press Office' (Mountfield, 1997, 8).

A number of new institutions have been established since 1997 to guarantee and enforce this control. The media monitoring unit prepares a daily
digest of news media content and identifies potential problems for consid
eration ('rebuttal') at the daily 9 am communications meeting which
prepares for the 11 am briefing of lobby journalists. The strategic communications unit (SCU), established in January 1998, is responsible for
'pulling together and sharing with departments the government's key policy
themes and messages': that is, keeping sources on message (Select
Committee on Public Administration, 1998, para. 19). The primary task for
the SCU is to co-ordinate the weekly media presentation of stories. It prepares 'the grid', a weekly diary of events presented each Thursday to a
meeting of heads of information from the Whitehall departments. The
purpose is to prevent unhelpful clashes between departmental news
releases; to prevent positive developments being overshadowed by 'bad'
news; and, on occasion, to 'slip out' any bad news on what is broadly a good
news day for the government. A memo from the head of the SCU to departmental heads of information, dated 9 November 1999, outlined the new centralised protocols for developing co-ordinated media coverage. 'From now
on,' it announced, 'for each major [news] event we will be using a planning
document (copy attached) for which the relevant Downing Street press

officer will be responsible. As you can see it sets out the key messages that should be communicated by the event, how they link to the government's overall message, and the methods we will be using to get wide coverage in the run up, launch and follow up to the event' (cited in Williams, 2000, Annex H).

In June 2000, the *Guardian* published a leaked copy of the grid which illustrated the SCU's role in co-ordinating the media presentation of four speeches planned for the third week in May: each policy is accompanied by a soundbite encapsulating the 'message'. A memo attached to the grid confirmed that the prime minister wished ministers to stress that the government had a 'clear mission and purpose' by 'referring to each other's work':

> Monday, Chancellor, child poverty: 'no child need grow up in poverty'; Tuesday, Prime Minister, economy: 'families are protected from boom and bust and enjoy rising living standards'; Wednesday, Home Secretary, police training and recruitment: 'people need not live in fear': Thursday, Secretary of State for Health, medical school expansion: 'we can get an NHS fit for the twenty-first century'. (cited in Jones, 2001, 145)

The attached memo underscored the overall message 'Big goals. Big arguments. Serious government versus opportunistic opposition' (Jones, 2001, 145). A senior press officer in one Whitehall department claimed the SCU had been a great success in shaping relationships with journalists. 'By organising the diary so strictly,' he suggested, 'the SCU has played a critical role in the government's efforts to dominate the news agenda' (cited in Williams, 2000, 15).

This centralised structure regulating relationships between politicians and journalists has prompted predictable tensions in the Labour ranks, but also between special advisers and civil servants working in the GICS. In March 1998, for example, Harriet Harman (then Secretary of State for Health) was chastised by Campbell for giving media interviews without his approval. A leaked fax demanded that she explain 'why the interviews with the *Guardian, Women's Hour* and *World At One* were not cleared through this office' (*Guardian*, 30 March 1998, 5; Jones, 2001, 145). In the Department of Transport more recently, and more spectacularly, a special adviser and the head of information 'resigned' following a 'feud' over communications supremacy. Each began to brief journalists against the other, prompting 'mixed' and contradictory 'messages', which in turn caused embarrassment to No. 10 and triggered journalists to question the capacity of 'Downing Street's once fabled spin operation ... to offer consistent explanations' of events: such questions 'sealed the fate' of both and underlined the centralised communications control exercised from No. 10 (*Guardian*, 16 February 2002, 13).

**Keeping on Top of the Media Circus: Labour's
Relationships with News Media**

Relationships between journalists and politicians 'have been transformed
over the past ten years' (McNair, 2000, 170; Barnett and Gaber, 2001, 99).
Certainly since 1997, Labour's uncompromising news management strategy has presented journalists and broadcasters with 'tough choices'.
Compliant journalists will be rewarded with the occasional 'exclusive', but
the 'awkward squad' will be denied interviews with senior politicians, will
no longer receive tips about 'breaking stories and exclusives', and will find
their competitors being favoured when government press officers 'place'
significant stories (Gaber, 1998, 14). In short, the government is playing an
old-fashioned game of carrots and sticks (see Bernard Ingham, in *Select
Committee on Public Administration*, 1998, 9–14). One senior lobby correspondent claimed that the ambition was to create 'a political press corps
which is ready to report government in the terms it wishes to be reported
and within parameters set by Downing Street itself' (Oborne, 2002, 33).
Guardian editor Alan Rusbridger describes how this game of carrots and
sticks was played out before the 1997 election, claiming that Campbell
'used to ring up to cajole, plead, shout and horse-trade'. Rusbridger recalled
that 'Stories would be offered on condition that they went on the front page.
I would be told that if I didn't agree they would go to the *Independent*. They
would withdraw favours, grant favours, exclude us from stories going elsewhere ... Now we have almost no contact' (cited in Oborne, 1999, 184).

Sticks are undoubtedly more commonplace than carrots. In October
1997, Campbell circulated a forceful memo to GICS heads of information
arguing that 'media handling' must become more assertive. 'Decide your
headlines,' he insisted, 'sell your story and, if you disagree with what is
being written, argue your case. If you need support from here [Downing
Street] let me know' (Timmins, 1997, 1). For journalists writing against the
government line, the consequences are problematic. Journalists are bullied
in private, harangued in public and excluded from off-the-record briefings.
There are 'very few journalists' whom Campbell 'has not attempted to
abuse or humiliate' (Oborne, 1999, 181). Labour spin doctors, moreover,
have 'never hesitated to destablise journalists by going behind their backs to
their bosses' (Oborne, 1999, 182). The most celebrated such occasion
involved Andrew Marr, then editor of the *Independent* and a Labour ally.
Marr wrote an article critical of Labour's European policy, prompting
Campbell to contact David Montgomery, then chief executive of Mirror
Group Newspapers, which owned the *Independent*, to insist that Marr be
sacked (Cohen, 1999, 153–4): Campbell told Marr 'you are either with us or
against us' (McGwire, 1997, 11).

What Seymour-Ure (1968) describes as 'press–party parallelism' is influential here, with relationships based on shared political commitments more likely to be congenial. Consequently, Campbell displays a particular courtesy during lobby briefings to *The Times* correspondent Philip Webster, and Trevor Kavanagh of the *Sun* (both owned by Murdoch's News International). Campbell's golden rule 'is that he leaves the *Sun* well alone' (Oborne, 1999, 181). But George Jones of the critical *Daily Telegraph* (favoured by previous Conservative administrations) finds himself in 'the wilderness' and 'starved of the oxygen of information which alone can sustain the dedicated political reporter' (Oborne, 1999, 174).

Perhaps what was most noticeable about relationships between politicians and journalists during New Labour's first term was the extent of career 'cross-over' between the two groups. Nicholas Jones neologises the term 'journo-politicos' to describe the new generation of policy advisers who have been at 'the sharp end of the hard sell' characterising New Labour's approach to the media. These hybrids – whose background is in 'media, publicity or politics' and whose 'success is judged in terms of their effectiveness in political presentation' – symbolise the degree to which 'demarcation lines have become blurred' (Jones, 2001, 68–9). For their part, journalists are increasingly being appointed to senior GICS posts, or as special advisers to ministers. The political editor of the *Daily Mirror* noted that 'Blair's government is stuffed with journalists' (Routledge, 2001, 34). And the appointment of senior BBC producers and broadcasters to government posts prompted one description of the BBC as 'a regular target for the Downing Street raiding party' (Jones, 2001, 79). Similarly, politicians and government sources are increasingly behaving like journalists. The *Independent*, for example, claimed that in the first two years of the first term, 166 articles were published with Tony Blair's byline: only thirteen less than *Sun* columnist Richard Littlejohn across the same period (*Independent*, 8 June 1999). The great majority of these articles were written, of course, by Alastair Campbell and former journalists working in the SCU. In these different ways, the roles of politicians and journalists are increasingly overlapping.

Civil Service Culture and Getting the Message Across

Since winning office in 1997, Labour has enjoyed access to the resources and services of the Government Information and Communication Service, staffed by 1,200 civil servants whose press and public relations activities are governed by a code of conduct (The Whitehall Red Book) designed to guarantee their political impartiality. 'Press officers' according to the Red Book, must 'establish a position with the media whereby it is understood that they stand apart from the party political battle, but are there to assist the media to understand the policies of the government of the day' (Cabinet Office, 1997, para. 11). By contrast, special advisers are 'not bound by the usual requirements that civil servants should be ... impartial' (Select Committee on Public Administration, 1998, xv). The Select Committee on Public Administration, investigating concerns that the Labour Government might be politicising the GICS by ignoring these distinctions, concluded that there 'is a very fine line between the promotion and defence of government policy and the promotion and defence of the ruling party's policies' (Select Committee on Public Administration, 1998, xv). Since 1997, however, civil servants have expressed growing concerns that this 'line' is crossed too frequently. Senior information officers have warned about the 'creeping politicisation of the GICS', with significant consequences for their relationships with journalists (Select Committee, 1998, 80). The government's response is that it wishes only to 'modernise' the GICS to ensure that 'it is equipped to meet the demands of a fast changing media world' (Mountfield, 1997, para. 2). Four recent trends have triggered civil service concerns.

First, the government has appointed unprecedented numbers of special advisers, whose main priority is press relations and the promotion of government policy. Every Cabinet minister may appoint up to two advisers, 'political' or 'expert', but in practice, as the Neill Committee observed, this restriction has not always been observed. Ministers, moreover, may appoint an unspecified number of unpaid advisers (Select Committee on Public Administration, 2001, para. 5). The thirty-two advisers previously in post were replaced by sixty within the early days of the Labour's 1997 victory, at an additional annual cost of £600,000, a 44 per cent increase over Conservative expenditure (Franklin, 1998, 11). By January 2001 there were seventy-eight advisers, with twenty-six based at No. 10, and costing £4.4 millions annually (HC Debates, 22 January 2001, col. 467). One observer described this growth in special advisers as 'near rampant' (Peter Hennessy in evidence to the Select Committee on Public Administration, 2001, para. 19). At the time of writing there are eighty-one advisers, three times as many as under the Major Administration (Jones, 2002b, 5).

Second, by 2001 *all* the 44 civil service heads of information who were in post in 1997 had resigned or retired. The lighthearted civil service phrase used to describe these departures was 'gardening leave'. The valedictory procession began in the first year of Labour's first term, prompting the Select Committee reviewing the procedures of the GICS to describe these staffing changes as 'an unusual turnover' (Select Committee, 1998, xviii). The reasons behind these civil service changes were evidently wide-ranging but included 'the desire of ministers for information officers to be less neutral than they thought was compatible with their regular civil service terms of employment' (Select Committee, 1998, xviii). The retired head of information at the Northern Ireland Office spoke of a 'culling' of heads of information and their replacement 'by "politically acceptable" temporary bureaucrats', a process he labelled the 'Washingtonisation' of the civil service (Select Committee, 1998, 86).

Third, this growth of special advisers has created a 'two-tier structure of information' in which the advisers have become the dominant partners over civil servants (Select Committee, 1998, ix). Advisers are selected by ministers, and are typically close and trusted friends who have worked with the minister outside as well as inside government. By contrast, heads of information are an inheritance of government, and judged to be rule-driven and unduly 'impartial' in their relationships with journalists. Consequently, the significant communications tasks are allocated to the adviser, leaving the civil service press officer to deal with more routine matters. GICS officers suggest that the 'enormous increase in the power of the special adviser' is 'widely acknowledged'. In one department, the arrival of the minister's 'workaholic mouthpiece' meant 'every single press release, and there were to be a lot more of them, had to be cleared by a special adviser'. Constructing the crucial weekly 'grid' is also acknowledged to be the adviser's priority. One head of news conceded 'there are no two ways about it, [the special adviser] decides what goes in the diary and when ... Officials can object, but at the end of the day the decision is his' (Williams, 2000, 27–9). Tensions between political advisers and civil servants abound. There have been a number of very public spats since 1997. The departure of Treasury civil servant, Jill Rutter, early in the first term, reflected the tensions in her relationship with Charlie Whelan. And the acrimonious mutual 'resignation' of Jo Moore and Martin Sixsmith, discussed earlier, illustrated the most dramatic and protracted conflict between a civil servant and a special adviser (Jones, 2002b, 367).

Finally, the most significant change at the GICS has been the concerted government pressure to get the service 'on message', that is, to propagandise for government. In October 1997, Campbell sent a memo to heads of information confirming that the central task of GICS information and media relations work was to ensure that the 'government's four key messages' were 'built in to all areas of our activity'. Labour is 'a modernising government', a government 'for all the people', which is 'delivering on its promises' with 'mainstream policies' providing new directions for Britain (*Financial Times*, 9 October 1997). Some information officers have preferred to resign rather than to comply with centrally-issued dictates that appear to show so little regard for the civil service's traditional professional commitments to neutrality. For those who remain, the pressures to comply are acute.

When Alan Evans, for example, resisted special adviser John McTernan's requests to draft press releases in ways that Evans judged to be party-political, McTernan briefed the press. Evans, he claimed, was 'dead meat'. Evans told a parliamentary committee 'the drafting of press releases was closely scrutinised to the point of obsession by specialist advisers. They sought to reproduce the tone of the Labour manifesto and repeat its election commitments as emerging news'. He claimed, 'I would suspect there are a number of senior members of the GICS who feel they are very much on trial with ministers and who will be concerned that giving unpalatable advice may result in them losing their job. I regard living under pressure of this kind as being politicised' (quoted on *Control Freaks*, Channel 5 TV, 28 September 2002). A senior GICS officer commented that the growing power of special advisers reflects, at least in part, a 'lack of leadership, poor leadership by permanent secretaries which undermines the ability of the system to resist being bullied and pushed around by advisers'. The relationship between special advisers and civil servants goes wrong when the former 'look as if they have become unassailable and when they become gatekeepers to the minister. It defeats the whole purpose of having a section, an objective agency, which should advise' (interview with the author, July 2002).

A number of parliamentary select committee inquiries since 1998 have examined the numerous conflicts between the advisers and the traditional civil servants who staff the GICS. In 2001, as part of its broader inquiry into 'Making Government Work', the Select Committee on Public Administration published the report *Special Advisers: Boon or Bane*, which concluded that 'All the available evidence suggests that special advisers can make a positive contribution to good government', and that their involvement in government need not 'be threatening to the traditional role of the civil service', but suggested that 'it is time to put the position of special advisers on a firmer footing' (Select Committee on Public Administration, 2001, para. 81). This committee endorsed the Neil Committee's recommendation for a code of conduct for special advisers, which should offer clear guidance on the relations between advisers and members of the GICS. All adviser appointments, moreover, should be advertised and competitive, and consideration should be given to establishing a fund to pay the costs of advisers not recruited under civil service rules, and Parliament should at the 'earliest opportunity' debate a code for regulating the activities of special advisers (Select Committee on Public Administration, 2001, xxv).

A year later, concerns about the politicising of the civil service were still being voiced. Sir Richard Wilson, the outgoing Cabinet secretary, used his retirement speech to warn of the possible dangers. Given civil servants' legendary reputation for understatement and measured language, Wilson's remarks might be judged to be acerbic: 'It is fundamental to the working of our constitution,' he claimed, 'that governments should use the resources entrusted to them, including the civil service, for the benefit of the country as a whole and not for the benefit of their political party ... the non-political character of the civil service underpins that convention.' His prescription for change was threefold: a limit on the number of special advisers should be 'set by Parliament at the beginning of each new Parliament'; special advisers should be banned from managing permanent civil servants; and, in a barely veiled reference to Jo Moore, 'special advisers should not behave illegally or improperly', nor should they 'ask civil servants to do anything improper or illegal ... [and] they should not do anything to undermine the political impartiality of civil servants or the duty of civil servants to give their own best advice to Ministers' (Sherman, 2002, 10).

Advertising Government Policies

Labour's commitment to using publicly-funded advertising and marketing to promote its policy ambitions develops a trend initiated by Conservative Administrations in the 1980s. It was Lord Young's radical suggestion that 'Government programmes are like cornflakes – if they are not marketed, they will not sell' (*PR Week*, 16 March 1988), which marked a watershed in political communications by articulating a new approach that addressed voters less as citizens than as consumers. Young's arrival sparked an explosion of publicity expenditure from £1,785,000 in 1986–7 to £31,276,000 by 1988–9 (*Labour Research*, November 1991). By the end of the 1980s, the government had become the nation's largest spending advertiser (Franklin, 1994, 103).

Critics began to highlight a number of radical shifts in government campaigning and advertising expenditure that were prompting anxieties: more than a hundred parliamentary questions were posed on this subject during the 1987–8 session (Blair, 1989, 1). First, there had been a striking increase in advertising budgets: expenditure (at constant 1987–8 prices) more than doubled from £60.5 million in 1982–3 to £141 million in 1987–8 (*Hansard*, 15 January 1988, col. 404). Second, there was a marked shift from overseas to domestic publicity: the former declined from 34 per cent of budget in 1984–5 to 14 per cent in 1987–8. Third, there was an increase in expenditure related to economic and social policy, from 2 per cent of domestic expenditure in 1978–86 to 26 per cent in 1987. Fourth, a pattern emerged of increased expenditure in the year prior to a general election. Central Office of Information (COI) data reveal that such increases are evident for every election since 1964 (Scammell, 1991, 315–25). An unprecedented surge in expenditure was evident in the months before the 2001 general election (*Panorama*, 26 May 2002). Finally, but significantly, government advertising appeared to move away from the uncontentious social persuasion campaigns of the 1980s – for example, encouraging drivers to 'Clunk Click Every Trip' – towards highly contested areas of policy such as the Conservatives' privatisation programmes. Advertising expenditure promoting these privatisations was unprecedented – £76 million alone for the sale of electricity (Blair, 1989).

Blair, then shadowing the Department of Trade, alleged that, 'It is no coincidence that the areas of largest increase in [publicity] spending are those of most political sensitivity for the government' (*Financial Times*, 30 March 1988). A year later, his comments were more explicit. 'You can see quite clearly that the purpose [of these government advertising campaigns] is not to give us the public the facts,' he alleged, 'but to sell the government's political message. And that's quite wrong' (*Panorama*, 1989). But Blair's governments have continued this trend. The next section considers government advertising under New Labour, including the highly contentious campaigns prior to the 2001 general election. It details concerns that New Labour, like its Conservative predecessors, may be crossing the line between advertising to provide the public with information and its use to promote public support for particular policy choices: the line which separates policy *marketing* from *propaganda*. The review of recent advertising and campaigning activities offers little support for Blair's second-term contention that the party is seeking 'to engage in the political debate in a different way'.

Labour, Advertising and Marketing

The period since 1997 has certainly witnessed a sharp increase in advertising expenditure. COI statistics (the clearing house for the purchasing of government advertising) reveal a striking increase in advertising-related and expenditure, from £110.8 m in 1997–8 to £173.4 million in 1998–9, a year on year rise of 57 per cent. By 2000–01 the government's marketing and publicity activities required an unprecedented budget of £295.4 million, a near threefold increase in expenditure over four years (COI, 2002, 4). This expenditure reinstated the government as the largest buyer of advertising in the UK. It spent almost twice as much as its second (Unilever) and third place (BT) rivals combined (Watt, 2001, 13).

A number of factors make this substantial expenditure even more noteworthy, and some suggest that it may underestimate actual levels of government marketing activity. First, expenditure has expanded despite the radical shrinking of the state sector. Most of the Thatcher Government's advertising budgets during the 1980s funded the privatisation campaigns, which no longer happen. Privatisation has diminished the state sector but with no visible effect on the size of advertising budgets. Second, bulk purchasing of advertising through the COI secures a 27 per cent discount, so that the above-cited figures underestimate by approximately a quarter the media value as well as the quantity of government advertising. Third, since April 1984, the COI has been obliged to bid for departmental publicity work in competition with private agencies. In 2000–01, only ten departments purchased such services through the COI, signalling an even greater publicity expenditure by the government, as many departments 'outsource' promotional campaigns (COI, 2002).

New Labour's advertising budget has generated a flurry of marketing activity with expanding range, scope and audience reach. In 1998, for example, the COI implemented a regional campaign to market the 'New Deal' employment policy. The multi-media campaign involved all aspects of promotion, from 'securing media coverage on regional television and in the press' to 'delivery of the New Deal in Job Centres and the development of relevant web site materials' (COI, 1998, 3). In the same year, the National Year of Reading was launched by David Blunkett on the set of *EastEnders*. With a £2 million budget for television advertising, its celebrity backers included the Spice Girls, Chris Evans, John Cleese and Linford Christie, and 'free' coverage was promised in a wide range of popular programmes including *Brookside, Ready Steady Cook, Esther* and *Big Breakfast* (Franklin, 1999, 23–7). In 2000 and 2001 there were further campaigns to reduce teenage pregnancy and to promote the working families tax credit, as well as campaigns to reduce levels of smoking (Shaeffer, 2000, 4; Watt, 2001, 13). Further campaigns in 2001 focused on reducing benefit fraud, lone parent benefits, the National Health Service, and ethnic minority recruitment to the police and navy. During 2001, the COI conducted 383 research studies for departments, completed 2,000 jobs with print runs in excess of 20 million, organised 2,056 ministerial visits, raised £8 million value added from private sponsorship, received more than 100 million hits on its news delivery website, and achieved discounts on advertising worth in excess of £52 million (COI, 2001, 4). A noteworthy element in the COI's campaigns has been pre-recorded tapes, known as 'fillers' or 'COIs', distributed free to radio and television broadcasters (Gardner, 1986; COI, 2001, 13). The format is typically an interview, often with a minister, discussing proposed or recent legislation. By 2001, the COI annual report claimed that 'over the past year they [fillers] have been transmitted 708,000 times. That's 11,800 hours of donated airtime – the same as 151 years of episodes of *EastEnders*'. And the COI now targets 'ever wider audiences by broadcasting fillers via a diverse range of media from football clubs and shopping centres to buses and Internet TV' (COI, 2001, 13).

Concerns about the levels of expenditure, combined with the potentially partisan character of some government advertising, grew apace during the saturation advertising immediately prior to the 2001 general election. The BBC *Panorama* programme entitled 'Tony in Adland' (26 May 2002) analysed expenditure in the run-up to the 2001 election, replicating a *Panorama* programme broadcast on 4 September 1989 which had featured extensive criticisms by Blair of the Conservative Government's advertising expenditure. Two media analysts from the original programme, were invited to comment on three prominent advertisements featured in television-based advertising in 2001. Each publicly-funded advertisement focused on a 'politically contentious topic': nurses' pay and the state of the NHS; benefit 'cheats'; and benefits for lone parents.

The programme levelled three criticisms. First, the unprecedentedly high level of government advertising expenditure was inappropriate, especially given the proximity of the general election. Between April 2000 and March 2001, government advertising expenditure increased by 70 per cent over the previous year, and totalled £192 million. More than half (54 per cent) of this expenditure occurred in the last three months of the financial year. The government spent £29 million on advertising in January, £19 m in February and £49 million in March. March represented a record for expenditure in a single month; the election was planned for early May (Watt, 2001). Media analyst Hurdwell claimed that 'to spend a quarter of your budget in the last month of the financial year suggests bad financial management or a significant plan to spend the money in that month' (quoted on *Panorama*, 26 May 2002). Neville Taylor, director general of the COI between 1985 and 1988, commented that, 'To concentrate expenditure and impact and message ... in the run up to an election' he argued 'has got to smell. It has to indicate another motive for doing it' (quoted on *Panorama*, 26 May 2002).

Second, much of the advertising targeted the wrong audience. One advertisment focused on nursing recruitment but, *Panorama* alleged, it was more concerned to boost the image of the NHS. The advertisment, which ran in February and March 2001, related the story of a young boy injured in a road accident, listing the twenty-two specialist nurses 'who saved Joe's life'. But the media analysts suggested that, at a cost of £3 million, which 'put them in the same league as B&Q', the advertisement targeted the wrong audience. Lord Bell, previously of Saatchi & Saatchi, and a former Conservative adviser, suggested that 'these advertisments were occupying a lot of airtime to communicate the values of the NHS but they are nothing to do with recruitment'. Bell also suggested that television advertising was 'not the most efficient way of recruiting nurses. TV is a mass market, a blunt instrument that costs a great deal of money. It is not an efficient means of identifying a target audience and getting them to apply for a job' (quoted on *Panorama*, 26 May 2002). The government's own research concluded that 'disappointingly, interest in finding out more about nursing declined' across the period of broadcasting the advertisements. *Panorama* alleged the 'campaign may have been just what the doctor ordered for new Labour – a soft sell for the NHS' (*Panorama*, 26 May 2002).

Third, the timing of the advertisements so close to the election might represent crossing the line between 'general government advertising and tax-payer-funded "puffs" to promote the Labour cause' (White, 2002, 9). Certainly this was the view of a number of distinguished civil servants such as Sir Michael Partridge, permanent secretary at the Department of Social Security (1989–95), who claimed that the advertisment about nurse recruitment 'only really had nurse recruitment tacked on the end. The rest of it you could mistake for a "party political" saying, now we've got a good NHS'. He denounced an advertisement about benefits for lone parents as 'an improper use of taxpayers' money' since it was insufficiently factual and amounted 'to a general puff for government policy ... It seemed to me to be crossing the line' (quoted on *Panorama*, 26 May 2002). If the three criticisms can be sustained, moreover, they suggest government advertising might subvert the new limits on election expenditure imposed in 2001. Lord Armstrong, former Head of the Home Civil Service, argued, 'there are very strict rules about election expenses and this could be a way in which ... the party in government could be spending more on purposes related to the campaign than the law allows ... If I were the opposition I think I would be asking a good many questions about this' (quoted on *Panorama*, 26 May 2002).

But despite these loudly-mooted concerns, critics believe there is little effective control of the government's marketing and public relations expenditure and activities. In February 2002, in a little publicised move, the government's director of communications assumed unprecedented and overall control of government advertising. A quinquennial review of the COI, to which all government agencies are subject, concluded that the chief executive of the COI should report directly to Alastair Campbell when co-ordinating government publicity campaigns. The move triggered some predictable huffing and puffing from opposition politicians. Tim Collins, shadowing the Cabinet Office, claimed that 'for an unelected hack to be put in charge of the largest publicity budget in the UK is a gross violation of the traditional principles of independence for the civil service and strict neutrality for government advertising' (*Independent*, 25 May 2002, 5). In July 2002, Carole Fisher, the chief executive of the COI, resigned.

A Damascene Conversion?

New Labour has instigated radical changes to the structures and processes of political communication since 1997, by building on the legacy of Bernard Ingham and successive Conservative administrations which bequeathed an increasingly centralised system of government communications based around the No. 10 Press Office. Since 1997, the government has attempted systematically to influence and shape the media reporting of its activities, policies and key personalities; to replicate in government the highly successful news management strategy that served it so admirably in opposition. To that end, the government has created a number of new organisations committed to effective news management, including the media monitoring unit, the strategic communications unit and the daily 9 am meeting chaired by the director of communications. One consequence of this news management effort has been the emergence of a more robust and, on occasion, highly adversarial relationship with certain political journalists, especially those who tend to stray 'off message'. New Labour has also modernised the GICS in ways that have made the service more vulnerable than previously to the suggestion of partiality.

During its second term in office, Labour has announced publicly that this strategy may have been misguided and prompted too great an emphasis on presentation. Blair confessed to the Liaison Committee of the House of Commons that Labour may have mistaken the presentational word for the policy deed. But there is little, if any, evidence since his statement in 2002 to suggest that Labour's emphasis on presentation has been substantially revised or reversed. Sceptics challenge the genuineness of Blair's Damascene conversion. Charlie Whelan, Gordon Brown's former spin doctor, remains unconvinced: 'There are people predicting this is the death of spin,' he claims, but this is 'Nonsense. They're still doing it: and probably with a push from Alastair Campbell' (*Daily Mirror*, 29 May 2002). Indeed, since 2001 the government has strengthened its news management activities by 'rolling out' its computer-based rebuttal system, known as the knowledge network, into more government departments. Alastair Campbell has also changed the protocols governing lobby briefings in ways which many senior journalists believe will make the government less susceptible to critical questioning by influential and specialist political correspondents (Kavanagh, 2002; Oborne, 2002).

New Labour has also revealed a commitment to television and newspaper advertising to promote new policy initiatives. Labour has undoubtedly been a reforming and innovative government, initiating a good deal of legislative change which in turn suggests a justifiable rationale for the increased expenditure on public information and 'public awareness' advertising. But from the particular perspective that opposition alone seems to engender, Conservative politicians have expressed concern about the extent and scale of Labour's commitments. Critics have suggested that this growing use of advertising to promote *awareness* of Labour policy has, in reality, been used to promote *support* for Labour policies and, in turn, for the Labour Party. The accusation against Labour is that its use of advertising constitutes nothing less than propaganda: precisely the same charge that Blair levelled against successive Conservative Governments when he was a member of the opposition. But under New Labour, government advertising has grown in scale and subverted the conventions that traditionally govern such expenditure. In 1998, for example, government publicity expenditure rose to £165 million (Franklin, 1999, 23), but in 2001 New Labour spent a record £295 million on publicity and advertising (COI, 2001, 4). Undoubtedly more significant was the government's unwillingness to acknowledge the convention that advertising should be limited during the period immediately prior to a general election.

But while there is little evidence to suggest that Blair's 'Damascene conversion' may be genuine, recent political developments and media changes signal that New Labour should perhaps reconsider its reliance on spin and the 'packaging of politics'. First, the partisanship of the national press, which Blair and Campbell courted so assiduously and effectively, is shifting decisively. The *Daily Mirror*, which in 1997 seemed so editorially supine and loyal has turned feral and, post '9-11', reassumed the mantle of a previous editor, Hugh Cudlipp, to become the government's harshest and most insightful critic. The *Daily Mail* is unrelentingly critical of the Blairs, while Rebekah Wade, who succeeded David Yelland as editor of the *Sun* in January 2003, announced a change in the paper's political allegiance in her first editorial: 'it's time to say that we're very disappointed' about New Labour's failures on crime, education, welfare, health, tax and immigration. Wade warned the prime minister that 'six years of promises have turned out to be empty': the 'big smile and warm words are wearing thin' (cited in *Press Gazette*, 17 January 2003)

Second, what came to be dubbed as 'Cheriegate' by the tabloid press in December 2002, involving Cherie Blair's relationship with a 'lifestyle guru' whose boyfriend was a convicted fraudster, illustrated the inability of the No. 10 Press Office to prevent certain stories gaining 'legs' and running out of control. More significantly, the affair created an unprecedented degree of mistrust between political journalists and the No. 10 Press Office, as journalists became convinced that Campbell and his two senior colleagues, Godric Smith and Tom Kelly, may deliberately have misled them during lobby briefings about the affair. What also remains uncertain is whether

Blair took Campbell fully into his confidence about 'Cheriegate'; the extent of any subsequent rift between the prime minister and the director of communications strategy; and the possibly corrosive impact of events on the very close relationship between these two central figures in New Labour's political communication arrangements. Third, spin is not homogeneous in direction nor ambition, and members of the Cabinet continue to brief against each: supporters of Brown brief against their Blairite colleagues, and vice versa. The very effectiveness of spin and the continued leaking and trailing of stories and rumours to the press might prove increasingly damaging to New Labour in a climate where the press is less supportive of the government. Fourth, the Jo Moore/Martin Sixsmith dispute exposed the increasingly public rift between special advisers and members of the GICS, and the widespread public opprobrium for certain aspects of some special advisers' activities.

Finally, in January 2003, the government announced an independent inquiry into the government's media relations: its brief includes consideration of the Moore/Sixsmith row at the Department of Transport as well as MPs' concerns about the plagiarised Iraq dossier produced by staff in Campbell's communications office but masquerading as an intelligence document. A *Guardian* editorial expressed some scepticism about the effectiveness of the inquiry, suggesting that 'no government, least of all one with such a reputation for control freakery in its media relations' is likely to 'willingly hand over any meaningful authority over such a subject to a committee consisting largely of outsiders'. More probable is that 'Mr Blair wants his government to shake off that well-deserved reputation for spin' (*Guardian*, 17 January 2003, 23). But the members of the committee are hardly 'outsiders'. Chaired by Bob Phillis, chief executive of the Guardian Media Group, members include David Hill (a former director of communications for the Labour Party), a public relations adviser to John Major, and the prime minister's two official spokespersons, Godric Smith and Tom Kelly (*Guardian*, 12 February 2003, 13). The *Guardian* is evidently sceptical about the genuineness of Blair's Damascene conversion. But given the changes in the broader political and media scene identified above, New Labour might wish to reconsider whether to revoke its reliance on spin and the packaging of politics: to retreat from the preoccupation with 'issues of process and personality', and to adopt a new mission to 'try to engage in the political debate in a different way' to overcome 'what is perceived, often unfairly, as issues to do simply with news management' (Blair, 2002d). Strategically, the time may be ripe for a genuine Damascene conversion.

7

The 'Hybrid State': Labour's Response to the Challenge of Governance

DAVID RICHARDS AND MARTIN J. SMITH

Introduction: Labour and the Pathology of Governance

Even before the present Labour Administration entered office, a pressing issue the Party had been trying to resolve was a challenge presented in the form of governance – the perceived inability of elected governments to control and co-ordinate policy across and beyond Whitehall (see Richards and Smith, 2002). In 1992, Labour accepted the governance narrative that, in the course of the previous three decades, the policy arena had become a much more crowded environment, with numerous actors competing for political space. The net effect has been the curtailment of the government's ability to maintain some semblance of control by appealing to the traditional form of governing through state hierarchies (see Blair, 1996; Mandelson and Liddle, 1996; Gould, 1998; Newman, 2001; Richards and Smith, 2002). From 1979, internal pressures, in the form of the Conservatives' attack on the state and, with it, a greater neo-liberal emphasis on markets as a form of self-regulating governance, coupled to external factors associated with increasing pressures in the form of globalisation and internationalisation, had concentrated Labour minds on the search for alternative models of state delivery (see Mandelson and Liddle, 1996; Richards and Smith, 2002).

The governance narrative proposes that the policy process had evolved in such a way that, by 1997, policy was developed in a much more isolated and segmented manner than, say, in the more corporatist era of the 1970s. Furthermore, this problem was exacerbated by what can be referred to as the 'pathology of departmentalism' (see Kaufmann, 1997; Marsh *et al.*, 2001): for example, policy may be developed in one area without taking into account, or inspite of, the (un)intended or (un)foreseen impact this might have in other parts of the policy-making arena. In opposition, Labour recognised that, at a general level, the government was seen to have lost the ability to operate in a single, unified and co-ordinated manner across the whole policy spectrum (see Mandelson and Liddle, 1996). In office, the initial response of the Labour Government was to try to wire the system back up, and to bring together the many, often disparate, elements that constitute the contemporary policy arena. Indeed, Labour's antidote to the pathology of governance has been a programme of 'joined-up-government' based on a model of strong central control from No. 10 and the Cabinet Office (see Cmnd. 4310, 1999; Cabinet Office, 2000; Richards and Smith, 2001).

Yet, two years into their first term in office, the Labour Government had become frustrated at what it saw as institutional inertia on behalf of the bureaucracy in the face of demands to reform itself. This frustration was articulated clearly by Blair in a speech to the British Venture Capitalist Association in London on 6 July 1999, when he alluded to the forces of conservatism in the public sector, observing: 'You try getting change in the public sector and public services – I bear the scars on my back after two years in government. Heaven knows what it will be like if it is a bit longer!' (*Guardian*, 1999). This speech marked a change in both rhetoric and style by the government, who, while continuing to pay lip service to its goal of achieving joined-up government, from then on stressed the need for much greater improvement in the delivery of public services. Furthermore, having learnt the lessons from the frustrations over joined-up-government, the leadership decided that, in order to drive its programme of enhanced delivery forward, it was up to the 'centre' to really push for change. Reflecting on his first term in office in 2002, Tony Blair observed in evidence to the Select Committee on Liaison:

> The public sector for this Government is not simply a necessary evil we have to negotiate with, it is at the core of what the Government is about. Therefore, delivering public service reform in a coherent way it is, in part, absolutely vital for the centre to play a role. (*Select Committee on Liaison*, 16 July 2002, 5)

Confirmation of the importance that Labour placed on improving delivery was reflected in the address given by the soon-to-be head of the civil service to the Civil Service Management Board on the 24 June 2002. Andrew Turnball's (2002) paper – *Cabinet Office Reform and Delivery in the Civil Service* – stressed the need for the Civil Service to be respected for its capacity to deliver as much as for its traditional policy-making skills. As we highlight below, since 1999, Labour's programme for enhanced delivery has seen a frenetic period of policy-unit creation, in areas of strategy, delivery and performance, corporate development, e-transformation, public service reform and commercial reform. Yet an unintended consequence is that the centre has been in a state of flux, as Labour has striven for improved service delivery.

Joined-up-government and enhanced public-sector delivery are both stories that remain unfinished. Indeed, one possible conclusion may be, that both prove to be elusive goals within the context of the existing Parliamentary system (see Kavanagh and Richards, 2001; Ling, 2002). Nevertheless, since 1997, Labour has embarked on a complex and varied programme of state reform which presents a number of interesting challenges. If it is intended to ensure that ministers once again regain control of the policy process, what are the implications for the nature of power in future? Furthermore, to what extent have Labour been able to steer a course successfully between traditional state hierarchies, networks and markets? How has the centre been able to cope with the rapid pace of institutional restructuring since the late 1990s? To what extent have traditional Whitehall networks been renegotiated or even broken up in response to the extent of change that has taken place?

In order to address these questions, we first assess the ideas behind Labour's programme of state reform; and in particular, the themes associated with the third way. We then examine Labour's programme of reform, where we identify two stages: stage one (1997–9), where the emphasis was on achieving joined-up-government; and stage two (1999–present), where the focus of Labour's strategy turned to improved policy delivery. We then analyse the effect of the changes Labour has wrought; first, on core executive relations, and then on the nature of the state. Finally, we conclude by suggesting that the overall process of reform has taken place without a proper re-examination of the Westminster model. The result is that Labour's programme contains a number of unintended or unforeseen contradictions and has led to the creation of a 'hybrid state' – which contains elements of both Thatcherism and social democracy.

Labour and the Governance Narrative: The Third Way, State and Society

Elsewhere, we have argued that, historically, Labour's attitude to the state has been based on two principles: that the state is neutral, and that it provides an effective mechanism for achieving Labour's policy goals (see Richards and Smith, 2001). Yet in the eighteen years that Labour was in opposition, the traditional hierarchical, top-down model of state delivery was being eroded (see Richards and Smith, 2002). A shift occurred from a unitary state to multi-level governance (see Jessop, 2002a; Perri 6 *et al.*, 2002;

Richards and Smith, 2002). The impact on the power of the core executive of this shift is marked, because a key tenet of multi-level governance is the dispersal of authority and decision-making to a wide range of bodies through a process of negotiation. The net effect is that policy-making has been transformed from a being state-centred and state-driven activity to become a complex mix of hierarchies, networks and markets. If Labour rejected the option of turning the clock back to a 1970s model of state-centric delivery, then to understand its response to the newly emerging political climate, one needs to turn to the ideas informing New Labour's reappraisal of the state.

New Labour, the State and the Third Way

The 'third way' is the label that is most regularly attached to accounts detailing the ideas underpinning New Labour thinking (see White, 2001; Fielding, 2003). It is not a coherent, ideological package, but instead, as Newman (2001, 2) argues, the third way should be understood as a metaphor for centre-left parties in both Europe and the US to help them to forge 'political settlements that combined a recognition of the increasing importance of the global economy with attention to the importance of social cohesion ... creating an alternative to the state and the market ... addressing issues of civil society and cultural values'.

Anthony Giddens (1994, 1998, 2000), author of *The Third Way*, has argued that the growth of economic and political internationalisation, combined with much greater social diversification, has undermined the traditional state's ability to promote and control social and economic outcomes. He contends that rigid, hierarchical state structures (most often associated with Weberian models of bureaucracy) in conjunction with large, cumbersome welfare states, are incapable of meeting the aspirations or fulfilling the needs of an increasingly heterogeneous society. In the 1980s and 1990s, the New Right's response to these problems was the pursuit of a neo-liberal programme that advocated a less important role for the state in society, and a shift in emphasis from collectivism towards individualism. Giddens avers that these changes, pursued under Thatcherism, presented a number of unintended consequences. It became increasingly obvious that unfettered markets did not guarantee economic success, and that they produced a number of unacceptable social outcomes (see Marsh and Rhodes, 1992; Hay, 1999).

In many respects, the third way attempts to resolve a crucial dilemma within the Labour Party – the need to accept some of the key reforms introduced by Thatcherism, while not turning away from the tenets of social democracy (see Heffernan, 2001; Newman, 2001; Fielding, 2003). If the post-war, Keynesian welfare state represented the high-water mark of collectivism, the period since the 1980s has witnessed the rise of individualism. Where once the state provided the basis on which social relations were formed, by 1997 the market had increasingly usurped this role. Labour had to come to terms with this, and reappraised its traditional understanding of a society based on a hierarchical, bureaucratic state and universal welfare.

Whatever the importance of the notion of a 'third way', it is clear that the Labour Party was willing to embrace a more flexible approach to solving society's ills, than the traditional response by the left of imposing a state-centred, top-down solution. Labour's new realism advocates the idea of networks of institutions and individuals working together in 'mutually beneficial' partnerships based on trust. Labour is not seeking the outright abandonment of central bureaucracy, nor does it advocate the wholesale use of markets; instead, it embraces a mixture of both. The aim is to use a combination of hierarchies, networks and markets, the mix of which is determined by the nature of the particular service to be provided. This position is designed to overcome the problem associated with the later Conservative years, in which there was a failure to develop the notion of an evolving or mutually beneficial relationship between the public and private sectors. Instead, services were simply contracted out by the former to the latter.

The key elements of the new thinking about policy are set out in the 1999 White Paper, *Modernising Government* (Cmnd. 4310). For Labour, good policy-making is expected to be, among other things, strategic, holistic, focused on outcomes and delivery, evidence-based, inclusive (in the sense of taking into account the impact of policy on different groups) and, finally, possessing clearly defined objectives. Labour advocates a position in which the public and private sectors collaborate, in order to deliver the required services. The key to binding the various relationships together is trust. Moreover, no formal structure should be adopted to condition this collaboration; rather, different options should be available, in order to ensure flexibility and responsiveness.

New Labour argues that this strategy will lead to the creation of an 'enabling state' based on responsive relationships within society. However, as we argue throughout this chapter, the risk in this strategy is that unintended consequences occur through appealing to a flexible and variegated response to service delivery. For example, in order to meet the diverse needs of a complex society, and by relying on the creation of numerous 'delivery-agencies' at the centre of government to enhance policy implementation, Labour has exacerbated the complexity at the heart of the core executive that could undermine its overall strategy. In the next section, we analyse the changes Labour has introduced at the centre and assess their impact.

Changes at the Centre – Labour's Permanent Revolution
Stage One: Strengthening the Centre 1997–99

In the first term, Labour made a number of significant changes to Whitehall which to some extent built on the reforms of the Conservatives but also took the reform process in new directions. Three principles underpinned the changes: the first was the need for greater co-ordination, the second was a belief in a strong centre (in the context of increasing fragmentation), and the third was a distrust of the Civil Service.

The need for greater co-ordination was met through the attempt to create joined-up government. The Labour Government has been faced with a persistent dilemma – the desire to multiply the sources of policy advice, pluralise service delivery and decentralise power, while at the same time ensuring that it achieves a coherent set of goals. Furthermore, the constitutional mechanism for ensuring departmental co-operation, the Cabinet, seems to have been undermined to the point that it is now a symbolic part of the constitution. Consequently, one of the mantras of the Labour Government is the need for joined-up-government at the policy-making and delivery level. From the government's perspective:

> The 'tubes' or 'silos' down which money flows from government to people and localities have come to be seen as part of the reason why government is bad at solving problems. Many issues have fitted imperfectly if at all into departmental slots. Vertical organisation by its nature skews government efforts away from certain activities, such as prevention – since the benefits of preventive action often come to another department. It tends to make government less sensitive to particular client groups whose needs cut across departmental lines. It incentivises departments to dump problems on each other – like schools dumping unruly children on to the streets to become a headache for the police ... Over time it reinforces the tendency common to all bureaucracies of devoting more energy to the protection of turf rather than serving the public (Mulgan, 2001, 21).

Consequently, the government created a range of bodies such as the social exclusion unit, task forces, the delivery unit, tsars and the forward strategy unit to overcome departmentalism. In some ways, this has further extended the reach of No. 10 into departmental affairs under the guise of ensuring a co-ordinated approach.

Changes at No. 10

For Blair, creating joined-up government was a mechanism for increasing control by the centre, because it was a way of ensuring that strategies developed in No. 10 were not undermined by the conflicting goals of departments. As Blair told the Liaison Select Committee in July 2002: 'I make no apology for having a strong centre, particularly in circumstances where, one, the focus is on delivering better services.' Since 1997, an important development has been the way in which the resources of the prime minister have increased. Initially, when Blair came into office, he expanded the size of the policy unit (now the policy directorate), almost doubling numbers of personnel compared to the Major years (see Kavanagh and Seldon, 2000; Greenwood *et al.*, 2002). Crucially, the role of the policy directorate has become one not so much of making policy but of ensuring that departments are aware of the Blair agenda and are delivering policy in line with No. 10's wishes. Blair reinforces this steering of policy through regular bilateral meetings with ministers which ensure that they and the prime minister are in agreement on policy objectives. This is an important development, because it means that there is an institutional relationship between departments and No. 10. Also, prime ministerial policy activism does not rely on the whim or attention span of the prime minister. No. 10 is developing capabilities to direct departments, based on the special advisers within No. 10 overseeing and commenting on the policy proposals coming from departments. Again, this is an important change in the patterns of dependency between departments and the prime minister, with departments becoming more dependent on the prime minister for policy initiatives.

While the role of the policy directorate is largely one of oversight, strategic policy capability is provided by the forward strategy unit (FSU) (located in No. 10) and the performance and innovation unit (PIU) (located in the Cabinet Office). Both units are headed by Geoff Mulgan, a former special adviser within the policy unit. The aim of the PIU is to develop forward-looking policy in specific areas. The policy development is intended to be rigorous, based on a high level of empirical data and analysis. Some of its projects are initiated by departments and others by the centre. The body reports to the prime minister through the Cabinet secretary.

The third change introduced by Labour is related to the Party's distrust of the Civil Service. In the past, certain Labour minister have been wary of officials, seeing them as being sympathetic to the Right and undermining Labour's socialist goals (see Crossman, 1975; Benn, 1981). Similarly, a number on the Right, including Thatcher and Michael Joseph, saw the Civil Service as being too wedded to the post-war consensus. However, Labour's distrust was not related to the ideological disposition of officials, but instead it questioned their ability to develop and deliver policy. This distrust was revealed in significant changes in policy-making. Labour looked much more to outside sources for policy advice. More recently there seems to have been a greater use of task forces and special advisers.

The government has created an array of *ad hoc* bodies with the intention of crossing departmental boundaries and providing a range of sources of advice. The exact role, or indeed names, of these bodies is not clear, but according to a response to a parliamentary question, between May 1997 and October 2000 there were over 200 'live' task forces drawing on individuals from the private, public and voluntary sectors, including academics and civil servants. Some task forces are chaired by ministers, but others are not, and the topics they cover are diverse.

The second change was the increased role of special advisers. The way that special advisers have been used can be illustrated by looking at both No. 10 (as we shall see below) and the Treasury. In the Treasury, Gordon Brown has overseen an important change in the role of civil servants. Increasingly, policy is made in consultation with special advisers rather than the high flying officials of the Treasury. Brown's initial economic decisions on the independence of the Bank of England, windfall tax, welfare to work and public expenditure were essentially worked out between Brown, his economic adviser, Ed Balls, and the MP, Geoffrey Robinson. Balls and Robinson conducted detailed discussions, not with civil servants but with advisers in the City of London (Pym and Kochan, 1998). Pym and Kochan indicate the way in which the Civil Service was left out of the loop. They point out that when the permanent secretary in the Treasury, Sir Terence Burns, wanted to see the final windfall tax plans, and suggested that a Treasury civil servant and a senior Inland Revenue official should start wading through a forest of documents, Brown's team refused. Labour's desire to 'hit the ground running' resulted in the exclusion of officials from the policy process – a quite remarkable development. However, this change was not confined to the early months of the Labour administration. It has in some ways become the established pattern of policy making for the Treasury. According to a report in the *Guardian* (15 April 2002), Balls and Miliband 'act as gatekeepers, letting civil servants know what the Chancellor is interested in and acting as a filter for policy ideas coming from below. An official knows that he or she is getting somewhere when they get a half-hour slot with Ed Balls.'

Brown also has a collection of *ad hoc* advisers who undertake 'blue skies' thinking, their role being to keep the chancellor in touch with fresh ideas that are developing outside the corridors of the Treasury. Brown, like the prime minister, has also used people from business to undertake reviews of particular issues (such as the report on funding the health service). Brown clearly has a sense of an agenda he is trying to develop which does not owe its existence to the traditional concerns or standard operating procedures that exist within the Treasury. Hence the decision, which shocked senior officials, to give independence to the Bank of England without consulting the Treasury. In Labour's first weeks in office, there was considerable consternation within the Treasury that Brown was ignoring official advice.

Change in the Civil Service

Labour was also concerned to push on much further with the Civil Service reform that had been initiated in the Thatcher years. The view within the Civil Service was that they had already been subject to considerable reform: Sir Richard Wilson (Head of the Civil Service 1997–2002) pointed out early in the process that: 'Wave after wave of initiatives battered permanent secretaries and departments until we actually found ways of improving our efficiency and bringing our management up to date in a way which was just about good enough, though we're still fairly uneven in it' (Wilson, 1999).

The sign Wilson detected in the Labour Administration was that this was the beginning of a permanent revolution. Subsequently, he committed the Civil Service to six key changes that derived from Labour's modernising government agenda (Cmnd 4310):

  (i)   stronger leadership with a clear sense of purpose;
 (ii)   better business planning from top to bottom;
(iii)   sharper performance management;
 (iv)   a dramatic improvement in diversity;
  (v)   a Service more open to people and ideas, which brings on talent; and
 (vi)   a better deal for staff.

The reform agenda that derived from this *Modernising Government* White Paper suggested that past reforms: 'paid little attention to the policy process and the way this affects the ability of government to meet the needs of the people' (Williams, 1999, 452). Labour was doing more than trying to make the Civil Service more efficient; it was concerned with changing relationships within the government itself, and between the government and the citizenry. It was, in part, about reconceptualizing the role of the Civil Service. The problem is that these changes had implications that have never really been thought through in terms of relationships within the core executive and the constitution. As Flinders points out in Chapter 8, constitutional change has occurred within the context of the Westminster model – yet there are many elements of the reform process that undermine that construction of the constitution.

One relatively minor, but nevertheless important, element in the reform process has been the shift to what the government calls evidence-based policy-making. The foundation of evidence-based policy-making is:

The advice and decisions of policy makers are based upon the best available evidence from a wide range of sources; all key stakeholders are involved at an early stage and throughout the policy's development. All relevant evidence, including that from specialists, is available in an accessible and meaningful form to policy makers. (CMPS, 2002)

In many ways, this appears an almost uncontroversial and indeed, normal approach to policy-making. It is also a return to what was widely seen as a rational approach to policy-making in the 1950s and 1960s. The government has taken evidence-based policy-making seriously, and is now putting considerable resources into research that will be used to inform policy-making. To give one example, by establishing the National Service Framework for Older People, the Department of Health created an external reference group. This collects evidence through a wide range of mechanisms including literature reviews and controlled experiments (PIU, 2002). The important point about this process – which is one that has been repeated in a range of policy areas – is that it changes the process by which policy advice goes to the minister. In the past, much of the process of collecting evidence and delivering advice to ministers came through civil servants. Increasingly, it is the case that new evidence is being collected independently, and in certain areas the advice is not mediated by officials, but it goes direct to ministers.

Labour's first term saw some significant changes in the organisation of central government and the way that policy was made. The key changes included the emphasis on joined-up government, the multiplication of the sources of advice, the strengthening of the centre, and the shifting role of the Civil Service. However, these changes were not without contradictions. While the government was embracing diversity through its constitutional reform programme, there was a strong desire within the core executive to ensure that the goals of the centre were implemented. The government was simultaneously strengthening the centre and the periphery. Moreover, although Blair in particular appeared to want to ensure greater coherence within the government, the proliferation of bodies involved in the process appeared to further fragment it.

It is also true that the goal of joined-up government created tensions within Whitehall. The ability of departments to work together was constrained greatly by the continuation of departmental structures and the notion of ministerial responsibility (Marsh *et al.*, 2000). Further problems arose because these changes built partly on the reforms introduced by the Conservatives, but also reflected the concerns of Labour and the changing external environment. This produced contradictory demands – for example, between the notions of market mechanisms as a principle of reform through contracting out and empowering managers, and centralized notions of reforms through the use of targets.

Stage Two: Improving Delivery 1999–Present

Despite the extent of reform during Labour's first term, No. 10 was disenchanted over the pace of reform and the feeling that senior civil servants were not supportive of the changes the government wanted to introduce. Not for the first time, senior civil servants appeared to be concerned about their loss of a monopoly of advice, and about the increasing role of special advisers. Furthermore, Richard Wilson expressed concern over the Blair Government's lack of consultation with Parliament (see Benn, 2002) and there appeared to be conflict between No. 10 and the Cabinet Office, and between Brown's team and Blair's team. Consequently, the period from the end of the first term (from about 1999) and the beginning of the second term saw a reinvigoration of Whitehall's permanent revolution.

Three significant, interrelated developments occurred, particularly in the period between 2001 and 2002. What struck Blair and his ministerial colleagues in the run up to and after the 2001 election was that Labour had not delivered on a number of promises. Blair was increasingly frustrated with the slow progress of reform within the Civil Service and the fact that, despite many changes at the centre, there was still a range of implementation problems. In consequence, in 2001, Blair announced a further tranche of public service reforms, with a particular emphasis on delivery. In order to drive through this programme and improve significantly on the processes of delivery, changes were made in the organisation of government at the centre. The new agenda signified a continuation of the permanent revolution and prompted adaptations to the nature of the state.

Public Service Reform

Soon after the 2001 general election, Blair made a speech that both clarified and emphasised certain themes that had been germinating during the course of the first term. He was concerned by the extent to which the public sector was able to be transformed, in order to ensure a higher level of service (although he recognised that part of the problem stemmed from under-funding). Blair observed that:

> It is therefore on the basis of sustained investment, a frank appraisal of the good and the bad in our public services, and a non-ideological approach to reform, that we are embarking on the most ambitious programme of change since the 1940s.
>
> We are backing investment with reform around four key principles:
>
> - First, high national standards and full accountability
> - Second, devolution to the front-line to encourage diversity and local creativity
> - Third, flexibility of employment so that staff are better able to deliver modern public services
> - Fourth, the promotion of alternative providers and greater choice.
>
> All four principles have one goal – to put the consumer first. We are making the public services user-led; not producer or bureaucracy led, allowing far greater freedom and incentives for services to develop as users want. (Blair, 2001c)

A central tenet of this reform process is a changing emphasis on the role of the state that does suggest a third way:

> In developing greater choice of provider, the private and voluntary sectors can play a role. Contrary to myth, no-one has ever suggested they are *the* answer. Or that they should replace public services. But where use of them can improve public services, nothing should stand in the way of their use. In any event, round the world, the barriers between public, private and voluntary are coming down. (Blair, 2001c)

This was a theme that was re-emphasised at the 2002 Labour Party Conference, when, despite considerable opposition among members and unions; the government re-committed itself to the Private Finance Initiative (PFI). As Brown told the Conference, since 1997 Britain has had:

> The biggest programme of peacetime public investment in history and not private money replacing public investment as under the Tories, but private money additional to public investment helping us to provide in constituencies that desperately need them schools and hospitals that I have to tell you but for PFI we simply could not have started so many so quickly in so many communities. (Brown, 2002)

The reform agenda has some important implications for the way the state operates. The process, as described above, will further fragment the process of delivery and undermine the hierarchical nature of the traditional Westminster model. Also contained within this agenda is a clear indication of a 'third way state'; this retains a central role for the state in developing policy in relation to public goods, but the delivery of those goods can be through a range of public, private and third-sector organisations and at a range of central, regional, local and EU levels. At the same time, Labour appears to be rewriting the contract between the citizen and the state. The notion of the citizen that derives from the Westminster model and the Keynesian welfare state (KWS) is generally that of a passive recipient of standardised services. Under Labour's reforms, there is a rejection of the notion of 'one size fits all' welfare, and a recognition that the concerns of welfare should be driven by consumers rather than producers. Nevertheless, these shifts towards a more diverse third way state appears to be problematised by other aspects of the reform process (see below).

Improved Delivery

The focus of much public service reform has been on the issue of delivery. After the 2001 election, Blair announced that the next phase of reform is based on improving delivery. This involves: the implementation of national standards, the devolution of more power to those delivering services, and more flexible working – with the option of using alternative service deliverers. Thus the attempt to ensure delivery through central intervention seems to undermine the scope for diverse forms of delivery and devolution of decision-making.

The extent of this contradiction is illustrated through the creation of the delivery unit within No. 10. The aim of the unit, which reports to the prime minister, is to ensure that the government delivers on its priorities in terms of health, education, crime and transport. Here, the rationale is that the problem has not been the making, but rather the delivery, of policy, and so the public has to be aware of the government's changes on the ground. Again, a mixture of civil servants and outsiders staff this body. The role of the delivery unit is to check that progress is being made in reaching goals. This is achieved through bi-monthly meetings between the prime minister and the relevant secretaries of state, and through meetings with the Public Expenditure Cabinet Committee (PSX). The formal mechanism for overseeing this process is through the establishment of public service agreements (PSAs), whereby departments are set specific targets for the delivery of policy. In principle, this is another major change in the relationship between the centre and departments. Previously, departments had sole responsibility for the delivery of services. Now, the establishment of the delivery unit institutionalizes No. 10's role in overseeing what traditionally has been a relatively autonomous area of departmental activity. The delivery unit, in discussions with the concerned departments, agrees on the process of delivery and how success is to be measured. Of course, constitutionally, it is ministers who are responsible to Parliament for the delivery of services, but the PSAs create a new line of responsibility reaching directly to the centre.

The goals of the delivery unit are supported in a more general way by the office of public service reform, which is intended to push the public sector reform agenda, in order to improve the capacity of Whitehall to deliver services more effectively. The unit is intended to provide strategic oversight of the 'modernisation of Whitehall' programme (discussed above) and to ensure that departments are implementing reforms. Consequently, the unit ensures that a central element of the Blair agenda is transmitted to departments.

In January 2003, the delivery unit was transferred to the Treasury. This was seen in the press as a continuation of the battle between Brown and Blair. However, it is almost inconceivable that the prime minister would be forced to shift a unit from No. 10 to the Treasury against his will. The reality is that this is a recognition of the continuing weakness of the centre in relation to departments. While it is difficult for No. 10 and the Cabinet Office to control departments, the Treasury, through its control over public expenditure, has an important lever and oversight over departments. The Treasury is already linking expenditure to the meeting of targets.

However, the aim of improving delivery goes beyond Whitehall. The government is increasingly concerned with improving implementation on the ground. The achievement of this goal is based on two elements. The first is a significant shift to electronic delivery service (EDS), in other words, the on-line delivery of services. The government aims to bring all service delivery on line by 2005, arguing that this allows for more flexible and effective delivery which is also joined up. It has also planned a programme for the establishment of EDS in various services, starting with tax returns in 2000 and continuing through applying for student support, VAT registration, social security benefits, and even payments under the common agricultural policy (see Cabinet Office, 2002).

The shift to electronic delivery has important implications for the state. As the PIU report on electronic delivery indicates:

> In the past, government could only deliver services by establishing physical networks as delivery arms. These networks are generally arranged along functional lines, with each one delivering a set of services to the citizen. However, a number of other formal and informal networks exist wholly or partly to deliver government services to the public, including the Post Office network, public libraries and community pharmacies. (*http://www.cabinet-office.gov.uk/innovation/2000/delivery/organisingtodeliver/content.htm*)

The establishment of EDS means a shift away from physical organisations for the delivery of services, and this has significant implications for how the government operates, and indeed the number of civil servants.

The second element of the delivery strategy is through the devolution of decisions to those directly responsible for delivery. This is a continuation of the policy established under the Conservatives, through, for example, the local management of schools. The government has extended this policy in health and local government via a process of incentives. The government's position is that, if health trusts or local authorities perform well, they will be given greater freedom in making decisions. So, for example, in local government, the best authorities will find a much smaller proportion of their funding ring-fenced. 'Good' local authorities will be given freedom over borrowing, requirements of central government for plans and strategies will be cut, and inspection will be more proportionate. According to Gordon Brown, it is a 'new localism' with 'flexibility and resources in return for reform and delivery' (Downing Street Press Notice, 2002).

Changes at the Centre

Since 2001, the development of public service reform and the emphasis on delivery has led to important changes at the centre of government.

The creation of new units such as the FSU and in particular the delivery unit described above has affected the nature of the relationship between the centre and departments. It has systematised what in the past has always been an *ad hoc* process, increased the resources of No. 10 and consequently changed the patterns of dependency. In particular, relationships between the prime minister and official policy advisers has changed, and the pattern of relationships between No. 10 and departments have become more complex in both policy-making and policy delivery. Nevertheless, it continues to be the case that the institutional support for the prime minister is much less than in Britain's European counterparts. As Tony Blair pointed out to the Liaison Committee (2002): '[the] Number Ten Office has roughly the same or perhaps slightly fewer people working for it than the Irish Taoiseach's. To put this in context, there are far fewer than either the French Prime Minister, never mind the Elysée and the Prime Minister combined, or the German Chancellor.

One point of relevance is the instability of the arrangements at the centre. By 1999, a whole range of new government machinery had been put in place (see Figure 7.1). However, following Andrew Turnbull's appointment as Cabinet Secretary, the structure of the Cabinet Office and, hence, core executive relations were again changed (see Figure 7.1).

What is interesting about these changes, apart from their rapidity, is that they have created a distinct institutional structure concerned with issues of delivery and reform. Furthermore, under the initial structure, the lines of responsibility were somewhat blurred, because it was unclear whether units were reporting to the Cabinet Office or the Prime Minister's Office. Now, they clearly report to the Cabinet Office, perhaps indicating the way in which the goals of Turnbull and Blair are much closer than those of Blair and the former Cabinet Secretary, Richard Wilson.

The Impact of Change on Core Executive Relations and the Nature of the State

The changes described above have important implications for the core executive, as they effectively change the relationship between ministers and civil servants. Whereas, traditionally, the constitutional framework of the relationship between officials and ministers derives from the Haldane notion of symbiosis (see Foster, 2001; Richards, 1997), today there is a splitting of roles, with ministers concerning themselves with policy-making, and officials focusing on the 'management' of the policy process. What we are seeing is a significant change in the role of officials as their traditional monopoly of policy advice is being eroded, and ministers are turning to a myriad of organisations and advisers for policy inputs, thus mirroring the

FIGURE 7.1 *Cabinet Office 2002*

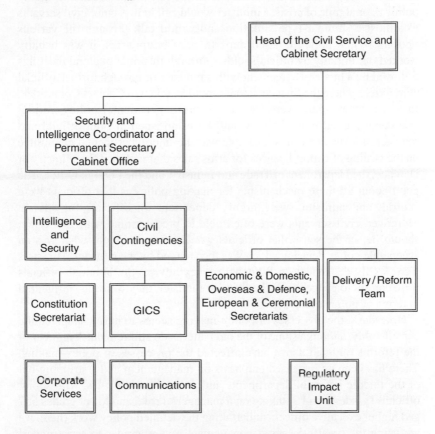

changes that are occurring inside Downing Street. Turnbull sees the Downing Street model of more advisers working with officials as a template for all departments (*The Times*, 1 May 2002). The traditional interdependent pattern of policy-making, where policy came out of a department rather than from a minister, is being replaced by very discrete roles for ministers and officials. As a consequence, ministers are much less reliant on officials than they were in the past. In the Haldane arrangement, officials were influential because they had permanence, and ministers relied on them for information and expertise (Foster, 2001).

Since 1997, there have been important developments in the processes of making policy. Traditionally, policy-making within Whitehall was made largely within departments: a senior civil servant would be placed in charge of gathering all the options and writing a paper. This would then be passed up the departmental hierarchy, often through the permanent secretary, before reaching the minister; in circumstances in which an issue was highly political, or at time of crisis, a minister would call in his senior civil servants to almost a seminar-type situation and would talk through the various options. When policy crossed departmental boundaries, it was usually worked out initially by officials, either through informal bilateral meetings followed by a bilateral agreement with a minister or through formal, official committees where the final decisions would be taken in Cabinet Committee. In areas where there were long-term interdepartmental policy, formal interdepartmental committees would be established at both official and ministerial levels. One such example was the interdepartmental committee on the issuing of export licences for arms sales that included the Ministry of Defence, the Department of Trade and Industry, and the Foreign Office. The point about all these mechanisms for making policy is that officials were central, and ministers were highly dependent on officials for advice. Moreover, civil servants were often able to predetermine what a decision should be, in the sense that officials would often work out what was an acceptable policy decision which was then agreed by the minister. Ministers were highly dependent on Whitehall policy advice. So, although officials were careful to gauge the wishes of their minister, they were also influential in terms of policy outcomes.

Nowadays, the processes of policy-making seems to have changed quite considerably, although some of the old patterns do still remain. A number of the reforms outlined above have affected the processes of policy-making. There has been an increased emphasis on management and a stripping-out of the middle layers of departments and the splitting of roles, with senior officials (grades 1 and 2) taking on a managerial role, and lower grades 5, 7 and higher executive officers undertaking the detailed policy work (here, we are using the pre-1995 senior management review grades to assist understanding). To some extent, top officials were excluded almost completely from policy-making – as seems to have happened with the previous Cabinet secretary, Richard Wilson – while, increasingly, policy advice has started to go directly from 'grade 7s' to officials. For some, like Foster (2001, 730), this has: 'diluted the quality of advice available to ministers'. Perhaps, more importantly, officials have become less important as a source of advice.

The developments we have described above are in many ways as significant, in terms of constitutional reform, as devolution and freedom of information. The role of officials, ministers, the prime minister and outsiders have all changed and, as a consequence, we are seeing new patterns of policy-making and new lines of dependence. Ministers and the prime minister have become more policy-active, and in particular the policy activism of the prime minister depends less on personal whim and preference and is being institutionalized by the development of No. 10.

All ministers are relying less on officials for policy advice and using a multiple of policy sources. There is an implicit recognition that officials are generalist administrators who are not experts on teenage pregnancy, global warming or managing the economy, for example. What the detailed investigations into the 'arms to Iraq' affair, the BSE outbreak and, more recently, the foot and mouth disease outbreak demonstrated was the poor quality of Civil Service advice. Indeed, much Civil Service advice was technically flawed and was concerned with how to present the minister and the respective department in the best possible light. So, in the case of arms to Iraq, officials were concerned with attempting to show that policy had not changed, when in fact it had; and in the BSE case, officials wanted to limited the information to the public, in order to avoid a scare and thus damage the beef industry. Andrew Rawnsley (2001) identified the failure of officials at the Ministry of Agriculture, Fisheries and Food (MAFF) to deal with the foot and mouth outbreak as being behind Blair's determination to reform the Civil Service in his second term. Their failure to act caused untold damage to the beef industry. The 'Rolls-Royce' machine – a perception that derives from their ability to support policy rather than to make it – seemed not to be working. Increasingly, the role of officials is to organize the multiple sources of advice and to some extent sift them for the minister.

Conclusion: The Contradictions of Labour's Reform Programme – A Hybrid State?

Labour has made significant changes to both the core executive and the wider state. Many of these changes have built on the reforms of the Thatcher and Major Governments, while others are important new developments. The impetus for Labour's reforms are twofold: one is internal, the need to overcome the failures of previous Labour Administrations. The second is external, the need to adapt the state in the light of the crisis of the Keynesian welfare state (KWS) (see Richards and Smith, 2001; Jessop, 2002b) and the pressures, perceived or otherwise, from globalisation. Of course, these two factors are closely linked; the failure of Labour to deliver in the past has been a consequences of the limitations and failures of the KWS.

The problem for New Labour is that, by attempting to develop an interventionist state that avoids the problems of the KWS, it has had to adapt the existing institutions, and this has produced contradictions and paradoxes. Labour has failed to recognize the continuing burden of the Westminster model (which, of course, is a comfort blanket to the party in power) or to shed the Thatcherite inheritance of managerialism and privatisation. Moreover, Labour, despite what many critics suggest, continues to shoulder a great burden through its commitment to the key elements of the welfare state – education, health and social welfare. Consequently, what is developing under Labour is a hybrid state that retains elements of the traditional Westminster model (a strong centre), Thatcherite reform (managerialism), social democracy (the welfare state) and New Labour (pluralizing policy-making, policy advice and delivery).

What we see within the Labour Government is a reform of the core executive and a complex mix of markets, hierarchy and networks in the wider state apparatus. Labour has introduced significant innovations, but in many cases, these have led to contradictions. First, a renegotiation of the relationships between ministers and officials, with ministers being less dependent on traditional sources of advice. However, this occurs within the context of the traditional definition of officials as neutral and permanent, and a continuation of the notion of ministerial responsibility (and so, within this context, is an acceptance of the precepts of the Westminster model). Second, a shift away from hierarchical forms of state organisation through the development of e-government, pluralistic forms of service delivery, delegation of management and the use of a range of public/private, local/national providers, but concomitantly, a strengthening of the centre and a clear policy agenda that is derived from the top. Again, this indicates the continuing importance of the Westminster model. Third, a shift to market and network mechanisms to deliver welfare goods in areas such as education, health, local government and transport. However, within these sectors, many hierarchical principles remain in place. For example, in education and health, a greater emphasis has been placed on local management and developing networks for service delivery. Yet, at the same time, there is pressure on local management to meet targets set by the centre. Fourth, the acceptance of many elements of a liberal, Thatcherite notion of the state (managerialism, privatisation and limited state responsibility), but coupled to strong, social democratic notions of welfare state responsibility. Probably one of the most striking aspects of the Blair/Brown agenda is a highly developed, progressive and modernist notion that the state has responsibility for improving the social conditions of groups in society; whether this is the reading ability of schoolchildren or the goal to abolish poverty. Fifth, the development of new patterns of representation through community participation, devolution, PR and elected mayors, but a failure to reform patterns of representation in Parliament, or to do anything to improve the ability of Parliament to scrutinize the executive. Finally, a rhetorical acknowledgement of new notions of sovereignty. Here, we would argue that, unlike the Conservatives, Labour avers that sovereignty can be enhanced through interdependence and acceptance of the shifting boundaries of the global. Yet, at the same time, it has embraced a cautious and traditionally British approach to issues of EU integration.

Since the 1970s, policy-making has undoubtedly become much more difficult. As Davis (2000, 242) observes, the key issue facing governments is that 'policy coherence becomes a problem as policies and interrelationships become more complex, and as the electorate fractures along multiple fault-lines. Finding the institutional capacity to take a longer view becomes *the* most difficult challenge.' As we have seen since 1997, Labour has addressed this challenge by embarking on a substantial programme of reform. It has explicitly rejected the 'corporatist solution' of the 1960s. Instead, it has compounded the changes introduced by the Conservatives, so further institutionalising the position of the prime minister, while also recalibrating the nature of the relationships between ministers and officials. Labour's reforms have affected the way the state operates, what it does and how it does it. These changes have produced contradictions for a number of reasons: they have occurred in an *ad hoc* manner – for instance, state reform has occurred without a real attempt to rethink the fundamentals of the Westminster model; the changes have been implemented within the context of an era where the 'liberal' or 'competition' state are seen as the dominant state forms; and, partly, because the Labour Government's goals have been contradictory, through its desire to run things from the centre, while at the same time devolving responsibility. Cumulatively, these contradictions characterise the dilemma at the heart of the Labour Government – it has tried to meet the ever more disparate needs of an increasingly complex and diverse society, while at the same time attempting to maintain its status as the most powerful actor in an increasingly fragmented policy-making arena. In trying to resolve this dilemma, we would suggest that Labour has created a 'hybrid state' – one that has not returned to the statism of the KWS, but neither has it maintained the neo-liberal, limited state aspirations of the New Right.

8

New Labour and the Constitution

MATTHEW FLINDERS

This chapter examines the progress of New Labour's constitutional reform agenda during the early stages of its second term of office. It seeks to unravel the paradoxes of Labour's constitutional reform programme and locate this analysis within the broader fabric of New Labour's project. The central argument of this chapter is that, contrary to ministerial and popular rhetoric, New Labour has largely failed to transform the British constitution in a radical way, preferring to accommodate reforms within a Westminster model that preserves executive dominance. In its second term, New Labour has largely failed to build on the far-reaching transformation promised by devolution and other constitutional reforms.

At the end of the last Parliament there were clear areas of 'unfinished business' in relation to the constitution. By examining the three main elements of constitutional policy that demanded early attention during New Labour's second term (reform of the House of Lords, the House of Commons and English regional government) the chapter emphasises concern regarding the lack of clear goals or principles in relation to constitutional policy as a whole. Moreover, the chapter argues that the constitutional elasticity of the Westminster model has been exhausted. Several of New Labour's constitutional reforms undermine central pillars of the Westminster model. While the enacting legislation may have been designed to maintain in theory the sovereignty of Parliament and the position of ministers, the actual operation of the new constitutional relationships increasingly reveal and underline the variance between constitutional fact and fiction. Although this divergence has been widely noted by constitutional 'anoraks', it is possible to suggest that the emerging constitutional fault lines have wider reverberations in terms of the public's confidence and trust in British government and politics. Finally, the chapter questions what is

'New' about the current Labour Government in relation to constitutional policy. Not only are a large number of the reforms rooted in Labour Party history dating back to 1906, but the pragmatism and essentially statist approach of Tony Blair's Government is straight out of the 'old' Labour governing manual. The constitutional project might therefore be seen as an aspect of 'old' Labour policy, and while it is possible to talk of a 'new constitutionalism' (Evans, 2001) within the United Kingdom, the degree to which this should be associated automatically with Tony Blair's leadership of the Party since 1994, and the 'New' Labour project, is disputable.

Although the British constitution is never static or immobile, viewed in retrospect, the second half of the twentieth century was a period of unusual constitutional quiescence (see Bingham, 2002). The Parliament Act 1949, Life Peerages Act 1958, Local Government Act 1963, Northern Ireland Act 1972 and the European Communities Act 1972, to name but a few, marked significant constitutional adjustments. But compared to the fundamental and often prolonged constitutional struggles of the nineteenth century, the latter half of the twentieth century, with the exception of the European Communities Act, can be interpreted as a period of relative constitutional serenity. This extended period of inertia ended with the election of the Labour Government on 1 May 1997. No less than twenty bills relating to constitutional reform were steered through Parliament during the first three parliamentary sessions. Evidence from the first parliamentary session of Labour's second term suggests that a high degree of constitutional fatigue has set in. This has resulted from a range of factors, not least international events and domestic policy pressures. But central among these factors is that the dilemmas and paradoxes of the constitutional reform project are increasingly visible.

New Labour's Second Term

It is clearly true that the British constitution has undergone a significant reform process because of a raft of reform measures that have been passed by Parliament since 1997 (see Box 8.1). This fact is reflected in a burgeoning literature on Labour's first-term reforms (King, 2001; Morrison, 2001; Forman, 2002; Trench, 2002). Although several members of the new government were constitutionally cautious, Tony Blair included, the 1997–2001 Parliament can be interpreted as being an unprecedented 'window of opportunity' in relation to constitutional reform. The Labour Party was heavily committed to certain reforms, and its commitment to stay within the previous Conservative Government's spending limits restricted policy development in the social and economic sphere. As a consequence,

---

BOX 8.1   *Labour's main constitutional measures, 1997–2001*

- Referendums (Scotland ands Wales) Act 1997
- Scotland Act 1998
- Government of Wales Act 1998
- European Communities Amendment Act 1998
- Bank of England Act 1998
- Human Rights Act 1998
- Northern Ireland (Elections) Act 1998
- Regional Development Agencies Act 1998
- Greater London Authority Act 1998
- Registration of Political Parties Act 1998
- European Parliament Elections Act 1998
- House of Lords Act 1999
- Freedom of Information Act 2000
- Local Government Act 2000
- Political Parties, Elections and Referendums Act 2000

---

the parliamentary timetable could accommodate a large amount of constitutional legislation without intense competition within the Cabinet for
legislative space.

Although the constitutional reform project is by no means complete it
was clear long before the 2001 general election that the Labour
Government's priorities had changed. It was also likely that the second
Blair Administration would be less ambitious while also having less time to
concentrate on constitutional reform. This is likely to suit the personal preferences of the prime minister, who has always been suspicious of constitutional reform. It is instructive to note that, as prime minister, Tony Blair has
never delivered a speech on constitutional reform but has delivered sixteen
on education policy. The only speech he has delivered on the constitution
was the John Smith Memorial Lecture in February 1996, and even this represented a nuanced attempt to retreat from several aspects of John Smith's
legacy that Blair had little choice *but* to see through.

Labour's second term was therefore not expected to match its first with
regard to constitutional reform. This would be a time for constitutional consolidation: to complete unfinished business, attempt to provide some form
of co-ordinated overview and monitoring capacity, and allow the reforms to
'bed in'. Morrison (2001) suggests that, towards the end of the previous
Parliament, several senior members of the Cabinet felt that constitutional
reform had taken up too much parliamentary and ministerial time.
Moreover, pollsters suggested that the public failed to attach high political

salience to constitutional reform, but were restless in relation to public services. Crime, employment, health and education would therefore receive priority during Labour's second term. This contextual change in environment is critical in understanding the manner in which constitutional policy has evolved during New Labour's second term. During the first term, some form of devolution was irresistible through a combination of popular pressures. In many ways the constitutional pressures of the broader public were satisfied to a greater or lesser extent. The second term agenda prioritised public services. Paradoxically, not only did this reduce the saliency of constitutional issues, but the pressure on New Labour to deliver on health, education and so on created an environment that demanded a strong executive. However, constitutional reform is still an important issue for New Labour during its second term, and in terms of 'unfinished business' (see Hazell, 2001a) parliamentary reform and English regional government stood out as critical aspects of the overall constitutional reform project that demanded attention. Moreover, New Labour's lack of progress on these issues during their first Government (1997–2001) attracted criticism, whereas developments during the first parliamentary session of its second term (2001–06) illuminate a great number of the paradoxes and tensions mentioned above.

Parliamentary Reform: The House of Lords

In line with the 1997 manifesto, stage one of the House of Lords reform was implemented with the passage of the 1999 House of Lords Act. This removed all but ninety-two hereditary peers from the House of Lords. The total membership of the Lords was reduced by nearly a half, from 1,295 in January 1999 to 694 in July 2001, by which time the non-hereditary component of the Lords' membership had risen from 41 per cent to 87 per cent. While this fulfilled a Labour Party pledge that dated back to 1968, there was no clear vision of the role, responsibilities or composition of a reformed second Chamber. This reflects traditional tensions within a Labour Party that, while committed to abolishing the hereditary principle, could not agree with what to replace it. For example, the 1983 Labour Party manifesto committed the party to abolishing the House of Lords. By 1989, this commitment had been replaced by one that favoured the creation of a wholly-elected second chamber. At the 1993 Labour Conference, as shadow home secretary, Tony Blair promised 'an end to hereditary peers sitting in the House of Lords as the first step to a proper, directly elected second chamber'. As leader of the Party in 1996, Blair hinted during the John Smith Memorial Lecture that, in addition to elected members, there may be room for 'people of a particularly distinguished position or record'.

The Labour Government's drift towards a nominated second Chamber became clear with the publication of its White Paper (Cm 4183) on the issue in January 1999. Moreover, it set the tone of the debate by stating that a revised second Chamber 'must neither usurp, nor threaten, the supremacy of the first chamber'. The White Paper announced the establishment of a Royal Commission to examine the future of the House of Lords under the chairmanship of Lord Wakeham, which reported in January 2000 (Cm 4534). The Wakeham Commission faced not only restricted terms of reference that prevented radical thinking in certain areas, but it also faced a very tight timetable. It recommended a largely nominated second Chamber, but with a minority of elected members to represent the nation and the regions. The Commission proposed three options for the elected element, of 65, 87 or 195 elected members, representing 12 per cent, 16 per cent or 35 per cent of a reformed second Chamber of around 550 members.

The government announced that it was broadly in agreement with the Commission's preference for a largely appointed body, and by February 2001 press reports suggested that the government favoured a middle option of eighty elected members, a position rejected by the Conservatives and Liberal Democrats, who favoured a greater elected proportion and a wholly elected Chamber, respectively. Consequently it was not possible during the previous Parliament to convene the parliamentary committee of both Houses.

The Labour Party's 2001 general election manifesto committed the Party to making the Lords 'more representative and democratic while maintaining the primacy of the House of Commons'. The government's proposals were published in a White Paper entitled *Completing the Reform* in November 2001 (Cm 5291). The document proposed that 120, or a fifth, of the reformed second Chamber of 600 members should be elected by proportional representation for a term of fifteen years, or possibly less. The rest of the membership is to be split between 332 members appointed by the parties and 120 appointed by a statutory Appointments Commission. The proposals received widespread criticism. An Early Day Motion was signed by 165 Labour backbenchers, supporting a wholly or largely elected second Chamber. Of particular significance was the rejection by the government of the Wakeham Commission's recommendation that the independent Appointment Commission should make all appointments, even those representing the political parties. This weakens the independence built into the Wakeham proposals, and maintains a critical source of party political patronage.

On 14 February 2002, the Public Administration Select Committee published a detailed critique of the government's plans (HC 494, 2001/2002). The committee recommended a smaller Chamber consisting of

350 members, with 60 per cent elected and 40 per cent appointed. Soon after this, the Conservatives announced their own plans, favouring a body consisting of 300 members, with 80 per cent elected. The Liberal Democrats favoured a similar model but based on proportional representation.

In May 2002, in an attempt to make progress on stage two of the Lords reform, the government supported the establishment of a Joint Committee of both Houses under the chairmanship of Jack Cunningham. The Joint Committee published its report on 11 December 2002 (HL 17, 2002) in which it put forward no less than seven options for both Houses of Parliament to choose between in a free vote. This vote took place on 4 February 2003. Although the House of Lords voted, by 335 votes to 225, for a fully appointed second Chamber, the House of Commons rejected all the options for change. This has left the government's plans in disarray. The lack of any agreed position within the Cabinet was particularly apparent, with Tony Blair and Lord Irvine coming out strongly in favour of a fully appointed second Chamber, and Robin Cook and several other leading ministers, including Charles Clarke and Patricia Hewitt, favouring an elected component. In another surprise, 172 MPs, far more than had been expected, voted to abolish the second Chamber completely. A joint committee of both Houses will now consider how to proceed, and realistically stage two of the Lords reform is unlikely to be completed until well into Labour's third term, should they win the next election.

Parliamentary Reform: The House of Commons

In the run-up to the 1997 general election, a survey of MPs indicated a high degree of support for far-reaching parliamentary reform (Weir and Wright, 1996). This support was fuelled by speeches by senior shadow ministers in which they committed themselves to 're-establish the proper balance between parliament and the executive' (Taylor, 1996). However, progress during Labour's first term was limited. Indeed, it is suggested that Labour's approach to reforming the House of Commons encapsulates many of the tensions and inconsistencies that are visible to a greater or lesser extent throughout its constitutional reform project. Moreover, during the first parliamentary session of Labour's second term of office the variance between the *principles* and *practice* of reform in this sphere had become increasingly crude and explicit.

A Modernisation of the House Select Committee was established shortly after the 1997 election. Although this was established with a remit to 'look at the means by which the House holds ministers to account' the committee concentrated on procedural and timetable issues during Labour's first term, and eschewed the more fundamental issue of the balance of power between Parliament and the executive (Flinders, 2002b). Hazell (2001a, 43) laments, 'parliamentary reform started with a bang and ended with a whimper. With no support from Downing Street, the initial momentum quickly dissipated'. The lack of significant reform in the House coupled with concerns regarding the style of the prime minister's leadership occasioned great parliamentary unrest. In March 2000, the Liaison Committee published *Shifting the Balance: Select Committees and the Executive* (HC 300, 1999/2000) in which the committee criticised the government's progress in this area and recommended the introduction of specific reforms. The government's response (Cm 4737, 1999/2000) was not accommodating, 'The Government are not convinced that a change to the current system is needed.' The Liaison Committee published a caustic critique of the government's reply, *Independence or Control?* (HC 748, 1999/2000), and were supported by an Early Day Motion, signed by over 250 MPs, supporting its recommendations. However, tight parliamentary control of the House by the executive thwarted further progress. Unperturbed, the Liaison Committee published *Shifting the Balance: Unfinished Business* (HC 321, 2000/2001) just weeks before the 2001 general election. This report was complemented by the publication of influential reports on the topic that were both critical of progress to date and set out similar reform proposals (Norton, 2000; Hansard Society, 2001) PROBLEMS/SET BACKS IN REFORM

Reform of the House of Commons therefore formed a critical component of the Labour Government's 'unfinished business' during its second term. A case could also be made that Labour's second term represented a 'window of opportunity' for significant parliamentary reform (Norton, 2000). For such an opportunity to arise, three conditions must usually be fulfilled: a general election must have recently been held; a clear reform agenda must have been published providing a coherent set of proposals behind which MPs could unite; and, there has to be political leadership and commitment. In theory, the beginning of Labour's second term provided a juncture of all these factors: a new Parliament; a large degree of overlap and complementarity between the various reform proposals; and, finally, the appointment of a senior and reform-minded figure, Robin Cook, as Leader of the House. BUT→ However, the government's second term began with an inauspicious start when the Committee of Selection announced the Select Committee memberships in July 2001. The composition of the committees, and particularly the removal of Gwyneth Dunwoody and Donald Anderson, and the appointment of former minister Chris Smith, caused controversy. The following week, in a calculated display of defiance, over a hundred Labour MPs voted against the government, to reject the proposed memberships. This incident intensified concern regarding the power of the executive to manipulate and control the scrutiny mechanisms of the House. It also fuelled the demands of the Liaison Committee for a severing of the link between the Whips and the Committee of Selection. A large group of disenchanted MPs from all parties united to form *Parliament First*, an internal pressure group for significant reform of the Commons.

The new Leader of the House distanced himself from the incident, but quickly announced a raft of reforms and reviews. Not only did he immediately empower select committees to appoint their own sub-committees and launch joint inquiries with other committees, but he also signalled his willingness to consider the proposals of the Liaison Committee, Norton Commission and Hansard Society (Cook, 2001b). The central pillars of these proposals centred on the need to reform the manner in which select committees are appointed, and possibly pay Select Committee chairs an additional salary in order to create an alternative career structure within the House. However, it was noticeable that Robin Cook's memorandum to the Modernisation Committee, published on 12 December 2001, failed to mention either of these reforms, and concentrated solely on procedural and timetable issues. However, the Modernisation Committee's first report of Labour's second term, *Select Committees* (HC 224, 2001/2002), represented a far-reaching attempt to reform radically both the structure of the House and the relationship between Parliament and the executive. In addition to the legislative and procedural reforms proposed in the Cook memorandum, the astute influence of the Liaison Committee, Norton Commission and Hansard Society was clearly visible. The Committee aimed to 'strengthen the independence, status and resources of Parliament's committees of scrutiny'. In order to diminish the executive's powers to appoint Select Committee members, via the Whips, through the Committee of Selection the Modernisation Committee recommended the creation of a new Committee of Nomination under the chair of Ways and Means. The bulk of the new ten-member committee would be drawn from the Chair's panel (the pool of chairs chosen by the Speaker to head standing committees and Westminster Hall debates). The Modernisation Committee also recommended a significant increase in the resources available to Select Committees, most notably through the creation of a new central unit of specialist research support. Crucially, the Modernisation Committee endorsed the Cook's proposal of paying Select Committee chairs. Within weeks the reform proposals received unqualified support from the Liaison Committee (HC 692, 2001/2002).

However, plans for the reform of the House of Commons received an unexpected setback on 14 May 2002 when plans for the new Committee of Nomination were narrowly rejected by an ostensibly free vote in the House (209 votes to 195). No Cabinet minister voted with Robin Cook, a fact

134   *New Labour and the Constitution*

glossed over by the Leader of the House in his speech to the Hansard Society the following week. This defeat for the reformers casts doubt on whether it will be possible to pay Select Committee chairs. The House did agree to refer the issue of additional remuneration to the Senior Salaries Review Board, but it is unlikely that MPs would approve such a plan as long as the appointment of committee members remains under the control of the Whips. Accordingly, the reform programme outlined by the Modernisation Committee in its second report of the first session (HC 1168, 2001/2002) was modest in both tone and ambition, concentrating solely on issues of procedure and timetabling, and with no mention of scrutiny or Select Committees. THINGS THAT WERE INTRODUCED

It would be misleading to suggest that the House of Commons has not been further reformed during the Labour Government's second term. In October 2002, the House voted to approve all the recommendations contained in the second report of the Modernisation Committee (HC1168, 2002). As a result, from 1 January 2003, late-night sittings were stopped and there was the introduction of a new parliamentary timetable beginning at 11.30 am and ending no later than 7 pm in the evening on Tuesdays, Wednesdays and Thursdays. The Common's calendar will in future be published a year in advance, and an experimental system was introduced that will facilitate the carry-over of bills between parliamentary sessions. Moreover, the Select Committee system is now based around an agreed set of objectives, annual reports have been introduced, a new central research unit has been established, and committees will benefit from more secondments from the National Audit Office. A new limit for chairpersons was introduced, of two Parliaments or eight years, whichever is the greater. Committees have also been given the power to exchange documents with devolved assemblies/Parliaments, which should facilitate joint working. An important development took place on 16 July 2002, when the prime minister appeared before a Select Committee: the first time a prime minister had done so since Neville Chamberlain regarding the Secrets Act in 1937. During Labour's first term the prime minister had consistently declined several invitations to appear before the Public Administration Committee, but has now committed himself to appear before the Liaison Committee twice a year (see HC 984, 2001/2002). Blair's decision establishes a precedent that will be difficult for future prime ministers to retreat from.

Devolution in England

The third major aspect of constitutional reform that remained 'unfinished business' at the beginning of Labour's second term concerned devolution in

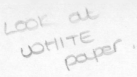

England – 'the gaping hole in the devolution settlement' (Hazell, 2000, 278). This relates not just to the development of regional government in England, but also the concomitant implications for sub-regional and supra-regional levels of government. During its first term, the Labour Government was clearly undecided about how to proceed. Media reports suggested internal Cabinet divisions on the issue, with John Prescott apparently struggling to convince sceptical colleagues. The resulting initiatives were confined to the establishment of nine regional development agencies and the emergence of consultative regional chambers composed mainly of nominated councillors. These regional institutions were to be created in addition to the government offices in the regions, and the various regionally structured public bodies, to create a dense and somewhat illogical regional topography (Tomaney and Ward, 2001). This 'thick' institutional layer has been further complicated by the creation of a range of area-based initiatives (ABIs) since 1997 (health, education and so on).

On 30 May 2001, the deputy prime minister announced that the government intended to produce a White Paper shortly after the general election, rather than the expected 'Green' consultation paper on regional government. However, the 2001 Labour Party manifesto barely mentioned English regional government, and the issue was not included in the Queen's Speech of June 2001. Despite this, English regionalism has emerged as a central issue during Labour's second term and continues to reflect serious tensions within the Labour Party. The post-election reshuffle exemplified these tensions as responsibility for regional policy was divided between three departments – the Cabinet Office, the Department for Trade and Industry, and the Department of Transport, Local Government and the Regions (DTLR). Despite this confusion, English regional policy has progressed steadily throughout Labour's second term, and in May 2002 a degree of institutional coherency was achieve with the dismemberment of the DTLR and the creation of a new Office of the Deputy Prime Minister, which combined some of the former regional responsibilities of the Cabinet Office and the DTLR. In July 2001, the government announced a £15 million package to enhance the capacity of regional assemblies to scrutinise RDA activities, and on 9 May 2002, after protracted wrangling within the new 'Nations and Regions' Cabinet Committee, the regional government White Paper was published (Cm 5511, 2002).

The White Paper offers an elected regional assembly, where there is clear public support, made up of around thirty members with responsibility for areas including economic development, the environment and European funding. The White Paper insists on wholly unitary local government being instituted at the same time as the regional assembly in any given region. The Electoral Commission will decide the pattern of unitary local government. It is clear that the White Paper's proposals represent a political compromise that seeks to assuage sceptical ministers, departments and business organisations. The proposed regional assemblies are hybrid institutions, in form a mixture of the London Assembly and the Welsh Assembly. The Labour Government is committed to enacting legislation to facilitate regional referendums at the earliest opportunity, and this commitment was included within the Queen's Speech of November 2002. However, a large number of significant hurdles still have to be overcome. First, there is little doubt that John Prescott lacks support within the Cabinet on this issue, notably from the prime minister. Second, the requirement of a unitary structure of local government below any regional tier is problematic because many policy responsibilities (for example, in the sphere of housing, transport and planning) may move from the county councils to the regional government. Opponents of reform have therefore characterised the government's proposals as a centralist rather than devolutionary reform. Third, it is also by no means apparent that there is overwhelming public support for regional government (see Bromley *et al.*, 2001). Finally, it is clear that the White Paper demands further refinement. The minister for Local Government and the Regions, Nick Raynsford, noted in June 2002 that the White Paper has a 'green tinge' – fuelling speculation that the government was far from decided on this issue. On 31 July 2002, the same minister adopted a cautious line in which he stressed that any plans were far from settled, emphasised the importance of local government's position, and underlined that it would be up to the government to decide when and which regions would hold the first referendums. Realistically, as with reform of the House of Lords, regional government is likely to be a third-term issue.

Regional devolution in England exemplifies the complexity of constitutional engineering and the dangers of proceeding without a coherent vision of how reforms in one area have implications, and often-unintended consequences, for other parts of the constitutional infrastructure. For example, it is unclear how the Labour Government's plans for regional government dovetail with their reforms in the sphere of local government. Many observers have noted that it is possible to identify the emergence of two competing models of regional governance in the UK: one based around regional assemblies, and the other based around elected mayors in large county cities such as Manchester, Leeds and Liverpool. The long-term consequences of asymmetrical regional governance are far from clear. Parts of England where the traditional counties are well established (for example, Kent and Norfolk) may well have no, or minimal, regional governance. In other parts of England, however, particularly in the North where the drive for regionalism has been strongest, a cogent tier of regional governance may evolve. The chances of the latter scenario are improved by the fact that the North East, North West, and Yorkshire and Humberside already have a predominantly unitary local government structure.

The Labour Government's second-term constitutional agenda seeks to continue and complete several aspects of the programme that was initiated during its first term. The three policy areas discussed above contain four common characteristics. First, it is clear that in relation to each policy the Cabinet is divided. There is no clear consensus, and individual ministers (for example, John Prescott in relation to English regional government and Robin Cook with regard to reform of the Commons) were left to persuade and cajole diffident colleagues within the Cabinet about the merits of any reforms. Second, the reforms are not designed or interpreted as aspects of a coherent and planned constitutional project. Each reform is viewed in isolation, with little appreciation of the inter-connected nature of the British polity or the law of unintended consequences. Third, there is an obvious and quite candid refusal to fetter the central position of the House of Commons' and the executive's dominance and control within that institution. This has been visible most notably in relation to New Labour's unctuous approach to its promise to hold a referendum on changing the electoral system to the House of Commons. Finally, because of all these factors it is unlikely that there will be major developments in any of the areas outlined above, with the possible exception of the House of Lords, during the second term of the Labour Government. They are all likely to become third term issues for New Labour.

Critically, it is clear that the consistencies and continuities between the 1997–2001 and the 2001–06 governments are solidly based around a refusal to challenge essential elements of the Westminster model. As noted in the introduction, the radical rhetoric of Labour ministers and talk of a 'constitutional revolution' must be viewed with caution. During its 1997–2001 term, the New Labour Government was criticised heavily for watering-down the provisions of many of its most significant constitutional reforms, particularly in relation to freedom of information and incorporation of the European Convention on Human Rights (Flinders, 2000b). A similar trend can be identified during New Labour's second term, as it continues to modify the Westminster model rather than to introduce a paradigm shift that would truly transfer power away from the executive. This is not to negate the positive dimensions of this reform process, nor the advantages of a strong executive, but it does raise questions about strategy and implications for the future should the constitutional reform process fail to achieve its ambition of reducing public apathy and increasing public trust in politics. These issues will be examined in the next and concluding section.

Governing as New Labour

During the first parliamentary session of its second term, the New Labour Government attempted to complete a number of pieces of its constitutional reform project. It also made several decisions in relation to reforms implemented during its first period in government. For example, to the dismay of campaigners, the government has announced that full implementation of the Freedom of Information Act 2000 will not take place until January 2005 (Flinders, 2000a). After reviewing New Labour's progress throughout the government's first term and the early stages of its second term, David Beetham *et al.* (2002, 401) conclude 'ministers are determined to hold onto all their traditional powers at the centre and to reject, delay or frustrate constitutional changes that would check or make transparent their exercise of those powers'. This statement exemplifies what Marquand (1998) has termed the 'Blair paradox'. How can a government that has set in train a great number of major constitutional reforms involving the devolution or transference of some degree of political power be seen, at the same time, to have a strong, centralising and controlling approach to governing that conflicts with the centrifugal thrust of many constitutional reforms. This section will examine this issue by reflecting on several of the points raised in the introduction to this chapter. These include the lack of a coherent statement of goals or clear framework that would offer a holistic view of the constitution as a whole. Arguably, this is related to the fact that constitutional reform has never been located clearly within the wider 'third way' project. Moreover, in the light of Labour Party history, it is possible to question the direct correlation between 'New' Labour and recent constitutional developments. This has clear ramifications for New Labour's approach to governing and may reveal, or at least suggest, explanations for its commitment to the Westminster model while implementing reforms that eviscerate the model's central components. Finally, it is possible to employ social survey data to gauge the degree to which New Labour's constitutional reforms have increased public confidence in British democracy. The findings of these surveys may well have critical implications not only for New Labour's constitutional reform project but also for the future structure of the British state.

In its attempt to complete its 'unfinished business', New Labour has been criticised for lacking a coherent approach to its constitutional reform programme as a whole. Whereas the 'third way' or 'revised social democratic strategy' has been employed as a vague conceptual umbrella to unite New Labour's social and economic policies, the link with its constitutional policy is far from clear. Labour ministers have made no attempt to link their constitutional measures with the rest of their so-called project. Not only does there appear to be little institutional capacity for appreciating the interconnected nature of the British polity, but there also seems to be very little constitutional cement in terms of a uniting ideological or theoretical framework or statement. Marquand (1999) has outlined the 'paradox laden constitutional revolution' and lamented the 'deafening silence about the rationale, implications and ultimate goal of the changes set in train'. This raises a broader question of the degree to which it is possible to isolate a core governing philosophy that underpins New Labour's approach to government in general, and constitutional reform in particular. The government has stated on many occasions that 'there is no intention to begin from first principles' (HL Hansard, 21 June 2001). Gamble and Wright (2000, 265) note, 'In its genesis and implementation the government's enterprise of constitutional reform deliberately eschewed any engagement with first principles, with grand plans and templates, or with the creation of new constitutional machinery to underpin the arrangements it was busily putting in place.'

The reform programme has generated a number of questions regarding the nature of governing arrangements in Britain. Yet the government seems uninterested in either asking or answering them. Many commentators now suggest that Labour's second term represents an opportunity to reflect on the reform process and underpin the emerging constitutional infrastructure with a supporting institutional and theoretical framework. The failure by the government to create a mechanism that can adopt a holistic approach to reforms has prompted an increasing number of constitutional experts to advocate the creation of a Royal Commission on the Constitution or an Independent Standing Committee on the Constitution (Gamble and Wright, 2000; Alexander, 2001). Such a mechanism, it has been suggested, would provide the capacity for a broader and more coherent appreciation of the manner in which the constitution is evolving, while also developing an expertise that may avoid negative unintended consequences. These demands have to some extent been addressed through the creation of the House of Lords' Committee on the Constitution. Nevertheless, several observers have suggested that the Lords' Committee lacks the necessary independence and practical resources needed to keep the constitution under review.

When seeking a core set of principles or governing philosophy with which to understand and unite the government's approach to constitutional reform it seems obvious to analyse what might be termed 'third-way theory'. Indeed, Tony Blair (1998) emphasised that a core goal of the 'third way' strategy was to end disaffection with distant political institutions and restore public trust in politics. Giddens (1998, 73–4) locates the need for far-reaching constitutional reform as a central component of any third-way strategy. Although the third way has complex theoretical roots it is clear, paradoxically, that a central aspect of the concept, and hence New Labour's governing strategy, is focused on results rather than on political philosophy. As Finlayson (1999, 271) notes, 'Policy is legitimated not by ethical principles but by the truth of certain social facts.' This approach is elaborated in Giddens' (1998) exposition of the third way. Major societal challenges demand a 'deepening and widening of democracy' but the evolution of a 'new politics' is based on a 'philospohic conservatism' which suggests a pragmatic attitude to coping with change and a respect for the past and history.

Beyond such rhetoric it is difficult to expose any central governing philosophy. Rather than being a hermetically sealed ideological family, New Labour is an amalgam that seeks to draw from liberal, conservative and socialist traditions (Freeden, 1999). Finlayson (1999, 277) concludes that 'any demand for New Labour to present a coherent political philosophy will not be met'. The New Labour approach is therefore a broad and flexible ideology. This need not make it vacuous or nonsensical, but it does risk accusations of multiple meanings, incompatible aims and policy drift presented as pragmatism. Freeden (1999, 51) notes this in relation to constitutional reform:

> the grammar of democratic devolution as applied to Scotland and Wales is countered by the practice of democratic centralism in England, and the grammar of democratic accountability ... as applied to the House of Lords is countered by the practice of controlled co-ordination of the entire legislative process in the best British manner.

The opacity of the New Labour project related directly to concerns regarding constitutional underpinning. William Hague's (1998) comment that 'Labour has embarked on a journey of constitutional upheaval without a route map' is not simply a partisan point. It reflects a deeper concern that the constitutional project lacked clarity with regard to both principles and outcomes. Lord Irvine (1998) sought to counter this criticism by arguing:

> The strands do not spring from a single master plan, however much that concept might appeal to purists. We prefer the empirical genius of our nation: to go, pragmatically, step by step, for change through continuing consent. Principled steps, not absolutist master plans, are the winning route to constitutional renewal in unity and in peace.

However, it is possible to identify a central strand of the New Labour project that had a direct relevance to the constitutional reform project – *institutional modernisation*. This concept was a consistent theme in ministerial speeches throughout the first New Labour term. Forman (2002, 367) notes that, in presentational terms, 'modernisation' has been a convenient way of encapsulating institutional and constitutional reforms without seeming to be too radical. Moreover, 'modernisation' has been used by senior ministers to associate their constitutional reforms with the future, while denigrating and dismissing their political opponents as being reactionary representatives of the past. The notion of 'modernization' suggests the adoption of a pragmatic agenda for updating what currently exists rather than fundamental reform. In this respect there is a clear link with the traditional evolutionary approach to constitutional change.

Consequently modernisation should not be taken as a synonym for 'democratisation'. Many critics believe that modernisation of the constitution under New Labour has always had more to do with making government more efficient and effective rather than accountable and democratic (see Flinders, 2001a; Forman, 2002). For example, in relation to the reform of the House of Commons, one suspicious MP noted, 'We all know what modernization means ... It is a euphemism for streamlining the House so that a quantity of legislation can be got through as quickly as possible' (Hansard, 9 November 2000). Sheldrick (2002, 141) concludes 'There is little in the Third Way, at least in terms of its practice in the British context, for those who hope for a more radical impetus towards democratisation.' This is a critical issue.

The principled pragmatism and emphasis on institutional modernisation within New Labour's constitutional project is highly restrictive. Moreover, the statism, pragmatism and preference for the Westminster model appear to be classic components of 'old' Labour philosophy. As Weir notes (quoted in Morrison, 2001, 527), 'New Labour is just a smokescreen. Broadly what we have is pretty Old Labour party in terms of its pragmatism and its acceptance of the status quo politically.' Historically, the Labour Party has always placed great weight on the capacity of the state to drive through and implement far-reaching social change. Essentially, the constitution creates a powerful executive unfettered by major hurdles that could implement its policies. This is exactly the core dynamic of the constitution that New Labour is reluctant to cede. It is instructive that, in his influential treaty on the third way, Anthony Giddens (1998, 68) insists that the New Labour government must be willing to use the 'tools of modernity' in order to drive through its social and economic reforms. It is this failure to dilute the central axis of political power that led Morrison (2001, 501) to conclude about New Labour that 'despite all the reforms to the periphery, the core of the British political system of elective dictatorship has remained intact'.

While speeches on New Labour's ideology frequently contained commitments to 'create a relevant and radical politics for the 21st century' (Blair, 2001b), it has been suggested that New Labour's failing has been a lack of imagination and a reluctance to introduce fundamental reform of a model of representative democracy that is widely viewed as being illegitimate by the public. Johnson (2001) asserts that Labour's constitutional project has not only been inchoate but it has also failed to challenge conventional notions of governing in Britain that are essentially elitist. Although there may be a certain utopianism in some of the new theories of democracy, they do at least offer an acute analysis of the limits of the existing state structures and a new perspective on how democratic relationships might be reorganised (Dryzek, 1994; Hirst, 1994; Held, 1995). It is this basic reappraisal that presents the source of the challenge to the reformers who concentrate on attempting to reinvigorate the traditional framework of representative democracy. Morrison (1998, 525) notes, 'Orthodox constitutionalism seems only to be about shoring up a liberal, individualist version of democracy that for many seems fundamentally incapable of delivering the legitimacy required to under-write government in a changing world.'

There is now a significant amount of critical literature that questions New Labour's commitment to the Westminster model. Much of this comment asserts that the government has been short-sighted in refusing to acknowledge formally and to reconstruct elements of the constitutional infrastructure that have been problematic for some time. In essence, there has been little tangible will in establishing a truly modern, or even post-modern, constitutional settlement. New Labour's approach to the constitution may well, therefore, be interpreted as suffering from a paucity in imagination not only about how the business of government has changed but also regarding the need for new frameworks of scrutiny and control. For Morrison (1998, 514), 'the genie of post-modern government cannot be returned to the bottle of the parliamentary state'.

Despite a lack of specific detail, a central and consistent theme of the New Labour project focused on the need to reconnect the public with the institutions of politics in order to reduce public apathy and increase electoral turnouts. Longitudinal public surveys therefore provide an opportunity to gauge the degree to which New Labour's constitutional reforms have achieved these goals. If surveys indicated an increase in public trust in government, this would undermine the arguments of those who have criticised New Labour for failing to adopt a more radical approach.

However, the British Social Attitudes (BSA) survey of 2001 makes depressing reading for New Labour strategists. The 2001 general election was itself disappointing, as turnout fell to its lowest point since 1918 (59.1 per cent). Turnout also fell to record lows in the local and European elections held between 1998 and 2000. However, the commentary about the reasons for this low turnout failed to consider the defects in New Labour's constitutional reform programme. The BSA survey suggests that there is no evidence at all of a decline in people's willingness to engage in politics, but there is a trend towards direct action and away from representative institutions. It appears that public trust in government and faith in the political structure's capacity to respond to public demands fell in the 1990s, recovered slightly in the wake of Labour's election in 1997, but have now fallen back to more or less what they were in the mid-1990s (see Dunleavy *et al.*, 2001). Bromley *et al.* (2001, 200) conclude, 'It appears that Britain faces a crisis of confidence and participation that is far deeper than any programme of constitutional reform is capable of reversing.' It is these declining levels of trust and political efficacy that are central factors in explaining falling electoral turnout. The question is, to what degree does this inability to increase the public's confidence in the government of the country reflect New Labour's failure to go far enough?

Conclusion

The central conclusion of this chapter is that New Labour has taken great care to implement its constitutional reforms, however precariously, within the traditional Westminster model of British government. Crucially, the conventional arrangements have not been replaced with any discernible conception of an alternative constitution. New Labour's constitutional reform project cannot therefore be interpreted as a fundamental paradigm shift. The sudden reforms of June 2003 reinforce many of the arguments of this chapter. The new Department for Constitutional Affairs creates a strategic capacity on constitutional issues. Abolishing the Lord Chancellor's judicial role addresses the lack of a clear separation of legislative and judicial powers. Abolishing the Secretaries of State for Wales and Scotland was not unexpected. The 2003 reforms may have far-reaching implications, but it is difficult to interpret them as radical. They create new anomalies, and fail to give Labour's constitutional programme clear underpinning principles. They represent a further example of the British Constitution 'muddling through', leaving several aspects of the constitutional agenda no clearer, and representing little threat to the domination of the executive. They will however, particularly the Supreme Court, place further pressures on the Westminster model.

It is, however, vitally important to appreciate that any process of reform will deliver both *intended* and *unintended* consequences. Constitutional reforms can never be viewed in isolation: it is more appropriate to view reform as a chain reaction or process. New Labour's reforms have set in train a critical momentum and dynamic that may well at some point force an explicit reconsideration of the structure and power relationships within Britain. This can already be seen in the patchwork structure of asymmetrical regional governance in Britain. The prospect of a full-scale debate on the constitution for Europe at the 2004 Intergovernmental Conference may force the government to clarify its ideas. The foreign secretary's support for a written constitution for the European Union, as outlined during a speech in August 2002 (Straw, 2002), is a substantial proposal with far-reaching implications. It will be difficult to promote seriously a written constitution for the European Union without the argument spilling over into the need for a similar document for the United Kingdom. It is these constitutional fuels, falling electoral turnout and weakening public trust that may force a future New Labour government to adopt a more radical approach to the constitution. At the heart of such a reappraisal would have to be a formal acknowledgement that parliamentary sovereignty has become a relative rather than an absolute concept.

9

Economic and Welfare Policy

CLAIRE ANNESLEY AND ANDREW GAMBLE

Since the Labour Government's election in May 1997, its economic policy has had two main strands: a strategy for delivering macroeconomic stability; and a one for providing employment and economic opportunities to all by tackling supply-side barriers to growth (Balls, 1998). Establishing strong and stable public finances was seen as the pre-condition for achieving sustained economic growth and improvements in productivity and investment, and economic growth in turn was regarded as the pre-condition for increasing spending on public services and tackling poverty. The important political point was that sustained economic growth and stable public finances took priority over spending; the government made it clear that it would only increase spending when it was prudent to do so.

In this, as in many other aspects, the Blair Government has been different from previous Labour Governments, which were prone to increase spending ahead of achieving either growth or stable public finances, and were then obliged to cut spending to placate the financial markets and re-establish confidence. Labour was determined to avoid lurches from boom to bust, both in the economic cycle and in public finances, and accordingly announced in 1997 that it would stick to Conservative spending plans for the first two years, and concentrate on reducing debt. This stance was unpopular with the Party and meant that in its first term Labour increased public spending at a slower rate than the Conservatives had done (Mullard, 2001). But it had the priceless political advantage of establishing the credibility and competence of the government in the financial markets and averted the normal mid-term crisis that every previous Labour Government had endured. This enabled the government to claim that it had overcome the cycle of boom and bust in economic policy, and had laid the macro foundations for sustained, long-term, incremental investment in public services.

Labour's commitment to strong and stable public finances has had severe implications for welfare spending and social policy. Its economic approach has meant that welfare spending has been held under tight reins in some areas, and yet public funds have also been made available for increased spending in others. Since 1997, Labour has consistently focused its attention on moving people of working age from welfare and inactive benefits into active benefits and work. It has targeted welfare spending towards the poorest people of non-working age – children and pensioners, and at two public policy areas with universal programmes: education and health.

Opinion on Labour's economic and social policy since 1997 has been mixed. Some critics have argued that the policy has been little more than a continuation of the main lines of Thatcherite policy, and that it marks a substantial break with the social democratic policies of Labour Governments since 1945 (Hay, 1999; Heffernan, 2000; Arestis and Sawyer, 2001). Labour has also been criticised for having 'Americanised' the welfare state with its 'welfare to work' programmes (King and Wickham-Jones, 1999; Peck and Theodore, 2001). Friendlier critics have contended that the policy proceeds from a distinctive 'third way' approach, which avoids the mistakes of both 'old left' and 'new right', and represents a new social democracy (Driver and Martell, 1998; Giddens, 1998). Both these positions tend to assess the position in ideological terms, as to whether Labour can still be considered to be a social democratic party, or whether it has mutated into something else.

Other analyses focus on the tight limits within which modern governments operate. If it succeeds in maintaining the policies in place at the time of writing, the Blair Government at the end of eight years will have increased the percentage share of public spending in gross domestic product (GDP) back to the level it inherited from the Conservatives. Britain will still have substantially lower taxes and public spending than many other countries in the EU. Nevertheless, the change in direction is important, although many of the increases in health and education are being funded by a squeeze on social security (Glyn and Wood, 2001).

Another perspective on the Blair Government argues that the substance of economic policy is less important than its forms. Since 1975, there has been a transformation of the assumptions and institutions of economic policy-making which had dominated the previous thirty years. The main change has been the shift from a discretion-based to a rules-based system (Burnham, 2001). The hands-on and often highly politicised management of the national economy in the Keynesian era has steadily been replaced since 1975 by attempts to resurrect some of the main features of the rules-based liberal economic order that existed before 1914, centred on the gold standard. Such a regime for economic policy means that a government establishes sets of rules which preclude its direct involvement in many decisions.

Discretion-based systems and rule-based systems both have their advocates, and there may well be a strong cyclical element in their adoption and rejection, as there is in other styles of public policy (Hirschman, 1985). What is important to note is that a rules-based system does not in itself exclude a social democratic programme, though neither does it guarantee it. The Labour Government's economic policy since 1997 has been puzzling to interpret, partly because its true character has taken time to emerge. The fiscal caution of the first few years gave way by the 2002 Budget to a renewed emphasis on improving universal welfare programmes and providing the long-term funding to achieve welfare improvement through modest increases in taxation. This small but significant change in the direction of economic policy has altered the political landscape, but critics on both left and right doubt that it can be sustained without much larger increases in taxation, especially if prospects for the world economy continue to deteriorate. Furthermore, the Treasury's own figures (HM Treasury, 2001a) show that the basic structural weaknesses of the British economy (low investment, low productivity and low skills) have still not been addressed, making the foundations of the new policy precarious (Arestis and Sawyer, 2001; Coates and Hay, 2001).

Economic Policy

Macroeconomic Stability

After its election in 1997, Labour set out to demonstrate that it could deliver the commitments it had made in opposition, and pursue a sound money policy, which would then become the bedrock for other policies such as welfare. By macroeconomic stability the new government meant both stable outcomes (principally, low inflation and sound public finances) as well as a stable policy framework (stability in economic instruments, such as interest rates). The principal means of achieving stability was the target for inflation. The chosen target of 2.5 per cent was symmetrical, which meant that monetary authorities were instructed to avoid allowing inflation either to overshoot or to undershoot the target by more than 1 per cent. Their actions were constrained by the need to meet the inflation target, but in order to meet it they had to exercise considerable discretion and judgement (Balls, 1998; Balls and O'Donnell, 2002). In the first five years of the Monetary Policy Committee (MPC), its judgements have apparently been vindicated, since inflation in 2002 was the lowest for forty years and the lowest in the EU, and growth had proceeded at an unspectacular but steady rate, with unemployment falling below one million, again the lowest level in the EU.

What the Treasury team wanted above all from its macroeconomic policy stance was *credibility*, which it sought by adopting long-term policies that the financial markets considered sound, by being transparent in its decision-making, and by making policy pre-commitments ruling out certain options. It adopted a code for fiscal stability containing two key rules; the 'golden' rule, which stipulated that over the economic cycle it is only legitimate for the government to borrow to invest and not to fund current spending; and a rule requiring public debt as a proportion of national income to be held at a stable and prudent level over the economic cycle (Balls and O'Donnell, 2002).

The most striking example, however, of the government's bid for credibility was Gordon Brown's unexpected decision to give the Bank of England a measure of independence. The party that had nationalised the Bank of England in 1946 handed power to set interest rates to the Bank's Monetary Policy Committee, which contained eight members, five of them appointed by the government. The MPC was charged with the responsibility of conducting monetary policy to achieve price stability as defined by the government's inflation target. At the same time, responsibility for supervising the banking system was removed from the Bank.

This change, deplored by some Keynesian economists but welcomed strongly by constitutional reformers as announcing a new openness and accountability in economic policy (Barnett, 1997), built on the greater openness that had been introduced into the setting of interest rates by the publication of the discussions held between the Conservative chancellor, Kenneth Clarke, and the governor of the Bank of England, Eddie George, but went further. The Bank had always been involved in giving advice on the setting of interest rates, but the final decision had rested with the chancellor. The symbolism of the change was all-important. Labour wished to demonstrate that it would not deviate from a macroeconomic stance which emphasised low inflation before other objectives. It wanted to reassure the financial markets that this was a different kind of Labour Government, one that would not be blown off-course by the kinds of financial pressures that had wrecked its predecessors. The recipe it chose for ensuring high and stable levels of aggregate demand and low inflation was a clear and transparent monetary objective, delegation of some powers to independent policy agencies (such as the Bank), and a willingness to tolerate unstable policy instruments (such as rapidly changing interest rates).

Another aspect of the government's bid for 'credibility' was electoral. It had given a pledge not to increase the standard or higher rates of income tax, and to keep spending within the planning totals bequeathed by the Conservatives, even to the extent of implementing cuts that the Conservatives had planned. In the early years, some of these backfired politically, such as the reduction in single mothers' benefit in November 1997 (inherited from the Conservatives), and the miserly 75p pension increase in 2000 (which resulted from the application of the standard inflation uprating of benefits), but the general message was maintained – Labour would not allow any dramatic rise in public spending to meet pent-up demands that would lead to substantial extra borrowing or increased taxation. The government even tried to underline the point by cutting some taxes with a high political profile, even though other increases meant that the overall tax burden was projected to rise. Corporation tax was cut in 1998, and income tax in 1999.

The early insistence on fiscal prudence and monetary credibility made the government appear far more orthodox than it was. As with previous Labour Governments, there remained a gap between the rhetoric of the government and the substance of its policy. For once, however, the substance was more radical than the rhetoric suggested. In its rhetoric, for example, the government never mentioned redistribution in its first term, dissociated itself from 'tax and spend' policies, and stuck rigidly to the spending limits it had inherited. But this did not prevent Gordon Brown from raising substantial additional revenue from other taxes, such as the one-off windfall tax on the profits of privatised utilities, intended to raise £5.2 billion, which was announced in the first budget in July 1997. Pension funds' tax credits for Advance Corporation Tax were also abolished, intended to raise £5.4 billion. The impact of this was largely hidden, and penalised those with personal pensions. In the 1999 Budget, various tax reliefs, such as the married couple allowance and mortgage tax relief, were abolished, National Insurance was raised for higher income earners, and an energy tax was introduced. Such measures raised revenues on a scale that was difficult to contemplate politically, through straightforward changes in the standard and top rates of income tax. After the 2001 general election victory, again fought on the promise that there would be no increases in the standard or higher rates of income tax, the government became bolder and, in the 2002 Budget, Gordon Brown announced increases in National Insurance contributions for higher rate taxpayers and employers, in order to fund large increases in spending on health and education. The effect was to raise the higher income tax rate to 41 per cent.

The drive to increase spending substantially on the core programmes of the British welfare state was clearly demonstrated in the Budget of 2002. But from the outset Brown had sought ways to increase spending in key target areas such as health and education, and to finance the welfare to work programme and other key government initiatives. From 1998, his spending plans had broken with the annual public spending planning totals that had dominated public expenditure reviews since the mid-1970s and instead committed the government to a planned programme of increased spending, initially totalling £57 billion over three years. By 2002, the government was committed to a five-year rolling programme, and planned to raise education spending to £69 billion per annum in 2008 (from £36 billion in 1979) and health spending to £106 billion per annum (from £41 billion in 1979).

The early plans were attacked as unrealistic because they assumed a rate of growth of the economy and associated levels of unemployment that many thought unlikely to be achieved, particularly as the effects of the turmoil on world financial markets were expected to translate into a slow-down in activity and possibly recession in Britain and the rest of Europe. But the Treasury claimed that it had built in sufficient flexibility to cope with any variation in the performance of the economy, and in the first five years its claims were vindicated. The government's plans were prudent and carefully costed, and have achieved a significant recasting of public spending priorities, a large reduction in public debt (from 44 per cent to 30 per cent of national income), and a modest redistribution of resources. The cumulative effect over a ten-year period, if the policies can be sustained, will be substantial.

The new fiscal rules meant no return to fiscal fine-tuning, but observers noted that the increase in public spending was planned to be broadly counter-cyclical, and that the government still talked about stabilising public-sector investment at a high level. Underlying its Comprehensive Spending Review was a policy approach that still had some links to Keynesianism, even as it was being criticised from the left for being monetarist. Perhaps the stance is best characterised as an eclectic blend between macroeconomic pragmatism (the rejection of doctrinaire approaches to economic management); monetarist ideas (particularly setting targets for inflation); and New Keynesian ideas, particularly the notion that policy activism can improve economic performance. It was a highly prudent approach which aimed to provide the conditions within which relatively progressive policies, including some counter-cyclical fiscal policy, an activist monetary policy, and increased investment in public services could be pursued.

Industrial Policy

Labour came into office in 1997 pledged to do something about the investment gap, the productivity gap and the skills gap between Britain and other OECD (Organization for Economic Co-operation and Development) economies. These gaps, it argued, had not been closed by Conservative economic policy, and were responsible for the persistence of a boom–bust cycle, and for the relatively low rate of growth of the British economy. But Labour had few ideas as to how to remedy the position beyond its determination to create financial stability and to link welfare to work.

The government's policy from the start was strongly pro-business and pro-competition. Following its preference for rules-based rather than discretion-based procedures, decisions on mergers and monopolies were removed from the remit of politicians. The government signalled that it did not wish to return to an interventionist industrial strategy, or to a pro-manufacturing stance (it was revealing that one of the five tests as to whether the UK should join the euro concerned the financial sector; no mention was made of manufacturing). The Competitiveness White Paper gave priority to sectors in the new knowledge-based economy and stressed the limited, if important, role that could be played by the government (DTI, 1999).

The problem for the government was that, at a time when the rest of the economy was growing, the industrial sector continued to suffer, many companies being squeezed by a high exchange rate and poor productivity performance: 180,000 jobs were lost in manufacturing in Labour's first term. There were some dramatic incidents, such as when BMW decided to pull out of Rover, exposing how little power the government had to influence such decisions. But the government did initiate some important studies: the Department of Trade and Industry (DTI) set up a Company Law Review to provide a comprehensive examination of the legal framework under which companies operate in the UK (DTI, 2002), and the Treasury looked in detail at productivity (HM Treasury, 2001). Both signalled an interest in investigating the links between existing structures of corporate governance and the supply of capital. The DTI also lobbied hard and successfully for a substantial increase in the science budget in order to protect the science base, and encourage partnerships between research universities and industry. The Review of Banking Competition was set up to look at ways in which finance for investment for small businesses could be improved, and Regional Development Agencies were created to act as catalysts for investment in the regions.

This pro-business policy was also carried forward with a major expansion of the Private Finance Initiative (PFI) programme established under the Conservatives for investment in public services, particularly in schools, hospitals and transport. The advantage to the Treasury and the government was that PFI schemes provided a means of increasing investment in public services by transferring the risk to the private sector, and did so in a way that did not add to public borrowing, so maintaining the strict budgetary rules. Critics alleged that many PFI schemes were more expensive than if the government had funded the investment directly through borrowing, reflecting the profits of the private companies, and that these extra costs would be borne by public-sector workers, whose conditions of work would be degraded, and by future generations of taxpayers, since many of the schemes ran for thirty years. The argument polarised into a public good/private bad debate, but the more interesting issue was the terms on which the public sector engaged with the private sector. A rigorous examination of the advantages and disadvantages of different forms of public–private partnerships, including PFI, showed the complexity of the relationships as well as the shortcomings of many of the PFIs that the government had negotiated (IPPR, 2001). The government had concluded that, if public services were to stay public, a higher level of private-sector involvement was essential, but there were doubts about whether they had yet got the procedures right for regulating that involvement to deliver both value-for-money and democratic accountability.

The pro-business stance of the Labour Government appeared at times to exclude the trade unions, but although not enjoying the kind of access and influence they had had previously, there were some noticeable steps in the unions' direction, including the introduction of a minimum wage, and the Fairness at Work proposals, which made union recognition easier. The trade unions also benefited from the steady fall in unemployment, and from the expansion of public expenditure. Released from these twin pressures, several public sector trade unions, particularly in the second term, began to rediscover some militancy, and strikes started to increase. The familiar problem of how to manage the expectations of workers without capsizing public finances loomed into view once more. For twenty years, British governments had done without incomes policies or any other corporatist means of managing wages. Unemployment and public spending cuts had maintained industrial discipline. But the situation after 2001 was substantially different. Labour's success in managing the economy was breeding problems of a familiar kind (Glyn and Wood, 2001).

Welfare Policy

Work-centred Welfare

Labour came to govern in 1997 with an explicit aim of moving people from welfare into work. This was consistent with the overarching aim to control the amount of public spending, but it was also consistent with a second aim, which was to tackle the problem of social exclusion. Following the conviction that employment is the best route out of exclusion and poverty, welfare reform set about reaching this goal by means of work-centred policy measures complemented by policies to improve the financial incentive of moving from benefits to work, and minimise the risk of in-work poverty. In addition, more emphasis was placed on offering practical support to ease the transition to work in the form of the National Childcare Strategy, career guidance, and training opportunities. More broadly, the Blair Government's first term was concerned with rebuilding a welfare consensus that had been eroded under successive Conservative Governments. In the first term, the Labour Government pursued specific, targeted aims to tackle the worst and most unacceptable issues of social exclusion. The apparent lack of ambition and lack of interest in wider redistribution was much criticised. Welfare policy in the second term has built on the aims and the achievements of the first term, but with some significant new developments. Whereas the first term concentrated first and foremost on moving the registered unemployed from welfare to work, the aim of the second term seeks, in addition, to move economically inactive claimants from benefits to the labour market. Labour's 2001 general election manifesto spelled out plans to create a 'Modern Welfare State' (Labour Party, 2001, 24–9) promoting employment for all people of working age; opportunities for those too young to work; and security for those who are over the age of retirement.

Labour's second term focuses on providing 'employment opportunity for all', or 'modern day full-employment'. This means continuing with the policy to reduce unemployment and finding employment for the approximately 1.5 million registered unemployed who still need jobs. In addition, though, in Labour's second term there is a clearly stated goal to increase levels of economic activity and to move into the labour market those who are not in work and are not registered as unemployed. Welfare spending on working-age claimants who are not registered for work – that is, claimants on so-called 'inactive benefits' – should be reduced (HM Treasury, 2002a, 36). The government calculates that there are 4 million claimants on 'inactive benefits', and these fall into clear categories: young people; the over-50s, lone parents; the sick and disabled; and people living in disadvantaged areas. These people are also characterised by low skill profiles, which reduces their chances of moving within the contemporary British labour market (HM Treasury and Department of Work and Pensions, 2001, 11–25). Labour's decision to encourage these claimants into the labour market is based on the joint premise that, on benefits, they are financially disadvantaged and particularly prone to poverty, that work is the best route out of this trap, and that many inactive benefit claimants want to work but are unable to because they are stuck in a dependency trap, or are victims of discrimination in the workplace.

The policies that are being used to tackle unemployment and increase economic activity are the same as in the first term. The second Blair Government is extending existing welfare policy to move people – both active and inactive economically – from welfare to work, to make work pay, to improve skills and to tackle discrimination against women, older workers, ethnic minorities and disabled people in the workplace.

In the first term, the New Deal policy was set up to help the young unemployed, the long-term unemployed, those aged over 50, lone parents and people with disabilities, but participating in the programme was only compulsory for the first two groups. What has changed in the second term is that it has been made compulsory for *all* benefit claimants of working age to attend 'work-focused' interviews, and other incentives have been introduced to encourage inactive benefit claimants to move into the labour market. The New Deal for Disabled People (NDDP) has been launched country-wide, and from April 2002 people claiming incapacity benefit will be allowed to work for up to 16 hours per week and remain on benefits (HM Treasury and Department of Work and Pensions, 2001). To tackle the regional dimension to economic inactivity, the government is setting up a Job Transition Service to help communities affected by large-scale redundancies, and a Rapid Response Fund to reskill people.

Another significant development in this direction was the creation of 'Jobcentre Plus' in October 2001. This new organisation grew from a merger of the Employment Service, which dealt with economically active claimants, with the Benefits Agency, which catered for people on so-called 'inactive benefits'. According to a Treasury and Department for Work and Pensions (DWP) document, this new organisation:

> Marks a dramatic change in the way in which Government helps working age citizens, delivering an active service to help people move on and become independent and move from welfare into work. All people, both unemployed and inactive, will on making a claim for benefit have a work-focused interview to discuss the opportunities available for taking up work. (HM Treasury and Department of Work and Pensions, 2001, 32)

The Labour Government has also been pursuing policies to make the transition from welfare to work financially worthwhile – in other words, to make work pay. It introduced the National Minimum Wage in April 1999, and in October 2001, at the start of its second term, this was raised to £4.10 an hour for workers aged 22 and over, and £3.50 an hour for 18–21-year-olds. These rates were raised again by 10p in October 2002. In October 1999, the Working Families Tax Credit (WFTC) was introduced, to provide continued benefits in the form of tax credits for people with families who were entering the labour market. An additional tax credit for people with disabilities (Disabled Person's Tax Credit) was introduced in parallel to the WFTC. In the second term, from 2003 the WFTC will be extended to address the issue of poor work incentives and in-work poverty among people without children or disabilities. The new scheme will be called Working Tax Credit.

Welfare for Children and Pensioners

Since 1997, the Blair Governments have been concerned about the high number of children and pensioners living in poverty, and openly boosted welfare benefits for these two legitimately economically inactive groups. Furthermore, the government has made a commitment to cut child poverty by half by 2010, and to eradicate it by 2020. The Government's policies to support families, children and pensioners in the second term are largely a continuation of those of the first term.

There has been a proliferation of households in which no one is economically active, and children are disproportionately represented in such households: one in five children were growing up in households without gainful work (Labour Party, 2001, 27). The Blair Governments' key policy strategy has been to reduce the number of jobless families, and to provide more childcare in order to make this possible. Families have been encouraged to return to the labour market by the Working Families Tax Credit, which offers in-work benefits as a financial incentive to take up employment. The National Childcare Strategy aimed to increase the provision of childcare with the aim that 'by March 2004 [it] will have created additional childcare places benefiting around a million extra children in England alone' (HM Treasury and Department of Work and Pensions, 2001, 28). Moreover, extra spending has been allocated for the period 2001–04 to improve childcare in deprived areas.

One of the most innovative ideas announced in Labour's manifesto for the second term are Child Trust Funds (or 'baby bonds', as the media dubbed them), which seek to provide a new universal benefit to begin to tackle the problem of the large number of citizens who are without any assets at all (Kelly and Lissauer, 2000). This is a proposal to 'extend to all children the advantages that come from reaching adulthood backed by a financial nest-egg' (Labour Party, 2001, 27). The policy proposes that 'all newly born children will have an interest-bearing Child Trust Fund set up in their name with an initial endowment from the government, with more for poorer children. The endowment will be locked until the child reaches adulthood'. The government plans to provide incentives for relatives and friends to invest in these funds, so that when the child reaches adulthood there will be substantial assets to 'invest in learning, buying a home or setting up a business'. If this policy is delivered, it will pioneer a new approach in Western social policy, by providing a new policy tool to tackle poverty and social exclusion, to invest in human capital, and to spread opportunity.

Pensioner poverty was tackled in the first term through a range of new policies and benefits, and the programme continued into the second term. The new means-tested Minimum Income Guarantee offers two million pensioners extra support. There was a manifesto pledge to raise this to £100 per week, £154 per week for couples (Labour Party, 2001, 29). In the second term the government published legislation for the new Pensions Credit to be introduced in 2003. This will bring pensioners up to a guaranteed minimum income, and will also reward pensioners for having built up savings during their working lives or for carrying on working beyond retirement age. Labour has retained the winter fuel payment for the over-60s and fixed the amount at £200 per year for the whole of its second term. This benefits eight million households. TV licences for the over-75s are free, a policy that benefits three million households. The Treasury website claims that by 2002, as a result of tax and benefit reforms since 1997, pensioner households should have been better off by £840 per year, and that around 1.8 million of the poorest pensioner households were over £1,000 better off. The government's strategy towards pensioners, however, has been widely criticised within the Labour Party, and by pensioners' groups, for focusing too heavily on means-tested benefits, for which there is a low take-up among the elderly, and too little on the level of the basic state pension. The government has refused to restore the link between pensions and earnings, which was broken by the Thatcher Government, although the Labour Party Conference voted to restore this link in September 2000. Labour was widely criticised for its meagre increases in the basic state pension – in 2001 it was raised in line with inflation by just 75p week, and in April 2002 by £5 a week for single pensioners and £8 a week for couples.

The government has also addressed the issue of long-term pensions reform. It has also set up an advisory service for present and future pensioners. It has reformed SERPS (the State Earnings-Related Pension Scheme), introduced a second state pension from April 2002, and stakeholder pensions. However, the success of these new initiatives is as yet unclear; the rolling out of the stakeholder pension was extremely slow, and many firms failed to set up schemes for their staff.

Second-term Welfare Policy

The policies of generous, albeit means-tested, benefits for those who are not of working age, and strong encouragement and incentives for those of working age to move from welfare into work are clear continuities from Labour's first term to its second. What is new in the second term is the explicit aim to achieve full employment and to encourage benefit claimants who have not been economically active – both men and women – to move into the labour market.

With this new policy emphasis on full employment, it appears that the government is promoting in Britain what has been labelled by Jane Lewis as an 'adult worker model' (AWM) welfare state (Lewis, 2001). This is one in which all people of working age are expected, and encouraged, to work.

This marks a fundamental change to the British welfare system, as previously it had always been accepted that the state would support certain groups such as lone parents, disabled people or older people with a range of benefits. If this is the case, then a key question remains: what kind of adult worker model will the UK become?

Lewis (2001) claims that there are currently two operating examples of the AWM welfare state – the USA and Sweden. They both expect all adults of working age to be economically active, but there are key difference between them in the ways that the economically inactive are encouraged to work, the financial incentives that exist for them, and the extent of the social infrastructure that is put in place to make a combination of work and other responsibilities feasible. The difference is also evident in the extent to which the state takes over responsibility for providing a social infrastructure to make this possible, and a legal framework to make it equitable.

There have been abundant criticisms that Labour's work-centred welfare approach is strongly influenced by American welfare, and that the UK is developing into more of a US-style AWM welfare regime. A number of accounts of Labour's approach to welfare have emphasised the influence of American welfare ideology, rhetoric and practice on UK social policy (for examples, see King and Wickham-Jones, 1999; Deacon, 2000; Heron, 2001; Peck and Theodore, 2001). These authors refer to two kinds of American influence: the New Right and Communitarianism. The New Right, informed by neo-liberal economic theory, emphasises the negative role of welfare in the macroeconomic performance of a state; it is argued that the welfare state erodes the work ethic and encourages welfare dependency. Communitarianism places social forces, community and social bonds at the centre of welfare issues, and Communitarians claim that it is the erosion of social bonds in American society, not markets or individual behaviour, that explains the phenomena of poverty and the underclass. They place civil society institutions and the family at the centre of the project to restore a 'moral voice' within communities, rather than the state (Annesley, 2003).

While the UK certainly imported many of its key welfare policy ideas from the USA, there is, however, more evidence that the Blair Government's approach is following a new social democratic strategy, and that it is developing more in the direction of a Scandinavian AWM. The new social democratic approach to welfare, still sees a significant role for the state in welfare. But, unlike old social democracy, it is not the state alone that provides welfare, and the state seeks to achieve different goals. A key feature of new social democratic welfare is that it promotes equality not through state redistribution but rather through and inclusion into the world of work, and the public sphere more generally (Giddens, 1998). It is anticipated that welfare spending should remain high, closer to European than US levels, but welfare spending should be 'positive' or 'active'. This means that welfare expenditure should be directed into human capital rather than into the direct provision of economic maintenance (Giddens, 1998, 117). The new approach to welfare also emphasises the promotion of sexual equality and of family-friendly workplace policies.

The Blair Government has made a determined effort to remould the welfare state to fit the new economic challenges of the new political economy. Esping-Andersen (1999) argues that welfare systems are made up of a triad of the state, the family and the labour market, and that each welfare regime adopts a mixture of these to alleviate social risks. As the economy, its labour market and family structures are transformed, the traditional balance of family, state and labour market no longer effectively alleviate the risks associated with the new era. The Blair Government's policy uses a new mixture of approaches to alleviate contemporary social risk. Men and women of working age are being moved from state dependency to the labour market, while the state is adopting the role of making the labour market fairer and developing policies to support families financially. The UK is not yet Sweden, but it appears to be moving in a new social democratic direction than towards the USA's ways of dealing with contemporary social risk.

The success of the Blair Government in its first five years has been to rebuild a consensus around the need for a high level of economic activity, universal welfare and public services, and for higher levels of taxation to fund them. The government at first cloaked its objectives in the vague language of the 'third way' to justify and explain this to the electorate, and refused to mention either redistribution or the need for higher taxes. In the second term this has changed, and the government has become more open and direct. Yet in many respects it continues to underplay its achievement. At times of welfare construction, governments generally tend to claim as much credit as possible for new welfare achievements. In contrast, at times of welfare retrenchment, politicians follow 'blame avoidance' strategies (Pierson, 1994) and try to dodge the blame for unpopular welfare cuts. The Blair Government has appeared to follow a peculiar strategy of 'credit avoidance': they have reshaped the welfare state, rebuilt a welfare consensus and in many instances have expanded welfare provision, but they have shied away from claiming credit for it. But this now appears to be changing. In its second term, the Blair Government is making a more confident use of the rediscovered welfare consensus by expanding spending in the fields of education and health, and there is evidence of more radical, universalistic welfare aims in policies such as the proposed Child Trust Funds.

Conclusion

Labour's economic programme depends, like those of previous governments, on achieving macroeconomic stability and at the same time increasing the long-run growth potential of the economy. The government needs the economy to keep growing at its current long-term potential growth rate in order to provide the minimum resources needed to fund the spending plans necessary to deliver Labour's wider policy commitments within the electoral cycle. This programme is often said to be a highly cautious one, but it is still high-risk, because it depends on assumptions about economic growth and unemployment that are not within the power of the government to deliver.

The government is determined not to commit macroeconomic mistakes which undermine its wider economic and social reform programme. It is keen to avoid the macro-adventurism and large-scale policy regime switches that characterised the Conservative era. In its first five years, the Labour Government was highly prudent and consistent in its policy choices. Macro-stability was seen as a condition for increasing the underlying growth rate of 2 per cent by 0.25 per cent. Although apparently small, this would be a large shift in historical terms if it could be achieved, and would make possible the aim of reducing the number of jobless households and sustaining the programme of increased investment in public services.

Before the Blair Government came to power, no previous Labour Government in the UK had won re-election to serve two full terms, one of the principal reasons for this was the repeated failure of Labour's economic policies, in particular its inability to reconcile its ambitions for greater public spending with the fiscal and monetary discipline needed to satisfy the financial markets. The Blair Government has tried to avoid the pitfalls of the past by establishing a credible set of institutions to govern fiscal and monetary policy. Previous governments of both parties often failed to ensure macroeconomic stability, lost credibility with both the markets and the electorate, and as a result failed to achieve many of their other policy objectives.

The policies Labour has pursued since 1997 have not signalled any abrupt change in the way economic and welfare policy has been conducted, and it is too early to say that a new social democratic model has been established. Nevertheless, it has been a distinctive approach that has linked economic and social policy more closely than before. At the heart of this approach are policies to encourage individuals to join the workforce. Welfare spending is only justified in this policy regime if it is active spending. Claimants and the economically inactive are being encouraged to return to work, and significant efforts have been made to improve incentives to work, the conditions of work and the reward for working, as well as extending these opportunities equally to men and women. This strategy for work feeds into and is underpinned by a macroeconomic policy whose goals are economic stability and sound public finances. Steady growth and modest redistribution are expected to secure increased investment in public services and the gradual alleviation of poverty.

Labour's policy regime was very successful in its first five years, but there remain difficult dilemmas ahead. One of these is how to respond to financial turmoil in the world financial markets. The government rode out the East Asian financial crisis in 1998–9 successfully, but by the end of 2002 the turmoil in the US and Japan, and continued stagnation in the EU, threatened to plunge the global economy into a major recession. The government's economic policy from the outset assumed that the international policy regime would remain broadly what it had been for the previous twenty years. A global depression would sweep such assumptions away, and introduce quite new considerations into national economic policy. Even a smaller recession would pose a severe test, probing the soundness of the fiscal framework erected by Gordon Brown and undermining his flagship policy, the New Deal. In the pre-Budget statement in November 2002, the government was forced to scale down its assumptions about future growth and future revenues, but stuck to its spending plans. For the first time, the commitment of the government to fiscal prudence as against its spending targets was questioned, and there was much media speculation that the government was returning to 'old' Labour habits.

A second dilemma is economic and monetary union. One of the advantages of joining the euro is that it would help to lock Britain into a regime that would deliver long-term macroeconomic stability. In this sense it would be a natural development of the policy the government has pursued since 1997. Business is divided on the issues, but the majority view accepts that being outside the euro imposes significantly higher costs, such as higher interest rates. Many large, transnational companies have been planning on the assumption that Britain will have joined the euro by 2006, but much City opinion is more cautious, believing that Britain is likely to stay out until 2010 (Talani, 2000).

The reason is not just the political difficulty of winning a referendum. There are also genuine doubts about when it will be most advantageous for Britain to join, as well as worries about the policy regime of the euro zone (Gamble and Kelly, 2002). In its early years, the European Central Bank (ECB) operated a monetary policy with an implicit inflation target of 0–2 per cent, in contrast to the symmetrical target in the UK. Unless this target is changed and the terms of the Stability and Growth Pact revised there is a serious risk of the monetary stance being too deflationary, which could lead to very high unemployment in some European regions. If the ECB is not properly accountable for its policy stance its legitimacy will also be undermined. With national governments constrained in their capacity to act, the political consequences could become explosive. Many supporters of European integration argue that the EU has to acquire an economic government alongside its monetary government which can ensure a monetary and fiscal policy mix that avoids a deflationary bias, and rewrites the Stability and Growth Pact, taking into account the very different context of the global economy in the first decade of the twenty-first century. Many of these arguments acknowledged in Brown's announcement in June 2003 on the results of the five tests. Brown's economic caution dominated the statement. Although the political desirability of joining the euro was once again forcefully stated by Blair, Brown's statement was widely interpreted as indicating that entry in the second term was off the agenda.

A third dilemma is the continuing poor productivity performance of the British economy, and whether a bolder supply-side strategy would have a greater impact on the problem. Labour's diagnosis of Britain's failings as an industrial economy was that it had become locked into low productivity, low wages, and low-skill jobs in too many sectors. Remedying the lack of investment in human capital through better training and education, the lack of investment in physical capital through better research and development, and an improved infrastructure, are Labour's solutions. Many on the centre-left question whether Labour can continue to deliver the kind of long-term improvement in economic performance that it seeks without broader institutional reform aimed at changing the vocational training system, the accessibility of lifelong learning opportunities, and structures of corporate governance, in order to develop more companies keen to train and retain workforces with high skills, and to establish long-term stakeholder relationships with their employees (Hutton, 1995; Coates and Hay, 2001).

10

New Labour and the Reform of Public Services

RAJIV PRABHAKAR

Introduction

The reform of public services is central to New Labour's domestic agenda in its second term in office. This is highlighted, for example, by its 2001 general election manifesto. This placed improvements in public services at its heart (Labour Party, 2001). Reform is thought to be necessary in order to respond to public concerns over the level and quality of services provided. An indication of this public discontent was seen in an incident when Tony Blair was harangued during the 2001 general election campaign by a member of the public over the state of the health services. The nature of New Labour's reform efforts is likely to be a key topic for future political debates. The leader of the Conservative Party, Iain Duncan Smith, for example, has promised to make any failure of Labour to deliver on pledges to improve services a key platform on which to attack the government.

This chapter sets out to do two things. First, it outlines the main elements of New Labour policy towards key public services since being elected to office in 1997. In order to assess whether New Labour will be successful in reforming public services, it is important first to consider what its approach constitutes. While there is not space here to do full justice to New Labour's approach by surveying policy towards all the public services and examining all the initiatives that emerge in these contexts, it is possible to identify the broad themes that structure policy interventions in core areas. Attention will focus in this chapter on the spheres of education and health. These realms have been chosen because New Labour rhetoric declares that these services are central to their reform effort. As such, a study of education and health is likely to capture the principal contours of the government's approach. Many early New Labour proclamations suggested that it would chart a 'third way' beyond the policies deployed by Labour and the Conservatives since 1945. Such claims generated much controversy and discussion within the academic literature. The examination of policy here suggests that important continuities throughout its period of office can be identified in Conservative and Labour policy since the end of the Second World War. This is manifested significantly with an emphasis on the use of targets and state expenditure in public policy. Although the claim that New Labour is fostering a third way is, accordingly, an exaggeration, this does not mean that it has no substance. The chapter contends that the attention paid by Labour to institutional diversity, as evidenced, for example, in public–private partnerships or attempts to integrate voluntary and community groups in policy, gives some content to the third way. However, as Stuart White points out, when analysing the third way it is important not to treat it as a homogeneous entity but to recognise that it is composed of different strands (White, 1998). Nevertheless, some weight can be given to the proposition that the government is forging a third way in public services alongside (rather than apart from) Conservative and Labour policy measures since 1945.

Second, the chapter considers what the different parts of New Labour's agenda distinguished above mean for the successful reform of public services. One pessimistic view is that the different parts of New Labour's approach amount to an incoherent jumble and will undermine the successful reform of public services. New Labour, from this perspective, uses a range of strategies without proper thought being paid to how they conflict with each other. Against this, the chapter proposes an alternative, more optimistic, reading. The complexity of reforming public services suggests it is likely that different instruments are appropriate in different circumstances. From this standpoint, features such as targets, state expenditure and institutional diversity simply represent different instruments used to reform public services. This does not mean, however, that no criticism can be levelled at New Labour from such a perspective. While there is no objection to the use of different instruments, the ways in which individual tools are fashioned are open to criticism.

The chapter proceeds, first, by briefly setting out what are the main facets of 'old Labour', Conservative and third way approaches to the reform of public services. This provides a framework for analysing the policy record that follows. This completes the first theme tackled in this chapter, namely, the broad elements of New Labour's approach. The chapter then moves to consider the second principal aspect of the chapter – that is, what this is likely to mean for reforming public services.

The Third Way: Modernising Social Democracy

This section starts by outlining some of the general features of 'old Labour', Conservative, and new approaches in social policy discourse. This will help to place the ensuing policy discussion within its context. New Labour pronouncements on public services often claim that they are forging a 'third-way' agenda. In a White Paper entitled, *A Modern and Dependable NHS*, published in 1997, for example, it was stated that there:

> will be no return to the old centralised command and control systems of the 1970s. That approach stifled innovation and put the needs of institutions ahead of the needs of patients. But nor will there be a continuation of the divisive internal market system of the 1990s. That approach which was intended to make the NHS more efficient ended up fragmenting decision-making and distorting incentives to such an extent that unfairness and bureaucracy became its defining features. Instead there will be a 'third way' of running the NHS – a system based on partnership and drive by performance. (Department of Health, 1997, 8)

The third way on this understanding constitutes an alternative to centralised command and control and a reliance on internal markets. For New Labour, centralised command and control is a feature of state-based welfare. This model stresses the importance of state funding and the provision of welfare services. A variety of rationales have been offered for this model. It has been argued, for instance, that the state is the only agency capable of satisfying egalitarian ambitions through its capacity for redistribution, or that through rational planning it is able to overcome the inefficiencies linked with anarchic market processes. The Attlee Administration of 1945 is usually credited as introducing many of the aspects of the welfare state into modern British politics. Although it can be exaggerated, this provided the basis for a social policy consensus between Labour and Conservatives for much of the period since 1945 (Marquand, 1988). During the 1970s this approach came under sustained attack from an assortment of 'New Right' intellectuals such as F. A. Hayek, as well as Conservative politicians such as Margaret Thatcher. A variety of arguments emerged within this context. Hayek, for example, alleged that public officials lack the necessary information to make efficient decisions.

Emphasis is placed, instead, on markets. It is thought that markets economise on the information needed for an efficient allocation of resources (Gamble, 1988). The attention to markets carried a series of implications. One important theme involved trying to limit government intervention in education by encouraging schools to opt-out of local authority control, thereby having control over their own budgets. Attempts were also made to enhance parental choice. One important way this was promoted was through the provision of information on the performance of schools through league tables. This dimension led, paradoxically, to a strengthening of certain government capacities. The government was involved in the formation and assessment of performance targets. This was manifested, for example, by intervention through the National Curriculum. One consequence of all of this was that the role of state spending as a way of financing public services was downgraded. Although the Conservatives found it difficult (despite their best efforts) to roll back the frontiers of the state, they tried to stem further rises which dampened down investment in public services. Therefore New Labour inherited a situation in which the public services were not in the rudest of health.

Many reformers connected with the third way have accepted the significance of Conservative criticisms of post-war social democracy. They reject, however, the emphasis on free markets seen in the alternative Conservative accounts. It is believed that markets may not ensure an efficient or equitable level of provision for the sorts of public goods provided by the public services. In such circumstances, collective institutions can address such failures, particularly in terms of co-ordination. But rather than simply fall back on the state, theorists of the third way examine alternative forms of collective provision. One salient theme has been to explore the realm of 'civil society' that broadly inhabits the space between the individual and the state. This points to an acceptance of institutional diversity (Giddens, 1998). Tony Blair argues that the

> Third way recognises the limits of government in the social sphere, but also the need for government within those limits, to forge new partnerships with the voluntary sector. Whether in education, health, social work, crime prevention or the care of children, 'enabling' government strengthens civil society rather than weakening it, and helps families and communities improve their own performance. (Blair, 1998, 14)

The attention paid to civil society leads to a focus on some form of government intervention, notwithstanding the limits imposed on it. Government has a role in helping to fashion civil society – for example, by instituting a legal framework conducive to the emergence of a variety of organisational forms. Another feature is an acceptance that this may involve a role for the private sector, in both the funding and delivery of services. Not all of the focus on institutional diversity is entirely new, however. At the beginning of the twentieth century many services were funded and delivered by self-help organisations and friendly societies. The approach outlined above renews this emphasis. Whether or not this conception of modernising social democracy is seen as a totally novel enterprise, it does consist of an alternative to the reliance on either state-centred or free-market approaches that have dominated discussions since 1945.

Policy

Government Intervention

Having looked at 'old' Labour, Conservative and third way approaches, the chapter now moves to examine the actual policy record of the government. This is split into the themes that emerge from the above discussion. Given space constraints, the examination will inevitably be selective. It looks at important dimensions of state, market and third way approaches rather than trying to characterise fully each of these strands. It studies, in particular, state intervention, targeting and institutional diversity. This section begins by contemplating state expenditure. Spending on public services has exhibited a number of twists under New Labour. One broad way of categorising the various changes is to note an initial period of fiscal restraint followed by a period of significant and sustained increases in government spending. Although this is a simplification, it nevertheless captures important elements of the trajectory of state expenditure. As discussed in Chapter 9, for the first two years in office, New Labour committed itself to honouring the spending commitments of the previous Conservative Administration. As the Tory government did not see increased spending as an important tool for reforming public services, New Labour's attachment to these spending plans damped down expectations that this would be an important instrument of reform. This fiscal stance was driven in important part by the desire of New Labour reformers to distance themselves from what they saw as the 'tax-and-spend' image of previous Labour Administrations. All this helped court controversy, and prompted claims that New Labour was adopting a policy of 'catch-up' to Conservative assumptions (Hay, 1999).

As time progressed, however, this policy of restraint has relaxed. State expenditure, particularly during the second term, has witnessed important growth. There are possibly a number of reasons for this, but one is probably the government's belief that without such increases New Labour risked alienating swathes of core Labour voters. This rise in spending, however, has not been distributed evenly across all departments. The pattern of changes can be seen in the three-yearly spending plans set out by the government. Announced in June 1997, the Comprehensive Spending Review was a close examination of expenditure across all government departments for the period 1998–9 to 2000–01. Health and education received the largest increases. Total health spending was to rise from £37.2 billion in 1998–9 to £43.1 billion in 2001–02. This meant a corresponding increase in the budget for the NHS from £36.5 billion to £42.4 billion (the average real increase being 4.7 per cent each year). Education spending was projected to rise from £38.2 billion in 1998–9 to £44.7 billion in 2000–01 (that entailed an increase in the Department for

Education and Employment from £14.17 billion to £17.29 billion)
(HM Treasury, 1998). The 2000 Spending Review announced a 5.4 per cent
real increase in funding for education over the three years taking total education spending from £49.46 billion in 2001–02 to £57.7 billion in 2003–04.
This increase was second only to health, whose departmental budget rose
from £49.46 billion in 2001–02 to £59.01 billion in 2003–04 (HM Treasury,
2000a). Of this, the total NHS budget was to rise from £48.2 billion in
2001–02 to £56.7 billion in 2003–04. The 2002 Spending Review notes that
spending on education will rise by £12.8 billion between 2002–03 and
2005–06. This implies an average rise of 6 per cent a year in the three years to
2005–06 (which means that education spending in 2005–06 would be 5.6 per
cent of gross domestic product (GDP) compared to 4.6 in 2000–01). With
regard to health, the Review flagged up the biggest sustained spending growth
in the history of the NHS, namely £40 billion extra resources committed by
2007–08 compared to 2002–03. This amounts to an average growth of 7.3 per
cent above inflation (HM Treasury, 2002a). The 2002 Budget noted that, to
help fund this increase, National Insurance contributions were to rise from
April 2003 (HM Treasury, 2002b). The Review argued that the rise in funding
was driven in part by the chancellor accepting many of the conclusions of an
investigation into the long-term funding of the NHS conducted by Derek
Wanless, former Group Chief Executive of NatWest bank (Wanless, 2002).
The report concluded that the amount of money spent on health care had to
rise to between 10.6 per cent and 20 per cent over the next twenty years if
future challenges are to be met. The 2002 Spending Review noted that total
UK NHS spending would rise from £68.1 billion in 2002–03 to £109.4 billion
in 2007–08, and that as a percentage of GDP total UK health spending would
increase from 7.7 per cent in 2002–03 to 9.4 per cent in 2007–08.

Much of state expenditure on education and health funds direct government provision of these services. For example, money earmarked for education in the 2000 Spending Review was directed in part at improving
the infrastructure of schools. Investment in school buildings tripled from
£683 million in 1996–7 to £2.1 billion in 2000–01. In 2003–04, spending
is planned to be £3.2 billion in school capital, £500 million of which will be
devolved to school bodies. In terms of the 2002 Spending Review, capital
investment in education will grow from £3.7 billion in 2002–03 to £7 billion
a year by 2005–06, with £1.2 billion being raised through the Private Finance
Initiative (PFI) (which involves a public–private partnership arrangement).
The resources dedicated to education will help pay for new grants (worth
£125,000) to support at least 1,400 schools in challenging areas; to expand
modern apprenticeships and work related qualifications; and to provide a
1 per cent real growth in funding every year to 2005–06 for further education
colleges committed to performance targets.

With respect to health, in recent times much of the money allocated helps to fulfil the NHS plan. Published in 2000, this set out the government's plan for reforming the health service in the following ten years. The plan identified decades of underinvestment as a key problem facing the reform of the health service. The resources earmarked for health were aimed at addressing this. Part of the new investment is targeted at improving NHS facilities. It will help pay, for example, for 7,000 extra NHS beds by 2004, over 100 new hospitals by 2010, and 500 new one-stop primary care centres by 2004. Money will also provide for 7,500 more consultants, 2,000 more general practitioners and 20,000 more nurses by 2004 (Department of Health, 2000). *Delivering the NHS Plan* (Department of Health, 2000a), outlined progress made on implementing the plan. In relation to investment in staff, it stated that, by 2008, the NHS is expected to have a net increase over September 2001 of at least 15,000 consultants and general practitioners; 35,000 nurses, midwives and health visitors; and 30,000 scientists and therapists. In 2008, there will also be 8,000 more nurses leaving training (an increases of over 60 per cent over the figure for 2001–02) as well as a rise of 1,900 medical graduates per year (a 54 per cent increase over 2001–02) (Department of Health, 2002a).

Targets

If higher government expenditure is an increasingly important component of policy, this exists alongside weight placed on the use of targets. For *Excellence in Schools* (Department for Education and Employment, 1997) (the first White Paper produced by this Labour Government), early learning was deemed to be critical for laying the foundation upon which lifetime learning would be built. For pre-school children, there was a commitment to nursery places for all 4-year-olds whose parents choose this option, with targets being set for 3-year-olds. In 2001, the Green Paper, *Schools: Building on Success* (Department for Education and Employment, 2001) noted that universal nursery education for all 4-year-olds had been put in place, plus an expansion for 3-year-olds (120,000 more places than in 1997). Moreover, 298,000 more new childcare places had been created between April 1997 and September 2000. For the future, a commitment was made to provide free nursery places for all 3-year-olds whose parents choose this option, as well as the provision of new childcare places benefiting a million children by 2004. A commitment was also made to establish up to 900 neighbourhood nursery centres in disadvantaged areas by 2004. To enhance quality, a star rating scheme would be introduced to provide better information for parents when making choices (Department for Education and Employment, 2001).

With regard to primary education, emphasis was placed on class sizes, since this was thought to be a critical determinant of human capital acquisition for early learners. The promise that there would be no classes with pupil numbers exceeding thirty for 5-, 6- and 7-year-olds formed one of new Labour's five key election pledges. Those infants who were in classes of more than thirty individuals were reduced from 500,000 to 30,000 between January 1998 and September 2000. By September 2001, this target was met (Department for Education and Employment, 2001). Within the curriculum, at least one hour each day would be devoted to basic literacy, numeracy skills and national targets set. These targets would be backed up by pupil assessment, and national guidelines for teacher training imposed. *Schools: Building on Success* required 80 per cent and 75 per cent of 11-year-olds to achieve standards set for their age in English and mathematics, respectively, by 2002. Emphasis was also placed on introducing sports, arts and citizenship programmes.

At secondary school level, emphasis was placed on targets at 14, since success here was thought to be an important determinant of success at GCSE level. Also, from the age of 13 or 14, attention was paid to the education system providing more vocational or work-based options (Department for Education and Employment, 2001). Budget 2000 announced that, from September 2000, the National Curriculum would make the links between education, employment and enterprise more explicit, and information about financial awareness and consumer education would be made available at both primary and secondary levels (HM Treasury, 2000b). Many proposals on secondary education are contained in the White Paper, *Schools Achieving Success* (Department for Education and Skills, 2001). Concern is expressed at the level of attainment between the ages of 11 and 14 (Key Stage Three). By 2007, it is expected that 85 per cent of pupils will reach Level 5 or above at the end of Key Stage Three in English, mathematics and ICT (information, communications and technology), and 80 per cent in science. Interim goals that 75 per cent should achieve Level 5 or above in English, mathematics and ICT, and 70 per cent in science are set for 2004. To help pupils reach these targets, schools and local education authorities will be asked to set goals for the performance of 14-year-olds, and the results will then be published.

Built on the above targets are proposals for education from the ages of 14–19, and attention here is paid to recognising the importance of vocational education. Schools and colleges are to implement reforms of advanced level qualifications, with the introduction of vocational AS- and A-levels. More generally, a new overarching award recognising both academic and vocational elements is to be developed. These proposals are backed up by a series of other measures, including the enhancement of the power of the Secretary of State for Education to intervene if a school is thought to be failing. Powers are introduced to allow the governing boards of failing schools to be replaced by an Interim Executive Board if the board itself is deemed part of the problem. The role played by teachers in fostering success is highlighted. There is a promise to recruit 10,000 more teachers and 20,000 support staff over the second term. Targets announced in the 2002 Spending Review encompass the aim to ensure that by 2004, 85 per cent of 11-year-olds achieve Level 4 or above, and 35 per cent attain Level 5 or above; by 2004, at least 28 per cent of young people start a modern apprenticeship by the age of 22; and to reduce the number of adults in the UK workforce who lack a National Vocational Qualification (NVQ) at Level 2 or equivalent by at least 40 per cent by 2010.

With regard to health, in an attempt to improve the efficiency and quality of NHS services, the 1997 White Paper on reform proposed to set up a variety of national standards and guidelines, captured in National Service Frameworks. To monitor these targets, the paper promised to establish some new national institutions. A National Institute for Clinical Excellence would study clinical performance and cost-effectiveness across the whole health service. A Commission for Health Improvement would be set up to oversee the quality of clinical services at the local level. The NHS plan also outlines new measures for monitoring the performance of local health services. It states that the existing Performance Assessment Framework (which encompasses outcomes from health care, access to services and the use of resources) will be extended from the focus on health authorities to cover from April 2001 all NHS organisations providing community services. Bodies will be classified as 'red', 'yellow' or 'green'. Red are those organisations that fail to meet a number of core targets, yellow are those that satisfy core targets but do not fall within the top 25 per cent of performers, and green are the remainder. While green organisations gain automatic access to funds, red bodies will get resources but with strings attached. Yellow institutions will be required to agree plans about how they intend to use their funds, though with less stringent conditions than red organisations. *Delivering the NHS Plan* (Department of Health, 2002a) outlines a commitment to reduce waiting times for an outpatient appointment to a maximum of three months by 2005 and to reduce waiting times for a hospital operation to a maximum of six months by 2005 (falling to three months by 2008). A proposal is made to establish a new Commission for Healthcare Audit and Inspection which will publish star ratings, inspect all NHS hospitals and license private provision.

Diversity

The attempt to promote diversity, in both funding and provision, is also a salient theme. As regards funding, an important aspect has been a stress on fostering public–private partnerships (manifested, for example, in the Private Finance Initiative (PFI)). An early initiative by New Labour (in addition to the PFI education arrangement noted in the previous section) concerned the setting up of Education Action Zones (EAZs). Here, under-performing schools and disadvantaged areas were targeted by local partner-ships involving local businesses, parents and the local education authority. These were set up in response to applications from groups of around 15–25 schools and partners. They set out plans for school improvements and new activities. Zones received up to £1 million per year: £500,000 baseline fund-ing from the Department for Education and Employment, with up to £250,000 in matched funds in return for contributions from zone partners. Zones are run by an Action Forum and managed by a project director. To foster innovation, zones have certain legislative freedoms. They can help to negotiate teachers' pay and conditions, and take advantage of flexibility in the curriculum. As of March 2001, there were 99 EAZs, with 82 'small' EAZs (eight to ten schools, including one secondary, and partners). While allowing existing EAZs to complete their five-year contracts, by 2002 the government wound up this programme, motivated by concerns that the scheme was not attracting sufficient levels of sponsorship (Evans, 2002).

This indicates that not all of New Labour's efforts have been undertaken without difficulty. This is not to say that the government is not interested in pressing ahead with involving civil society in the financing of public serv-ices, only that the success of different measures is mixed. The salience of this agenda is seen in the City Academy programme, that seeks sponsors from private and voluntary sectors to establish new schools, with the aim of achieving at least twenty City Academies by 2005. In relation to health, *Delivering the NHS Plan* (Department of Health, 2002a) notes that the Private Finance Initiative will be extended throughout health care, and that NHS bodies will be able to form joint ventures with private and voluntary sectors to help provide, for example, NHS-supported nursing homes. Use will also be made of spare capacity within the private sector, and the role of overseas providers will be accepted.

The stress on diversity is also exhibited at the level of provision. Within health, the 1997 White Paper on the NHS pointed to the setting up of Primary Care Groups which comprise all the general practitioners (GPs) and community nurses in a given area, and which would be charged with commissioning services for the local community (typically serving about 100,000 patients). Health Action Zones were touted as a way of improving the health of local people. Opened in up to ten areas from April 1998, these zones brought together bodies within and beyond the NHS to fashion and administer a strategy for improving the health of local people. The government also proposed that NHS Trusts should work alongside other

organisations (such as Primary Care Groups) in developing health improvement programmes, and provide detailed information about their arrangements for partnership. The NHS plan promised to set up regional and local
modernisation boards where local stakeholders, including hospital consultants and patient groups, contribute to improvements in the health service. The
plan also pointed to the establishment, in 2001, of a National Independent
Panel to advise on major changes. This is composed of one-third doctors,
nurses and health professionals; one-third patient and citizen representatives;
and one-third managers of green-light organisations. With respect to devolving power and resources, *Delivering the NHS Plan* notes that new Strategic
Health Authorities are being established to oversee local operations. It says
that Primary Care Trusts will soon increase their control from a half to
three-quarters of the total NHS budget. To improve mechanisms for
expressing patients' opinions, independent Patient Forums will be set up in
each trust to review local services from the patient's perspective (with one
member being represented on the NHS board). The paper notes that 2002
saw the setting-up of the first of the NHS Foundation Hospitals. Foundation
Trusts will have the freedom to develop their governance structures to
ensure more effective involvement among patients, staff, the local community and other stakeholders. The Department of Health published a concordat with the Independent Healthcare Association setting out some of the
general parameters of partnership arrangements between NHS organisations, and private and voluntary healthcare providers. The concordat
focused on issues of elective, intermediate and critical care. For example, in
relation to elective care, measures suggested included allowing Primary
Care Groups to commission accommodation from the private and voluntary
health care sector with services delivered by NHS staff under NHS
contracts, or allowing an NHS trust to sub-contract directly to a private or
voluntary provider (Department of Health, 2002b). Commitment to these
reforms was underlined in July 2002 in the government's response to the
House of Commons' Health Committee's first report on the role of the private sector in the NHS, when it was noted that working with 'providers
from the independent sector and from overseas is not a temporary measure.
They will become a permanent feature of the new NHS landscape and will
provide NHS services' (Department of Health, 2002c, 4). Such bodies will
play a role, for example, in a new generation of diagnostic and treatment
centres. The importance of fostering diversity was emphasised in the
Queen's Speech made on 13 November 2002. For instance, proposals were
announced to increase the accountability of hospitals to local communities,
as well as measures to give greater freedom to the most successful hospitals
(allowing them, for example, to borrow money from markets without
government approval). The 2002 pre-Budget report notes that £125 million

(in addition to £93 million over the 2002 spending review period) would be invested in a 'futurebuilder' programme. This provides financial help to involve voluntary and community organisations in the delivery of services such as education (HM Treasury, 2002c).

Assessment

A scrutiny of policy suggests that New Labour's approach to the reform of public services is characterised by a number of different facets. The deployment of state spending, targets and institutional diversity have been identified here. While this is not an exhaustive list, it does provide a flavour of the main components characterising New Labour policy. One possible objection to seeing policy in these terms is that it misses the extent to which New Labour may have a hidden agenda. In particular, although on the face of it policy is composed of a number of different strands, it is in fact gradually converging on one particular approach to reform. This is usually expressed in the charge that the emphasis on institutional diversity is simply an element of creeping privatisation. This view has difficulty, however, in explaining one of the most prominent features of New Labour's approach in recent times, namely the sustained increases seen in government spending. While it is probably the case that the amount of funds committed will not satisfy all observers, it is hard to reconcile the commitment to increased state spending with the view that the government is simply privatising public services. Rather than seeing reform as pointing inexorably to one particular logic, it is more useful perhaps to see the agenda as being composed of several different elements. One consequence of this is that understanding New Labour only in terms of one theme will be too crude an analysis. While there is truth in the allegation that, for example, New Labour exhibits catch-up to the Conservatives in the light of the continued stress on and consolidation of targets, seeing New Labour only in these terms obscures the extent to which the government has embraced elements of post-war social democracy through an emphasis on state spending. Equally, while there is some substance to the New Labour claim that it is charting a third way, this exists alongside (rather than in opposition to) the use of previous Labour and Conservative policy instruments. One implication of this is that, if debates on the merits of New Labour's policy programme are to be pursued properly, they ought to recognise the different faces of the government's approach. This means, for the government, that its rhetoric ought to shift to acknowledge the importance of post-war Labour and Tory policy alongside its advocacy of the third way.

What does the varied nature of the Blair administration's stance on the public services mean for their successful reform? In the space available here, it is not possible to explore all these issues in depth. Nevertheless, some general themes can be sketched out. It has been argued that the government's approach encompasses a focus on the state, market and civil society. While the origins of this trajectory may be the subject of debate (one question concerns, for example, how far this reflects accident rather than design), one important issue relates to how desirable the continuation of this stance is for reforming public services. One view is that the multi-faceted nature of policy points to confusion, and indicates the absence of a clear rationale for reform. An implication of this position is that reform ought to be based on one particular instrument (the market, state or civil society, depending on one's preference). I suggest that such a standpoint is too narrow. In particular, the complex nature of the reform of public services means that a similar instrument is unlikely to be useful in all contexts. Instead, the intricacies of reform suggest that the use of different initiatives is probably unavoidable. Reform of public services may be judged against a variety of principles. Two notions that are likely to command particular attention concern efficiency and accountability. It is suggested here that on both of these grounds a case can be made for the use of state, market and civil society in the reform of public services. With respect to efficiency, for example, one feature of importance in health and education relates to the importance of large-scale capital investments to help build hospitals and schools. As the government can often borrow funds from capital markets at more favourable rates of interest than can private-sector actors (reflecting, for example, the lower risk of defaulting on any loan), state intervention can foster efficiency where borrowing is needed. While the government can enhance efficiency in such a context, it is probably too far removed from end-users to be able to co-ordinate effectively the local information that is often required for efficiency. In such circumstances, collective institutions that inhabit the space between the individual and the centre can play a valuable role. There has been greater awareness in recent times of the ways that community and voluntary organisations can help to raise the 'social capital' within a community (Putnam, 2000). Elsewhere, any attempt to introduce incentives within public service will probably have to make some use of market mechanisms. This is not to say that a market ethic of self-interest is all-important, but that it will play a part in providing people with appropriate incentives (Le Grand, 1997). In terms of accountability, the need to have a system of national regulations points to the significance of national institutions. While such national bodies do not have to be conflated with central government, it seems reasonable to suppose that the government will have some role to play in regulation. National institutions are probably too remote to be fully sensitive to local conditions. Within this realm, the role of 'voice' provided by collective organisations as well as 'exit' fostered by markets are both likely to play a role in ensuring that services reflect the demands of end-users (Hirschman, 1970). It is true that the use of market, state and civil society is likely to engender various tensions. Government spending on education, for example, may 'crowd-out' private-sector investment. While not wishing to ignore such conflicts, the argument here is that pursuing policy initiatives on different fronts is valuable, notwithstanding the difficulties that such an approach also generates.

While it might be argued that policy has to be multi-faceted, it might be contended that the package of reforms should not encompass all the elements that have been identified above. The stress on civil society has been a particular target of criticism in recent times. The former health secretary, Frank Dobson, for example, has expressed concern over foundation hospitals, seeing diversity simply as a recipe for unequal provision. Dobson argues that the introduction of these hospitals will lead to the establishment of a 'two-tier' NHS that undermines the principle of universal provision upon which the health service was founded (Dobson, 2002). His campaign produced one of the most important splits among Labour MPs in recent years. David Walker generalises this in his critique of the emphasis on civil society, which he takes as being definitive of New Labour's approach. Walker argues that, historically, the left in Britain has been committed to promoting equality, and claims that the state is the only institution capable of delivering equality. He says that in turning its back on the state and embracing the 'new localism', New Labour is fostering inequality. Reversing this implies rejecting the new localism and stressing the role of the state (Walker, 2002).

Owing to its capacity for redistribution, it is likely that the state will be involved in any strategy to tackle inequality. It is questionable, however, whether New Labour is simply retreating from the state in the manner that Dobson and Walker suggest. As such, they exaggerate New Labour's break with equality. It is the case, nonetheless, that the government has used elements of 'new localism'. This may be defended on at least two counts. First, civil society may in fact play a role in combating inequality. Although the importance of the state in achieving equality has already been noted, it is nevertheless the case that the post-war welfare state left significant inequalities untouched. The middle class has often been more likely than the working class to avail themselves of the opportunities that the welfare state provided. One explanation for this is rooted in the idea that middle-class people are better-informed about benefits that are available, greater information encourages greater take-up. By involving wider stakeholders in the finance and delivery of policy, a focus on civil society might, by spreading information, encourage other groups to make greater use of available opportunities. Civil society, for reasons such as these, may have a useful role alongside the state in strategies to tackle inequality. It should not simply be dismissed. Second, new localism can help to serve other valuable ends. Although the state can help to support equality, it also suffers from various limitations that provide a rationale for going beyond the state. One concern is that relying only on the state is unlikely to promote adequate accountability of public services to end-users. This is the conclusion, for example, of an examination of accountability within the NHS conducted on behalf of the Association of Community Health Councils for England and Wales (Commission on the NHS, 2000). Localism can help to improve the responsiveness of services by creating practical realms where stakeholders can articulate their concerns.

Even though the weight New Labour places on involving civil society in the design and implementation of public services can broadly be defended, this does not mean that specific initiatives within these boundaries are immune from any criticism. Legitimate concerns may be raised, for example, about the ways in which programmes have been devised. For example, a study conducted under the auspices of a think-tank, the Institute for Public Policy Research, argued that one argument justifying public–private partnerships is the idea that using private finance to pay for capital investment allows the government to undertake more projects than would otherwise have been the case. It is contended that this is a spurious reason, since all PFI projects are publicly funded and incur future liabilities for the government. Instead, focus should be made on those situations where partnerships can offer value for money gains and increase the quality of services delivered (Commission on Public–Private Partnerships, 2001). Addressing this does not mean that all attempts at promoting institutional diversity have to be jettisoned, rather that there is room for debate about the way in which policy measures are constructed.

Implementing further reform based on market, state and civil society is unlikely to go uncontested, however. This raises the issue of how feasible it is to develop this approach. The problems the government faces over the private finance initiative helps to illustrate some of the problems faced. Many unions are opposed to attempts to go beyond state funding of public services. This is seen, for example, in a series of hostile resolutions on the Private Finance Initiative tabled at the annual Labour Party Conference in October 2002. Part of this opposition is likely to reflect proper concerns of the type raised by the Commission on Public–Private Partnerships. However, antipathy on the part of the unions probably also reflects their own sectional interests as they feel threatened by the involvement of private corporations in public policy. Some signs of Tony Blair's frustration with such opposition was indicated in a speech he made to Labour's Conference in Cardiff in February 2002, when he alluded to union opponents as representing 'forces of conservatism' to his efforts at 'modernisation'.

The existence of such difficulties means that reform is unlikely to go unchallenged. While it is unlikely that such opposition will derail entirely reform efforts based on the principles outlined above, it does suggest that the government will face defeats and have to make concessions as it presses on with reform. Accordingly, it is likely to have mixed success in its attempts at reform.

Conclusion

This chapter has examined two main things. First, it has offered an account of New Labour's strategy towards reforming key public services, such as education and health. It has argued that, in contrast to rhetoric that suggests the formation of a third way against policies adopted by Labour and the Conservatives since 1945, evidence of continuities can be seen in the recourse to direct state spending and targets. This does not mean, however, that claims to be modernising social democracy are unfounded. The attention paid to promoting the participation of the institutions of civil society in the finance and delivery of public services points to the existence of a distinct agenda. The criticisms of individuals such as Frank Dobson and David Walker lend credence to the reality of a new social democratic approach: they do not dispute its existence, but rather reject its worth. Although examples of new social democratic initiatives can be seen from New Labour's first term in office, many of these developments have gathered pace in its second term. The reason for this is probably linked to the fact that New Labour has dedicated its second term to the reform of public services. New social democratic reforms are likely to be consolidated as the government grapples with further reform.

Second, the chapter has sketched what the multi-faceted nature of New Labour's approach is likely to mean for the successful reform of services. It has suggested that the complexities of reform mean that New Labour's use of different instruments is probably justified, although the ways in which these instruments have been fashioned is open to criticism. It is important to address this point to assist future reform. Even if it is tackled, however, the government's reform agenda is unlikely to go unchallenged. New Labour's efforts will probably, at best, yield modest results.

11

Three Faces of New Labour: Principle, Pragmatism and Populism in New Labour's Home Office

NICK RANDALL

Introduction

If we are to employ both New and 'old' Labour as conceptual categories we need to admit that they represent complex and multi-faceted groupings of ideas, policies and strategies. Indeed, this chapter will argue, New Labour in the Home Office has implemented an eclectic, often seemingly contradictory mix of policies since 1997. Nevertheless, a closer examination of New Labour's criminal justice, civil liberties, asylum and immigration policies suggests that together they embody a governing strategy which deliberately presents three distinct faces of the New Labour project.

The first face of New Labour's policies in the Home Office is one that appeals consciously to principle, albeit in forms determined by New Labour's selective nostalgia. Accordingly, several policies have sought to appeal to the Party's liberal conscience, particularly its self-appointed guardians among the Party's remaining 'old' Labour membership. Similarly, certain immigration and race relations policies can be regarded as embodying the Party's supposedly instinctual commitment to racial equality. Yet elsewhere in the prospectus of measures introduced since 1997 we also discover distinctively New Labour principles and policies, not least in the Party's communitarianism, which has seen equal stress placed on both 'order' and 'law'.

However, such embodiments of both 'old' and New Labour principles have been accompanied simultaneously by policies of a pragmatic inspiration.

177

Accordingly, we shall see that New Labour's general pragmatic desire to modernise government and improve its efficiency has been incorporated into the Home Office's policies. Moreover, political events since 1997 have also led to pragmatic revisions of policy triggered by crisis management.

The third face of New Labour's policies in the Home Office presents a populist countenance. That this is a general characteristic of New Labour can be seen from the claim of the Party's 1997 manifesto, where it states that 'New Labour is the political arm of none other than the British people as a whole' (Labour Party, 1997). In the Home Office, such populism has been manifested in a series of measures designed to respond to, and tap into, presumed electoral prejudices on matters of crime, immigration and asylum-seeking.

The extent to which these three dimensions of New Labour carry over into other policy areas cannot be explored here. However, for several reasons, the particular character and broader political context of the Home Office's responsibilities expose these three faces of New Labour into particularly sharp relief.

First, the institutional responsibilities of the Home Office generate a political division which in part accounts for the fractured nature of New Labour's policies. As H. Young has observed, the Home Office 'is responsible for the police, immigration control and prisons – all three of them activities in which the State, any State, is obliged to exhibit its hard heart and stony face' (Young, 1983, 87). Yet, by the same token, 'the Home Office is the department of government whose work most centrally addresses individual rights and civil liberties' (Young, 1983, 94), responsibilities which are pressed by reform groups which 'beat on the ministerial door in a ... public, confrontational way' (Downes and Morgan, 1997, 114). Such groups welcomed the 2003 reforms that promised a supreme court and hinted at a future ministry of justice.

That New Labour exhibits a pragmatic face can be attributed in part to the further characteristic of the Home Office that, in the words of Herbert Morrison, its 'corridors are paved with dynamite' (quoted in Callaghan, 1983, 12). As James Callaghan, another Labour incumbent of the office of Home Secretary, has attested, the responsibilities of the Home Office are apt to generate 'continuous crisis management', diverting its ministers from 'the long term to deal with what ... [is] urgent in the short term' (Callaghan, 1983, 15).

The origins of the populist tendencies of New Labour's policies in the Home Office can be located in the broader political context. As Downes and Morgan (1997) have noted, until the 1970s crime lacked political salience as an issue. Thereafter, however, New Right attacks on the law-and-order record and underpinning criminology of post-war governments saw crime emerge as an electoral issue. This development, reinforced by the pre-existing disposition of the media to generate 'moral panics' around the issues of crime and race, displaced the liberal progressive consensus and its associated rehabilitative policies. Yet where both Roy Hattersley and Gerald Kaufman, as Labour Shadow Home Secretaries, positioned Labour within the perimeters of the progressive paradigm, Tony Blair's and then Jack Straw's determination to wrest control of these issues from the Conservatives triggered a 'Dutch auction' between the parties, with each seeking to outbid the other in the 'toughness' of their policies.

However, these imperatives, and New Labour's willingness to accommodate them, have not been applied consistently throughout all the policies for which the Home Office is responsible. Accordingly, this chapter will chart their impact in the three main areas of the Home Office's responsibilities: civil liberties, immigration and asylum, and crime and criminal justice. The latter will be the point of departure for our analysis.

Crime, Criminal Justice and Community

In virtually no other aspect of policy is the distinction between New and 'old' Labour posited as sharply as it has been with regard to crime. The post-1992 revision of the Party's criminal justice policies was predicated upon a vision of the Party's past approach as one focused exclusively on environmental causes and rehabilitative solutions to crime. In contrast, New Labour promised to 'insist on individual responsibility for crime' (Labour Party, 1997, 22) thereby ending the Party's endorsement of an 'excuse culture' with regard to criminality. However, the records of the Attlee and Wilson Governments suggest that this fundamental premise is something of a caricature.

Given the political context of the period noted above, law and order was not a major element of the Attlee Government's programme. Nevertheless, two principal themes have been identified: that social order demanded the reconstruction of British society, particularly measures to check poverty and 'the defence and extension of the upright morality of the nuclear family, dominated by the respectable working man' (Taylor, 1983, 44) through state support for the nuclear family, and economic policies providing personal and social security.

However, the legislative implementation of these themes proved to be somewhat contradictory in the Attlee Government's 1948 Criminal Justice Act. A progressive dimension was evident: hard labour was abolished, the courts were prohibited from ordering corporal punishment, and remand centres were introduced. Yet the 1948 Act was simultaneously a 'penological dinosaur' (Morris, 1989, 77) in so far as it sought to combat recidivism via preventative detention, corrective training for young offenders, and the creation of detention centres designed to administer a 'short, sharp shock'.

The criminal justice policies of the 1964–70 Wilson Government was shaped fundamentally by the report of the Party's Longford Committee, established in 1963 (Labour Party, 1964). It continued to identify the roots of crime in poverty and family breakdown. The poor were held to be more vulnerable to crime, since 'the strain of their living conditions must tend to weaken their resistance to such temptations … On the whole, however, criminals do not come from stable and closely knit working class families, however poor their circumstances' (Labour Party, 1964, 5). Accordingly, the preferred solution was 'social measures designed to remove or reduce the factors which predispose people to crime' (Labour Party, 1964, 5). However, in contrast to the Criminal Justice Act 1948 the report held that the 'object of our penal system … cannot be merely to punish, teach the criminal a lesson, make him expiate his offence – and set him "free" again to prey on society' (Labour Party, 1964, 6). Rather, the aspiration was the 'transformation of prisons into institutions for social learning' (Labour Party, 1964, 2). Indeed, such progressive ambitions underpinned the Criminal Justice Act 1967, which introduced the parole system and suspended sentences, extended the use of fines in place of custodial sentences, and provided easier conditions for bail. Moreover, the 1969 Children and Young Persons Act has been recognised retrospectively as the apotheosis of progressive criminology, with its removal of all children under the age of fourteen from the jurisdiction of the courts.

As these examples demonstrate, 'old' Labour's criminal justice policies were somewhat more diverse than New Labour admits. Nevertheless, there are clear echoes of these past criminal justice policies in New Labour's own prospectus. Thus, despite New Labour's insistence on individual responsibility for crime, the guiding axiom of 'tough on crime, tough on the causes of crime' retains within it a characteristically 'old' Labour emphasis on the importance of environmental determinants of crime. The broader contours of New Labour's social policies are considered elsewhere in this volume. However, New Labour's commitment to tackle such environmental causes of crime is evident, for example, in the £2 billion New Deal for Communities, which recognises explicitly that in deprived areas, issues of unemployment, housing and the physical environment all interlink, and interact with patterns of criminality.

New Labour's criminal justice policies also contain an emphasis on preventing re-offending and rehabilitation that would be familiar to 'old' Labour home secretaries. Indeed, the prime minister himself has declared that New Labour seeks 'a Criminal Justice System that punishes the criminal but also offers those convicted of crime a chance to rehabilitate and get their way out of the life of crime' (Blair, 2001a). For example, the 1998 Crime and Disorder Act establishes that the 'principal aim of the youth justice system is to prevent offending by children and young persons', an objective realised by empowering the courts to issue parenting orders, providing practical counselling and guidance sessions for the parents of young offenders. Furthermore, this legislation also introduced Drug Treatment and Testing Orders for drug-dependent offenders, in an effort to reduce drug-related crime. Similar rehabilitative aspirations are also evident in the provisions of the 1999 Youth Justice and Criminal Evidence Act, to refer first-time young offenders to youth offender panels charged with drawing up a programme of action with these offenders that is designed to prevent re-offending. Moreover, the unified National Probation Service for England and Wales established by the 2000 Criminal Justice and Court Services Act has been charged specifically with preventing re-offending, and has seen its funding increased from £426.5 million in 1997–8 to a scheduled £713 million by 2003–04. Finally, New Labour has extended significantly literacy and numeracy programmes for prison inmates, and invested an additional £20 million in prison education, which has provided for an increase in the average number of hours of education and skills training in prisons from just over four hours to over six and half a week.

However, while such policies resonate with those of past Labour Governments, the communitarianism at the heart of New Labour's 'third way' appears to have provided for a more distinctive trajectory to policy, one that has been as attentive to social disorder as it has been with regard to crime. Indeed, New Labour has defined the social causes of crime not just in terms of material socio-economic deprivation but has also extended its ambit to include a perceived decline in family and community cohesion.

This has led New Labour to the conviction 'that crime runs in certain families and that antisocial behaviour in childhood is a predictor of later criminality' (Muncie, 2002, 146). Accordingly, inept and irresponsible parenting has been identified as an important determinant of crime, and this has led to initiatives to educate parents, such as those noted above. However, New Labour's determination to tackle irresponsible parents has seen more punitive interventions: the government has increased the fines that courts can impose on the parents of truants from £1,000 to £2,500, and is reviewing the withdrawal of social security benefits from the parents of young offenders and truants.

New Labour has also isolated anti-social behaviour as a precursor to later criminality, and has sought to punish such moral and social transgressions as a means of crime prevention. Although David Blunkett subsequently distanced himself from the approach (Burrell, 2002), during New Labour's first term this saw the Conservative Government's 1996 experiments in zero tolerance policing of low-level disorder, such as graffiti and vandalism, extended. In addition, the Crime and Disorder Act 1998 empowered the police and local authorities to apply for anti-social behaviour orders which, if breached, carry a maximum five-year custodial sentence or a £5,000 fine. And this legislation also introduced powers for local authorities to declare dawn-to-dusk curfews for all children under the age of 10, powers subsequently extended under the Criminal Justice and Police Act 2001 to include children up to the age of 15. However, such provisions have so far been underused: just 654 anti-social behaviour orders had been imposed by November 2002, far short of the 5,000 a year initially anticipated (Burney, 2002), while no applications had been received to impose child curfew orders by the end of 2001.

Underused or not, such innovations embody a conservative and conformist communitarianism. Yet, while their configuration may be novel, their underlying rationale is not entirely alien to the Labour Party. At the heart of these policies lies a distinction between the respectable working classes, who deserve the state's support, and an irresponsible, undisciplined 'underclass'. In many respects this is not far removed from the Attlee Government's defence of the 'morality of the nuclear family, dominated by the respectable working man' (Taylor, 1984, 44).

However, one aspect of New Labour's criminal justice policies that is more emphatically novel is its introduction of restorative justice into the criminal justice system for young offenders. Restorative justice aims to bring together offenders and their victims to encourage offenders to accept responsibility for their actions, make amends to their victim(s) and reintegrate themselves into the community. The 1998 Crime and Disorder Act introduced 'reparation orders' to make young offenders confront their crimes and their consequences by requiring such acts as apologising to their victims or repairing criminal damaged property. Similarly, the referral orders for young offenders introduced in the 1999 Youth Justice and Criminal Justice Act require similar acts of restitution, but also allow for victims to participate in determining an appropriate form of reparation by the offender.

However, this mix of both old and new principles has been overlaid with a consciously pragmatic managerialism. In tune with its broader aspiration to engineer 'joined-up government', much of New Labour's criminal justice legislation has been premised on recognising that the causes of crime are multi-dimensional, and that adequate responses must bring multiple agencies together. Such aspirations were particularly evident in the 1998 Crime and Disorder Act, which obliged local authorities, police and voluntary sector organisations to work in partnership, not least in conducting local crime audits and creating local teams to deal with young offenders. Similar motivations can also be held to underlie the provisions of the 2001 Criminal Justice and Police Act to improve disclosure of information between government departments and public bodies in criminal investigations.

Such efforts are also representative of a further pragmatic edge to New Labour's criminal justice policies. Not only has New Labour brought multiple agencies together, but the design of policy has been shaped consciously by a philosophy of seeking 'what works' in preventing crime and recidivism. This desire for 'evidence-based' policy-making has seen a fresh appetite for assimilating criminological research into policy. For example, Labour's measures to foster multi-agency approaches and fast-track punishment of young offenders have their origins in the Audit Commission's 1996 report entitled *Misspent Youth*, and the Home Office's 1991 report called *Safer Communities: The Local Delivery of Crime Prevention through the Partnership Approach* (Muncie, 1999; Pitts, 2001), while the restorative aspects of Labour's policies towards young offenders have been identified as being influenced by NACRO's 1997 report *A New Three Rs for Young Offenders* (James and Raine, 1998, 95)

Yet such aspirations to manufacture 'joined-up', empirically based and effective policy has been accompanied by pragmatism triggered by crisis management. Nowhere has this been more evident than in relation to Britain's prisons. In May 1997, the prison population in England and Wales stood at 60,300. By June 2002, this figure had risen to 71,220, with the Howard League for Penal Reform calculating that 64 per cent of prisons were now overcrowded. One response has been to increase prison capacity, but as James Callaghan has noted, the 'inability to build new prisons has been a continual headache for every Home Secretary' (Callaghan, 1983, 16). For New Labour, circumventing such limitations has required an abandoning of the hostility the party expressed during opposition towards private prisons. Accordingly, four new privately-managed prisons have opened since 1997, with a further two being planned. However, in addition, the Labour Government has extended the use of electronic tagging and the early release of prisoners. The Crime and Disorder Act 1998 introduced an early release programme of 'home detention curfews' for certain categories of prisoner with two months (extended to three months in February 2002) of their sentences left to serve. By October 2002, 56,000 prisoners had been released early under this scheme. Yet the impact of such measures has been counter-balanced by the increasing willingness of the courts to issue custodial sentences. This has necessitated more radical measures. Accordingly, the 2002 White Paper proposes a host of new forms of incarceration, including 'Custody-Plus' sentences of three months in prison followed by supervision in the community; 'Custody-Minus' sentences, in which a custodial sentence is suspended while the offender undertakes community supervision; and sentences of 'Intermittent Custody', in which custodial sentences are served during weekends or during the week, with the remainder of the sentence discharged in the community.

Such pragmatism has also encroached into drugs policy in Labour's second term. As is perhaps to be expected from someone who reportedly demanded a crackdown on cannabis users while himself a student at Leeds University, Jack Straw was deaf to arguments supporting the relaxation of Britain's drug laws, and rejected the Police Federation's calls for the reclassification of cannabis in 2000. However, the subsequent praise for the Police Federation's report from *The Times*, *The Daily Telegraph* and the *Daily Mail* provided a window of political opportunity. Accordingly, David Blunkett took advantage of the opportunity provided by the Home Affairs Select Committee's May 2002 report on Britain's drug laws to reclassify cannabis as a 'Class C' drug to enable the diversion of police resources to more serious drug offences.

However, such developments have to be viewed not only in the context of an authoritarian and conservative communitarianism, but also of a 'populist punitiveness' (Bottoms, 1995) which has sought to tap into the public's perceived desire for punitive criminal justice policies. As such, New Labour's period in the Home Office has been marked by a host of headline-grabbing initiatives embodying a populist zeal for punishment. Thus, notwithstanding the introduction of rehabilitative and restorative policies, young offenders have discovered that New Labour is considerably less tolerant of repeat offences. Juvenile cautions have now been replaced with 'reprimands' and a 'final warning', with the consequence that opportunities for education and rehabilitation are forfeited much earlier.

More generally, this 'punitive populism' has manifested itself in a proliferation of tougher sentences for adults, not least in the introduction of 'three strikes' mandatory sentences for certain offences. Accordingly, burglars now face mandatory three-year sentences, and drug offenders seven-year sentences if convicted of third offences, while an automatic life sentence now accompanies a second serious sexual or violent crime. Encouraged by the signals sent by such sentencing policies, by the accusations of lenient sentencing issued by the previous Conservative Administration and Labour's subsequent refusal to repudiate them openly, the courts have resorted increasingly to custodial sentences. Consequently, the percentage of offenders who received cautions from the courts declined from 37.3 per cent of offenders in 1997 to 31.8 per cent in 2000, while those receiving custodial sentences rose from 22.6 per cent to 24.9 per cent over the same period.

Nor has this populist reflex been limited to serious offences. To widespread derision, Tony Blair proposed in June 2000 that 'a thug might think twice about kicking your gate, throwing traffic cones around your street, or hurling abuse into the night sky if he thought he might get picked up by the police, taken to a cash-point and asked to pay an on-the-spot fine of, for example, £100' (Blair, 2000a). However, after the furore accompanying these comments evaporated, the Criminal Justice and Police Act 2001 introduced a series of fixed penalty notices of £80 for offences including wasting police time or making hoax emergency calls, while £40 fines accompany being drunk and disorderly, throwing fireworks and trespassing on railways.

Nevertheless, there have been clear limitations on New Labour's populist flirtations. The populist ties between Labour and the Conservatives were starkly severed in April 2000 over the case of Tony Martin, a Norfolk farmer who shot a 16-year-old burglar in his home, with Jack Straw intransigent in response to Conservative calls for the abolition of the mandatory life sentence in such murder cases. Furthermore, although the government pledged to improve dissemination of information about the release of paedophiles in the wake of the abduction of Sarah Payne in July 2000, and the subsequent 'naming and shaming' of convicted paedophiles by the *News of the World*, it nevertheless refused to countenance controlled public access to the Sex Offenders Register in view of the dangers of vigilantism and of driving sex offenders underground.

Civil Liberties

Amid such developments, New Labour's record on civil liberties in its first five years in power has attracted considerable attention. One development of enormous significance has been the Human Rights Act of 1998, which incorporated the European Convention on Human Rights into UK law.

However, New Labour's period in the Home Office has seen other, albeit more specific extensions of civil liberties. This is evident, for example, in New Labour's general promotion of the rights of homosexuals, which echoes Roy Jenkins' assistance in the decriminalisation of homosexuality in 1967. Although New Labour failed to carry out its first-term promise to repeal Section 28, which prevents the promotion of homosexuality in schools, it has pledged to make parliamentary time available for amendment to deliver this commitment in early 2003. At the third attempt, and after invoking the Parliament Act against a recalcitrant House of Lords, the government succeeded in equalising the heterosexual and homosexual ages of consent in February 2000. Moreover, immigration rules have been changed to grant homosexual partners the same rights as heterosexual couples, while the pledge in the 2002 Queen's Speech to implement the recommendations of the Home Office's 2000 review of sexual offences will further extend equality in the laws between heterosexual and homosexual sex.

Yet such developments have to be seen within the broader context of New Labour's reforms to criminal justice. Accordingly, New Labour's pragmatic managerialism and desire for efficiency in the criminal justice system has convinced many that due process and justice have been significantly eroded during New Labour's term in office. In particular, New Labour has become convinced that the existing provisions for jury trials allow defendants to delay criminal proceedings unduly and create unwarranted additional costs in the criminal justice system. Undaunted by being twice thwarted by the House of Lords in its attempts to restrict the right to jury trial, a third attempt was included the 2002 Queen's Speech, in tandem with proposals to abolish the 'double jeopardy' rule and disclose previous convictions during court proceedings. However, lest such initiatives are identified as the exclusive property of New Labour, it should not be forgotten that Roy Jenkins also tampered with the sanctity of the jury trial by introducing majority verdicts in 1967.

New Labour's communitarian aspirations to restore individual responsibility for crime and reorientate the criminal justice system in favour of the victims of crime has also been held responsible for the erosion of civil liberties. Of particular note is New Labour's abolition of *doli incapax* – the legal presumption that 10–13-year-olds are incapable of distinguishing between right and wrong, leaving England and Wales with one of the lowest ages of criminal responsibility in Europe (albeit still higher than the age of 8, which applies in Scottish law). In addition, New Labour's anti-social behaviour orders have attracted the ire of civil liberties campaigners, not least because the general definition of 'anti-social' has made these orders available for potential misuse against harmless but otherwise marginalised and unpopular individuals and groups. Furthermore, curfew orders, although unused, have none the less been rebuked for their blanket coverage and subsequent potential to restrict severely the liberty of young people innocent of social disorder.

New Labour's 2000 Regulation of Investigatory Powers Act has also been damned variously for substantially eroding the right to privacy; for extending the powers of law enforcement and security agencies without compensating measures for authorisation and oversight; and as unworkable. Among its provisions are powers for the security services to monitor the internet habits of individuals on their own authority and, after personal approval by the home secretary, intercept and decode data where they suspect criminal activity. In particular, critics have argued that provisions to compel individuals to surrender data encryption keys under threat of a two-year jail sentence reverse the burden of proof in British law. Yet here there has been some evidence of belated pragmatism, with Blunkett withdrawing proposals in June 2002 to extend the powers to access information under the Act to a miscellany of government departments, local councils and quangos.

The opening of a domestic front in the 'war on terrorism' has triggered further alarm, much as did 'old' Labour's notorious 1974 Prevention of Terrorism Act. The 2000 Terrorism Act had already provoked disquiet among civil liberties campaigners, not least for its introduction of wider powers to proscribe organisations, and a new and broader definition of terrorism which, given its inclusion of damage to property, led to concerns that forms of direct action such as that undertaken by environmental protestors could be identified as terrorist acts.

However, in the aftermath of 11 September 2001 the already formidable powers of the 2000 Act were considerably extended in the 2001 Anti-Terrorism, Crime and Security Act. Most notably, the Act empowered the home secretary to derogate from Article 5(1) of the European Convention on Human Rights to detain indefinitely foreign nationals suspected of terrorism whom otherwise could not be prosecuted or deported. At the time of writing, nine men were approaching the twelve-month anniversary of their internment under these provisions.

Race Equality, Immigration, 'Britishness' and Asylum

In addition to its responsibilities for public order and individual liberties, the Home Office also has responsibility for issues of immigration and asylum. In these areas too, the relationship between 'old' and New Labour is complex. The Attlee Government introduced the 1948 British Nationality Act, which guaranteed all Commonwealth citizens the right to enter and settle in the UK. Yet it gave no consideration to racial equality, since 'racism was viewed as the proper concern of those involved in colonial affairs; it was something external, not germane, to the mainstream of the labour movement' (Joshi and Carter, 1984, 55). Subsequent Labour Governments however, were guided by a philosophy summarised by Roy Hattersley as 'Integration without control is impossible, but control without integration is indefensible' (*Hansard*, 23 March 1965, cols 378–85). Accordingly, the 1964–70 Wilson Government abandoned Labour's opposition to the 1962 Commonwealth Immigrants Act and introduced further restrictions in the 1968 Commonwealth Immigration Act. Yet the same administration was responsible for introducing the 1965 and 1968 Race Relations Acts, while Labour's return to office in the 1970s saw these provisions extended further in the 1976 Race Relations Act.

Since taking office, New Labour has introduced a number of principled and progressive policies that have extended integration and even reversed the tide of control. For example, New Labour is responsible for the introduction of an annual Holocaust Memorial Day while its 1998 Crime and Disorder Act introduced a host of new racially aggravated offences. In addition, despite Jack Straw's obduracy in 1995 that there should not be 'as much as a cigarette card ... between the Labour Party and the Tory government on immigration' (quoted in Saggar, 2001, 761), there have been some minor but progressive changes to immigration procedures. Accordingly, the 'primary purpose rule', which required those joining a spouse in Britain to demonstrate that the marriage did not have as its primary motive a desire to live in the UK, was abolished.

Furthermore, the Immigration and Asylum Act 2002 permitted 35,000 British overseas citizens the right to take full British citizenship, thus 'righting a historical wrong' (Home Office, 2002a) created by the 1968 Commonwealth Immigrants Act. Moreover, New Labour has discreetly encouraged economic migration into the UK. In 2002 it introduced a programme designed to attract highly skilled migrants to the UK and has increased the number of work permits issued during its period in office significantly from 62,795 in 1997 to 108,825 in 2001 (Home Office, 2002b, 21).

However, such initiatives have not attracted widespread public attention. In contrast, Jack Straw's decision, three months after the 1997 election, to appoint Sir William Macpherson to head an inquiry into the police's handling of the murder of Stephen Lawrence in April 1993 placed both New Labour's and broader societal attitudes to racial equality under intense scrutiny.

When the Macpherson inquiry reported in February 1999 it offered an excoriating critique of professional incompetence, institutional racism and failures of leadership. Labour's response was to extend the legislation concerning racial discrimination for the first time in a quarter of a century. Although it took the threat of rebellion in the Lords to include measures prohibiting indirect indiscrimination, the Race Relations (Amendment) Act 2000 nevertheless extended the coverage of Race Relations Act 1976 to the police and public authorities in general, a measure which, as S. Saggar notes, represented 'a major legislative achievement that the party would have habitually vetoed from consideration whilst in opposition' (Saggar, 2001, 772).

Despite parading 'Fitz' the bulldog during its 1997 election campaign, New Labour also entered office with a broad aspiration to redefine the British national identity. Here we discover more distinctive developments. Initially, such efforts were focused on a widely derided portrayal of Britain as 'Cool Britannia', which reduced 'national identity to a corporate brand, as if Britain were a political corporation needing a new image to sell itself abroad' (Parekh, 2000, 12). However, a rash of apocalyptic analyses of the implications of devolution and the publication of the Parekh report (2000), *The Future of Multi-Ethnic Britain*, elicited more substantive definitions, not least from Tony Blair, who identified Britishness with the 'core British values of fair play, creativity, tolerance and an outward-looking approach to the world' (Blair, 2000b).

However, David Blunkett's appointment, the civil disorder in Oldham, Burnley and Bradford during the summer of 2001 and the events of 11 September 2001 saw an understanding of Britishness emerge in New Labour's second term in office which challenges the multi-culturalism of the first. Following the Cantle report, which identified 'the depth of polarisation' (Home Office, 2001, 9) between communities as one factor responsible for the 2001 riots, an increasingly communitarian concern has developed that has questioned the reach of common 'core British values'. Where Jack Straw described Labour's vision to the 1999 Labour Conference as 'one that makes no apologies for people's differences, but instead celebrates the rich diversity of multi-racial Britain' (Labour Party, 1999, 114), David Blunkett offered a critique of 'an unbridled multicultur-alism which privileges difference over community cohesion' (Blunkett, 2002, 75). This led Blunkett to call upon ethnic minority communities to speak English at home, for arranged marriages to be encouraged among partners already resident in the UK, and for the children of asylum seekers to be educated separately to prevent 'swamping' of local schools. Despite the controversy of such remarks, Blunkett did not temporise in giving them legislative substance. Accordingly, the 2002 Nationality, Asylum and Immigration Act introduced English language requirements for those seek-ing naturalisation as the spouses of British citizens, and a requirement that all applicants demonstrate 'sufficient knowledge about life in the UK'. In addition, public citizenship ceremonies will be introduced and will include a citizenship oath that requires naturalised British citizens to respect democratic values and the rights and freedoms of the United Kingdom.

New Labour's approach to asylum has also occasionally seen progressive and principled initiatives. For example, from January 2002, asylum seekers have no longer been detained in prisons, and from April 2003 the govern-ment will accept refugees nominated by the United Nations High Commission for Refugees. Nor has New Labour's approach been without pragmatic dimensions. For example, its voucher system of asylum support, introduced in the 1999 Asylum and Immigration Act and widely perceived to stigmatise and impose additional hardships on asylum seekers, has now been abolished. Moreover, New Labour has portrayed much of its asylum policy in terms of a managerialist concern to introduce efficiency into the

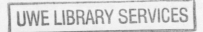

asylum system, not least given the large backlog of asylum applications that awaited New Labour on its entry into office in 1997.

However, the pressures generated by the Conservative opposition, the portrayal of asylum seekers as 'folk devils' in the tabloid press, led by the *Daily Mail* (see Statham, 2002), and, latterly, the electoral successes of the British National Party in Labour heartlands have generated a dynamic which has seen principle and pragmatism outstripped by a succession of populist initiatives designed to appease such pressures by further deterring asylum applications.

Accordingly, the 1999 Immigration and Asylum Act extended the restrictions introduced in the Conservative Government's 1993 Asylum and Immigration Appeals Act. Opportunities to appeal against asylum decisions were reduced, and the right of clandestine asylum seekers to appeal was totally removed. In addition, the entitlement of all persons subject to immigration control, asylum seekers included, to non-contributory social security benefits was withdrawn and a policy of dispersal of asylum seekers from the main ports of entry was initiated.

However, the 2002 Nationality, Immigration and Asylum Act, the fourth major overhaul of the asylum system in a decade, further embellished and refined this system of controls. Among its provisions were the further segregation of asylum seekers from the indigenous population through the creation of self-contained accommodation centres and the separate education of refugee children. In addition, the asylum application process was further 'fast-tracked'. Procedures for those denied asylum were further simplified, and the right of in-country appeal removed for refugees originating from a 'white list' of 'safe' countries. Finally, the Act also introduced a system of financial incentives for the resettlement of asylum seekers outside the UK under a 'Voluntary Assisted Returns Programme'.

Nevertheless, such initiatives have not prevented New Labour from associating itself repeatedly with Britain's ostensibly exemplary record of providing refuge to the persecuted. However, it is none the less reasonable to conclude that its policies since 1997 ultimately have little resemblance to Labour's previous approach to asylum as embodied in the Attlee Government's European Voluntary Workers programme, the 1974–9 government's resettlement of Chilean refugees, and its disavowal of the 1993 Asylum and Immigration Appeals Act.

Conclusion

All but the most cursory of analyses of New Labour's tenure in the Home Office must quickly frustrate those who seek a single, coherent and unifying principle that underpins its initiatives in relation to criminal justice, civil liberties, immigration and asylum seekers. In this respect, Muncie's assessment of the 1998 Crime and Disorder Act may usefully be extended to many of the measures introduced since 1997. As such, New Labour has been responsible for an 'amalgam of "get tough" authoritarian measures with elements of paternalism, pragmatism, communitarianism, responsibilisation and remoralisation. And all of this is worked within and through a burgeoning new managerialism' (Muncie, 1999, 169).

Moreover, the further we retreat from caricatures of 'old' Labour the more difficult it becomes to offer an easy and definitive adjudication as to whether these policies demonstrate the novelty of New Labour in office. Restorative justice is perhaps the most novel of New Labour's measures but has thus far proven tangential among its broader criminal justice policies. New Labour's stringency in regard to asylum controls is also novel amongst the record of Labour Governments. However, any comparison must recognise the distinctive character and context of contemporary asylum politics, not least the mounting electoral salience of the issue. The communitarian analysis and policies of New Labour are also distinctive, but principally by virtue of explicit and overt presentation rather than because such ideas and policies were unknown to previous Labour Governments. Elsewhere, as we have seen, the distinction between New and 'old' Labour which underpins sound-bites like 'tough on crime, tough on the causes of crime' is less than clear-cut.

As such, any claims that New Labour's second-term policies embody the emergence of a distinctive modernised social democracy must be heavily qualified. However, such qualifications should not obscure nascent and subtle but none the less significant shifts in Home Office policy since 2001. Pragmatism, for example, has led to the abandonment of vouchers for asylum seekers. The events of 11 September 2001 in New York and the civil disturbances of the summer of 2001 in Britain have also triggered new developments. Furthermore, David Blunkett has brought to the Home Office a more overt and muscular communitarianism than that of his predecessor, one that may yet have far reaching consequences for multi-culturalism.

Yet in the second term, the nature of the responsibilities of the Home Office, the demands of New Labour's political and electoral bloc, the character of the broader political environment, and the inherited commitments amassed during the metamorphosis from 'old' to New Labour have continued to mean that New Labour has to present three different faces to its policies.

Thus New Labour's propensity to simultaneously deny and affirm its own historical antecedents has seen the presentation of a countenance of principle, whether in characteristically 'old' Labour terms of recognising the social-environmental determinants of crime, ambitions to rehabilitate criminals and promote racial equality, or in New Labour's vocabulary of communitarianism. Similarly, New Labour continues to present a pragmatic face ingrained with a desire to improve efficiency and modernise, but also simultaneously weathered by the demands of crisis management and policy learning.

However, throughout both terms, these faces of New Labour have typically only been glimpsed in profile and have been reserved for audiences with the Party faithful or practioners. Jack Straw's eruptions against 'Hampstead liberals' and 'BMW-driving civil liberties lawyers from the suburbs' and David Blunkett's condemnation of 'bleeding heart liberals' embody something more than rhetoric. Rather, they represent the populism which is the public and most prominent face of New Labour's policies in the Home Office.

12

Foreign and European Policy

JIM BULLER

Introduction

How should the Blair Government's record on foreign policy be assessed?
Potentially, a number of criteria would appear to be appropriate for the task.
One might judge Labour's performance in office against the policy pledges
in its manifesto. Alternatively, we could evaluate its achievements by charting its ability to realise a broader ideological programme or set of values. In
this context, we might want to gauge Labour's success in terms of its ability
to forge a third way or a moderate social democratic programme in foreign
affairs (see, for example, Spear, 2000; Vickers, 2000; Deighton, 2001).
However, to argue that ministers should *only be judged* on their ability to
translate general ideas or values into practice runs the risk of 'abstracting'
Labour's performance from the everyday constraints and challenges in
office (Taylor, 2001). Among other things, ministers are professional politicians concerned with re-election. They may sometimes use foreign and
defence policy to score political points, a tactic employed to great effect by
the Conservative Government in the 1980s. Alternatively, political leaders
may try to de-politicise external issues they know are divisive within the
party. One might add that international environments can sometimes produce unpredictable shocks which have to be managed so that they do not
have an adverse effect on the domestic political scene. Occasionally (and
more ambitiously) policy-makers will attempt to reform external structures
so that they complement national institutions and confer an added legitimacy to a domestic programme (Bulpitt, 1988). Whatever the tactic, the
point here is that parties in office may have a relatively clear conception of
their own political interests, which they can pursue counter to any notions

of ideological or policy coherence. Any assessment of the actions of a party in office should also take this factor into account.

It follows that an appraisal of the Blair Government's performance must avoid separating the actions of ministers from the structural context surrounding them. Lucky politicians will sometimes be blessed with a benign structural inheritance, but on other occasions, they may have little choice but to 'muddle through' in difficult circumstances. In other words, any given structural context may provide opportunities as well as constraints (with the balance between these changing over time). To complicate matters further, the properties of these structures will often be mediated by perception and interpretation: what counts as a constraint or an opportunity will be defined partly by the actor's own world view. Indeed, the way that structures and their (supposed) effects are understood and discursively constructed may be as important as their 'material reality'. A brief account of the structural context facing British foreign-policy-makers is therefore necessary before we assess the performance of the Blair Government.

External Structural Context

Since 1945, Britain has been a status quo power that (more often than not) has benefited from the bipolar structure of international relations that developed after the Second World War. Put more accurately, the Cold War helped Whitehall to disguise the reality of Britain's economic and political decline, a tactic that was often thought to contribute to domestic political tranquillity. To this end, ministers cultivated a 'special' relationship with the USA which provided them with status and prestige (not to mention nuclear capability) unrivalled in Western Europe at the time. In return, Britain stood alongside America in the fight against Communism, using this privileged position to offer wise counsel during moments of superpower tension (Louis and Bull, 1986). As the 1960s and 1970s proceeded, it was remarked increasingly that the 'special' nature of this relationship was waning, a sentiment that the Thatcher–Reagan axis could halt only temporarily in the 1980s. At the same time, this alliance came at a price. Britain was required to maintain a military presence east of Suez, which diverted valuable resources from economic modernisation at home (see for example Kaldor *et al.*, 1979). Moreover, this American connection distracted London from the nascent 'Common Market' in Europe and the potential trade opportunities this developing organisation provided (Denman, 1997). Nevertheless (with the possible exception of Heath), the utility of the special relationship was never questioned seriously by the Establishment.

In contrast, after 1990, Whitehall was faced with an international environment that was more fluid and uncertain than at any time during the post-war period. One manifestation of this changing situation was the decline of bipolarity, evinced by the collapse of Communism and the dissolution of the Soviet Union. The simultaneous reunification of Germany, re-emergence of Russia, and the development of a new set of regional problems in southern and eastern Europe, gave the international system a nineteenth-century feel. One problem with this historical parallel was the undisputed economic and military supremacy of the USA. Unfortunately, while it was hoped that this American hegemony would be a source of stability in the world, Washington's rather inconsistent approach to international relations only added to the uncertainty facing policy-makers in London. Initially, the multilateralism of the Bush Sr presidency and the early Clinton Administration posed no serious problems for British diplomacy. However, the failure of American-led peacekeeping missions in Somalia and Rwanda led to a new mood of isolationism in the USA (Hames, 1999; Schwenninger, 1999). Early promotion of the 'son of Star Wars' (Nuclear Missile Defence) programme by the Bush Jr Administration merely confirmed the fears of many across the Atlantic that the USA intended to disengage from its commitment to European defence (Krepon, 2001; Newhouse, 2001).

Events in Europe have contributed to the fluid nature of the external context facing British foreign-policy-makers. Initially, the ending of the Cold War and the reunification of Germany appeared to accentuate the pressure for European integration. Member states responded with institutional reforms aimed a 'tying down' the 'German Gulliver', most notably through the creation of a single currency. However, the dissolution of the Soviet Union set off counter-forces whose precise effect on the European Union (EU) remain difficult to gauge. Worried about the security threat of an emerging Russia, many former Communist countries applied for EU (and NATO – North Atlantic Treaty Organization) membership (Friis and Murphy, 1999). This enlargement process has compelled the EU to re-evaluate its decision-making structures to accommodate these additional members. While the outcome of these discussions remains uncertain, the shifting contours of Europe's institutions may provide new opportunities as well as constraints for British statecraft.

Finally, overlaying this fluid and uncertain geo-political environment were broader processes of 'globalisation', which were said to be challenging continually the capacity of nation states to implement a variety of policy goals. Commentators have highlighted how national strategies of economic management have been undermined by global flows of trade, production and finance. These economic trends have, in turn, had an impact on the social and political sphere, presenting decision-makers everywhere with new problems. The growth of multi-national companies has resulted in environmental degradation, while information technology has facilitated the development of global networks of terrorists and drug traffickers (Held *et al.*, 1999; Held and McGrew, 2000). It should be noted that the 'material reality' of globalisation is a matter of fierce debate among politicians and academics alike (see, for example, Hirst and Thompson, 1996; Pierson, 2001). Some critics doubt the novelty of these developments. For example, Labour Governments in the twentieth century often had to contend with currency speculation. Others have pointed out that, although globalisation may be 'hollowing out' the state, policy-makers have sometimes encouraged this process. Asserting the strength of these global forces (irrespective of their novelty) can be a handy method for political elites to discipline societal expectations and 'lock in' neo-liberal policies at home (Hay and Watson, 1999).

New Labour Foreign Policy?

How has the Blair Government responded to this external environment? Has it developed a distinctive New Labour approach to foreign policy? One initial problem is that discussion of the New Labour is concerned primarily with domestic issues. Of course, it could be argued that one of the main characteristics of a New Labour foreign policy might simply be the export of these domestic reforms abroad. Indeed, as we shall see, this has been one objective of Labour's statecraft since the end of the twentieth century. That said, it is possible to detect other themes and policy prescriptions in the work of Giddens, which may further clarify the conception of a New Labour foreign policy.

As with its domestic components, a New Labour foreign policy would appear to rest on the assumption that globalisation has altered the nature of state sovereignty radically. Consequently, any moderate social democratic diplomacy in the twenty-first century should work with the grain of this structural context, while trying simultaneously to develop policies designed to ameliorate the adverse consequences of interdependence. A problem of particular concern to Giddens is that global forces have undermined the legitimacy of the governing classes in many countries. Nation states need to respond by recasting their authority on a participatory basis, and the future role of international institutions could be crucial in this respect. Not only would a New Labour foreign policy recognise the necessity of playing an active, co-operative role at the global level, but reform of international institutions might constitute an alternative means of empowering individuals and civil society. In short, third way teachings in this area suggest a commitment to *internationalism* as a way of addressing some of the problems traditionally resolved at the nation-state level (Giddens, 1998).

However, some writers have interpreted New Labour not so much as an ideological programme, but rather as a particular method or strategy for achieving policy goals. This style rests partly on a belief in the power of language as a way of resolving conflict and achieving consensus. Of particular interest here is the tactic of 'triangulation'. Labour leaders attempt to displace and transcend opposing viewpoints by characterising them as being on the extreme ends of a continuum, and asserting the primacy of a more moderate approach (Vickers, 2000). Slight variations on this strategy exist. At times, Labour refuses to accept that it must choose between what appear to be contradictory alternatives facing it. This strategy has been used to good effect in foreign policy, where Blair denies that Britain has to side with either Europe or the USA in its response to external events; being at the heart of Europe helps to strengthen relations with Washington and vice versa. As we shall see, this approach served Labour well in its first term. However, the credibility of this discursive ploy may survive only as long as circumstances do not arise that expose its contradictions (see also Fairclough, 2000).

Faced with an uncertain and fluid context, the first point to note about the response of the Blair Government is that it *interpreted* these structures as an *opportunity* to make a 'fresh start' in British diplomacy. This new approach borrowed significantly at times from Giddens' third way writings. Intrinsic to this new statecraft was an acceptance (even glorification) of the 'discourse' of globalisation. Britain was now a member of a new international community in which states were mutually dependent on each other and the national interest was largely determined by intergovernmental collaboration. As participants in this 'new world order', all nations were bound by certain obligations, the most important being a respect for human rights (Cook, 1997b, 1997d, 1998). From this position came Cook's early declaration that, under Labour, British foreign policy would have an ethical dimension (Cook, 1997a). However, as the first term progressed, this philosophy became bolder. Blair used an important speech in Chicago in 1999 to suggest that the principle of non-intervention in other states' affairs should be qualified in instances where that state failed to respect its international obligations, and was quick to add that such intervention should be subject to conditions. Moreover, these rules were merely there to guide, and would only be effective if realised through international institutions such as the UN (Blair, 1999; see also Freeland, 2001; Blair, 2002e; Leonard, 2002). However, the change of tone from that of previous Conservative Governments was stark: whether this would translate into a change in the substance of policy was something that remained to be seen.

New Leadership in Europe?

Adopting such an internationalist approach also had implications for
Britain's relations with the EU. Plagued by intra-party divisions, the
Conservatives had for too long squandered British influence in Europe
through a policy of negative isolationism. The Blair Government would
reassert Britain's leadership role by adopting a more co-operative stance,
helping to construct alliances with its partners and forging joint solutions to
common problems (Cook, 1997c, 1997e; Henderson, 1997; Labour Party,
1997; Symons, 1997). More particularly, ministers aimed to penetrate the
Franco-German axis (often perceived as the driving force of the EU), thus
enabling Britain to become an equal partner in a powerful new triumvirate.
However, Labour leaders emphasised that this new approach would not
mean an uncritical admiration for everything that emerged from Brussels.
Speeches repeatedly pressed for democratic changes to make the EU more
relevant and understandable to the lives of ordinary citizens (Cook, 1997f;
Blair, 1997). Once again, echoes from Giddens' work can be detected in the
articulation of this theme.

Initial optimism that a change of government would herald a new chapter
in Britain's relations with the EU seemed to be well founded. Employment
policy was soon singled out as an area in which diplomats could play a leadership role. A manifesto pledge to reverse Britain's opt-out from the Social
Chapter was expedited quickly, and more ambitiously, ministers began to
articulate a compromise between an Anglo-Saxon emphasis on labour
market flexibility and the well-trained, but often highly protected workforce
that existed in many European countries. By reducing the burden of 'red
tape' on small businesses, encouraging the growth of venture capital and
reforming the dependency culture of welfare, Britain could show the way to
the 'Holy Grail' of job creation (Brown, 1997; *Financial Times*, 5 June
1997; Blair, 1998b, 1998c). At first, these ideas proved to be attractive as a
diplomatic tool in the complex and acrimonious negotiations leading to the
Amsterdam Treaty signed in June 1997. They helped to forge a compromise
between France and Germany over the inclusion of a commitment to job
creation within the European Monetary Union (EMU)-inspired Stability
Pact (*Financial Times*, 16 June 1997; 17 June 1997). Further successes were
revealed in Blair's announcement at the Cardiff European Council (1998)
that the British presidency of the EU had negotiated guidelines aimed at
promoting the development of a skilled, trained and adaptable workforce.
Labour has maintained this pressure by signing bilateral agreements with
Spain and Italy to push for further reforms in this area (for a full list of bilateral initiatives, consult the Foreign Office website at *www.fco.gov.uk*).
These efforts seemed to bear fruit at the Lisbon Summit, at which member

states promised to transform Europe into the most competitive and dynamic economy in the world by 2010.

While there have been successes, Labour has also experienced setbacks in its attempts to influence the policy debate in this area. Ministers have opposed Commission plans to extend the Works Council Directive to small and medium-sized enterprises (SMEs) with fewer than fifty employees. Similarly, the Treasury has not been enamoured by Brussels' insistence in delaying its proposals to set up venture capital funds in the English regions (such funds have now been approved) (*Financial Times*, 6 February 2001). Worst of all, perhaps, was the new European Charter of Fundamental Rights negotiated at the Nice European Council in December 2000. Its contents covered not only political, but also economic and social rights (including the right to strike). Even though British negotiators ensured that the Charter's final standing was only declaratory, the Confederation of British Industry (CBI) remains worried that it may still become part of the Treaty of Rome and therefore represent a legal challenge to the UK's flexible labour market (*Financial Times*, 29 March 2000; 27 May 2000; 3 June 2000; 21 September 2000; 27 September 2000; see also *European Voice*, 11–17 July 2002).

New Realism in EU Foreign and Defence Policy

After a year in office, a 'new realism' had set in within the Labour leadership concerning the possibilities for influence within the EU. A review of European strategy was announced, representing a tacit admission that it would take Britain at least ten years to establish itself at the heart of this regional organisation (*Financial Times*, 1 July 1998). One of the conclusions of this assessment asserted that all departments had to work harder to construct alliances across the whole spectrum of policy areas. It also suggested that alternative opportunities to pursue a leadership role might lie in foreign and defence policy. Shortly before the Amsterdam European Council, the British delegation had resisted Franco-German plans to merge the Western European Union (WEU) with the EU. Now Labour accepted the idea of scrapping the former as a way of augmenting the latter's defence capability. The WEU's military role would be transferred to NATO, thus strengthening the European pillar of this organisation. Conversely, the WEU's political role would be folded into the EU, thereby enhancing the authority of the new position of 'high representative' which was also created at Amsterdam (*The Times*, 21 October 1998). These efforts seemed to pay off in December 1998, when Britain and France signed the St Malo agreement to develop Europe's out-of-area defence potential. Twelve months later, the Helsinki European Council (1999) agreed to set up a 60,000 'rapid reaction force' (RRF) designed to engage in future peacekeeping and humanitarian missions in which NATO (that is, the Americans) did not want to participate.

While publicly claiming the credit for imbuing Europe's foreign and defence policy with a greater coherence, attempts by Labour to play a leadership role in this area have highlighted some awkward trade-offs facing Whitehall. On the issue of defence restructuring, this positive role has been undermined by the Ministry of Defence's decision to pull out of the three-nation military satellite programme and the Horizon frigate project. Just as embarrassing was British Aerospace's decision to purchase the defence arm of General Electric at the start of 1999. This move makes the British company significantly larger than its European competitors, while at the same time complicating plans to create pan-European ventures in this area (Nicol, 1999). Moreover, the development of the RRF led Madeleine Albright, secretary of state in the Clinton Administration to complain that this new European defence structure could discriminate against NATO members outside the EU, and might ultimately lead to the fragmentation of NATO itself (see also Seltzer, 2001). One of the reasons this development has not caused more tension is because progress towards the operationalisation of the RFF remains painfully slow. In this sense, the Blair Government has been fortunate that its action has not led to more adverse, unintended consequences (Dempsey and White, 2001).

Nevertheless, enlargement pressures are currently having an impact on the institutional architecture of the EU in ways that are difficult to predict, but which may open up future possibilities for creative diplomacy. This line of argument is perhaps best demonstrated by considering events at the Nice European Council, which dealt with a number of 'leftover' issues from the negotiations surrounding the Treaty of Amsterdam. To begin with, questions concerning the size and composition of the Commission needed to be broached. The limited number of portfolios meant that, after enlargement, member states would no longer enjoy guaranteed representation in Brussels. This prospect alarmed the smaller states, which regarded their permanent position on the Commission as a counter-weight to the Franco-German axis. Second, enlargement would clearly necessitate the re-weighting of votes in the Council of Ministers. It was here that the concerns of the larger states came to the fore. Their fear of being outvoted by coalitions of smaller states prompted a proposal to take the size of a country's population into account when operating qualified majority voting (QMV). Finally, the issue of how far QMV itself should be extended to avoid gridlock in the EU decision-making process had to be addressed.

Debates on these intractable problems have led some commentators to argue that the politics of intergovernmental bargaining have changed significantly (Barber, 2000; Graham and Groom, 2000). At Nice, Germany demanded more votes than France in the Council of Ministers to reflect its population growth after reunification. Paris rejected this request, a rebuff that was one of the factors contributing to the absence of the usual pre-joint summit letter. At the same time, Spain lobbied for voting parity with France, Germany, Britain and Italy in the Council of Ministers, a move that annoyed Portugal and led to talk of splits within the 'Club Med' alliance. Even the Benelux club was not immune from disturbances: Belgium in particular was said to be upset by Dutch demands for more votes in the Council. In short, the politics of EU diplomacy appear to have become more open and fluid. The ability to forge *ad hoc* alliances with different states over a variety of issues is now an advantage. As we have seen, this development suits the Blair leadership, which has forged alliances with Italy and Spain (employment) and France (foreign policy and defence).

While the possibilities for influence within this changing institutional terrain remain uncertain and contingent, British diplomacy has certainly flourished in this more 'open' intergovernmental environment. At Nice, Blair and Cook successfully negotiated a rise in Britain's voting weight in the Council of Ministers to twenty-nine (in line with France, Germany and Italy). They also supported the new 'triple majority' procedure for reaching decisions under the qualified majority vote. In future, supporters of a proposal will need to build a coalition comprising: (a) a majority of all member states; (b) a demographic majority of at least 62 per cent of the total population of the EU; and (c) a qualified majority of 258 weighted votes out of a total of 345 in an enlarged EU of 27 members. At the same time, London remained relaxed about the prospect of losing one commissioner under the 'deferred ceiling model'. This agreement gave each member state one representative at Brussels, until the pressures of enlargement rendered this arrangement impractical. Finally, Blair and Cook safeguarded the British veto on taxation, social security and border issues (Cook, 1999; Cm. 5090, 2001). For once, Britain was not seen as the 'awkward partner' in Europe. Most post-summit commentary instead focused on France's heavy-handed use of the chair and its more general anxiety about losing its pre-eminent position within the EU.

Single Currency

The biggest contradiction within this strategy has perhaps been the government's policy on the single currency. By October 1997, Brown had ruled out sterling's participation in the first wave, citing Britain's failure to meet the five economic tests he had allegedly constructed (with Ed Balls, his adviser) on the back of an envelope in a taxi. This decision was perhaps understandable. Britain's economic cycle remained significantly out of step with that of its European partners. However, the Labour leadership's reluctance to put its full weight behind a public campaign to educate the electorate about the benefits of this policy was something that politicians on the continent (and commentators at home) found increasingly incomprehensible (see for example, Stephens, 2000; Young, 2000; Howe, 2001). For them, participation within the single currency was *the* benchmark against which commitment to the EU project was to be tested. The longer Britain remained outside the euro zone, the more marginalised it would become in the debates concerning the EU's future development. These predictions seemed to be borne out as early as December 1997, when Gordon Brown found himself excluded from the newly formed Euro-11 committee. Set up as a counterweight to the European Central Bank (ECB), this body allowed Europe's political leaders to discuss matters arising from the operation of the single currency (Barber, 1997; Hutton, 1997; Stephens, 1997; Young, 1997b). Others warned that Britain's share of inward investment would also be hit, although reports provided conflicting evidence concerning whether exclusion from the euro zone had made much difference to investment flows in Labour's first term (Smith and Lorenz, 2000; Woolf, 2000).

One explanation for the government's inactivity over the euro is that there are short-term political gains to be had from this non-decision. Domestic opinion in the first term remained overwhelmingly sceptical, with two-thirds of the electorate consistently opposing abolition of the pound (Evans, 2001). This scepticism was reinforced by much of the press, particularly those papers owned by the Murdoch empire. At the same time, this 'prepare and decide' policy successfully de-politicised an issue that had the potential to divide the party more generally (Baker *et al.*, 1996, 358). This ploy was not completely successful. As the first term progressed, there were signs of a split developing between the increasingly enthusiastic Blair (backed by Cook at the Foreign Office and Byers at the Department of Trade and Industry – DTI) and the more cautious Brown. But, by and large, the leadership succeeded in preventing the issue from complicating party management and damaging Labour's re-election chances. In this task, Blair may have been assisted by a benign domestic context. Continuing Conservative divisions over Europe prevented Tory leaders from fully exploiting this theme in the party political debate. Discussion over membership of the euro intensified in the second term as the promised announcement on the Treasury's five tests approached. But Brown's declaration in June 2003 insisting that most of the tests had not yet been met made it unlikely that Blair could call a referendum during the second term.

Ethics and Arms Sales

Cook's early call for an ethical dimension to British foreign policy appeared to herald another break with Conservative practice. As some authors (see for example, Brown, 1998) have noted, the concept of an ethical foreign policy is difficult to define. In the context of Labour policy after 1997, it came to be associated particularly with placing human rights at the centre of all future diplomatic actions. By the end of the first term, ministers could list a number of achievements to match this oratory. These included: the nego- tiation of the Ottawa Agreement banning the production, import and export of land mines; playing a key role both in setting up a new International Criminal Court to deal with war crimes and drawing up a new EU Code of Conduct for arms exports; the creation of a new Department of International Development (DfID); and the exchange of personnel between the Foreign Office and non-governmental organisations (NGOs) such as Amnesty International and Save the Children. Meanwhile, decisions by both the Foreign Office and the DfID to publish annual reports detailing the govern- ment's record on human rights gave some added credence to Labour's claims to be opening up the foreign policy process and making it more transparent.

While these achievements were commendable, there were also a number of digressions from this policy. In the area of arms exports, critics pointed to the continued sale of Hawk training jets to Indonesia, even though they had been deployed against the independence movement in East Timor. Calls for Parliament to have the right to vet applications for export licences were also denied, despite the existence of this practice in other countries (Nicoll, 1998). More generally, Labour's 'softly, softly' line on China's poor human rights record was a source of continual disappointment throughout the first term (Hill, 2001). Since the 2001 election, this patchy record has continued. Straw has visited Delhi, lobbying for a £1 billion deal to sell Hawk jets to India at the height of tensions with Pakistan over Kashmir (*Financial Times*, 21 February 2002). Moreover, Claire Short rebuked No. 10 in 2002 for approving the sale of an £28 million air traffic system to Tanzania, arguing that such a deal would undermine the chances of sustainable development in that African country (*Financial Times*, 4 March 2002).

It is, of course, easy to pick holes in Labour's inconsistent implementa- tion of its ethical foreign policy. Of equal significance were examples of moral interventionism conflicting with traditional diplomatic patterns and resources. The government's policy towards the conflict between the Serbs and ethnic Albanians in Kosovo is a case in point. Blair's genuine determi- nation not to countenance the atrocities and evidence of ethnic cleansing during this war should not be doubted. However, the implementation of this policy was partly constrained by Whitehall's reliance on the USA for much of the military hardware needed to defeat Slobodan Milosovic. More to the point, President Clinton's unwillingness to commit American troops to the region appears to have produced unfortunate and unintended consequences. Faced only with the threat of Allied air strikes, Milosovic retaliated by stepping up Serbia's campaign against the Albanians. The Allies in turn simply responded by intensifying a strategy which resulted in more civilian casualties and contributed to the destruction of infrastructure, ecological damage and the humanitarian crisis that followed (Schwenninger, 1999; Bartlett, 2000; Clarke, 2000, 732). These outcomes might have been acceptable had the 'international community' as a whole supported them. However, the US insistence that NATO lead the Kosovo mission without further UN authorisation led to increased tension with Russia and China. British support for the Americans gave the impression that ministers were willing to sideline an organisation whose universal values it was so quick to endorse in principle (Benn, 1998; Nicoll, 1998a; Carlson and Ramphal, 1999).

Similar observations can be made concerning New Labour's support for the US bombing campaign against Iraq in 1998–9. Once again, Blair's sincerity about defending the 'international community' from the perceived threat of the Iraqi regime is not in question. Indeed, the bombing campaign against President Saddam Hussein, after the latter refused UN access to presidential sites suspected of containing biological and chemical weapons, was defended on these grounds. Unfortunately, however, what is 'good' for the 'international community' is always likely to be essentially contested at any particular time. In operational terms, Blair and Clinton found themselves isolated, with the British premier being the only leader to lend substantial military support to Operation Desert Fox. Not surprisingly, this Anglo-American interpretation of 'internationalism' was interpreted as cultural imperialism in other parts of the world.

Labour's Second Term

Despite the occasional rumours that Labour planned to fight the 2001 election on the issue of Europe (see, for example, the *Guardian*, 30 August 2000), foreign policy was not a dominant theme of their campaign. It was true that in the run-up to the polls, Blair announced (apparently without consulting Brown) that any assessment concerning the five economic tests for euro membership would take place within two years of a new Labour Government (*Financial Times*, 8 February 2001). But Brown was in charge of Labour's election strategy, and that meant an emphasis on the Party's domestic economic record. Hague's speech at the Tories' spring Conference warning that Britain was becoming a 'foreign land' signalled that the

Conservatives might look to exploit the European issue. However, the campaign theme of keeping the pound did not become a dominant one until the third week, after which it was played down because of a perceived lack of interest (Butler and Kavanagh, 2002, 97, 99, 103, 106). To the extent that the issues mattered, Labour's re-election was evidence of the importance the electorate attached to promises of better public services. How the party would fare in office during the second term would largely depend on progress on the 'home front'.

If the election result seemed to indicate a renewed emphasis on domestic issues, the conduct of foreign policy has become trickier since Labour's victory. One reason for this development is that the terrorist attacks of 11 September 2001 in New York have changed the external context facing Whitehall in a way that poses more problems than before. Of particular concern in London is the emergence of a unilateralist American foreign policy based on a doctrine of pre-emptive strike. It should be noted that evidence of this trend existed before the al-Qaeda attack. One could point to Washington's abrogation of the Strategic Arms Limitation Treaty (1972); plans to militarise space through the continual development of New Missile Defence (NMD) and its refusal to recognise the jurisdiction of the International Criminal Court (see for example, Krepon, 2001; Newhouse, 2001; see also *Financial Times*, 14 December 2001 and 2/3 March 2002). However, Bush's 'axis of evil' speech during the hunt for Osama Bin Laden in Afghanistan seemed to mark the advent of a critical juncture. In future, the USA would not necessarily wait to deter emerging threats to its security, but would eliminate them before they had a chance to develop. At the time of writing, this doctrine still remains largely at the level of theory. However, it clearly has awkward implications for Britain's ability to balance its multiple relations with the USA and the EU (Stephens, 2002).

At present, it is too soon to judge how these external developments have affected Blair's statecraft. One school of thought asserts that he has played a difficult hand well. Britain was able to contribute to the construction of a Grand Coalition of countries which undertook a military campaign against al-Qaeda in Afghanistan. Some commentators (Baker, 2002; Frum, 2002; Young, 2002) have also argued that Blair's advice at a meeting with George W. Bush in September 2002 was crucial in persuading the USA to go back to the UN to negotiate a resolution giving Saddam Hussein one last opportunity to disarm. One could add that Britain's ambassador to the UN, Sir Jeremy Greenstock, played a key role in bringing together conflicting proposals from Paris and Washington into a resolution which the Security Council could agree on. The main details of this resolution are summarised in Box 12.1.

BOX 12.1   *Key demands in UN Resolution 1441 on Iraq*

- Iraq has to confirm within seven days of adoption of the resolution its intention to 'comply fully' with its demands and co-operate with UN weapons inspectors.
- Iraq must declare within 30 days all weapons of mass destruction programmes and related materials, including items that also could be used for civilian purposes.
- Inspectors are to get unconditional and unrestricted access to any place they want to survey, including President Saddam Hussein's palace compounds.
- Inspectors may 'at their discretion' interview Iraqi scientists and other officials as well as facilitate travel for interviews outside the country.
- Inspectors can 'freeze' a site to be surveyed by declaring exclusion zones in which Iraq is to suspend 'ground and aerial' movements.
- The resolution recalls the Security Council has repeatedly warned Iraq it would face 'serious consequences' as a result of continued violations of its obligations.
- The resolution declares that Iraq has been and is still in 'material breach' of its obligations.
- 'False statements and omissions' in declarations submitted by Iraq and failure to co-operate fully in the implementation of the resolution would constitute a 'further material breach' of Iraq's obligations and 'will be reported to the council for assessment'.

Source: *Financial Times*, 9/10 November 2002.

However, it could be argued that subsequent events demonstrated the weakness of the British government's position within the international order and the failure of its strategy to build a bridge between the USA and the EU. Despite Blair's efforts to try to prevent war with Iraq without a UN resolution, he was unable to stem the USA's desire for a war. His unwavering belief in the Anglo-American alliance meant that he had little choice but to support the war without UN cover, and against strong opposition from France, Germany and other members of the UN Security Council. In addition, in the vote on the war in the House of Commons on 18 March 2003, despite the government winning the motion by 412 to 149 votes, 139 Labour rebels had backed an anti-war amendment – up from 122 in an earlier vote. And, at least before the war began, there appeared to be a high level of public opposition to the conflict.

The decision to go to war over Iraq had significant implications for Britain in terms of foreign policy. First, despite the apparent internationalism of the New Labour project, Blair was prepared to act without UN approval and against the wishes of a large section of the international community. Blair appeared to adopt a traditional, *real politik*, position rather than operate within the context of interdependency and international law. Second, Blair's default position was the established position of the British state: to support the US rather than stand within the European 'circle'. Consequently, he reinvigorated the Anglo-American alliance despite the presence of a right wing, Republican President. Third, the war seems to have long-term implication for Britain position in Europe. As we saw above, New Labour's initial strategy seemed to be to place Britain with France and Germany at the centre of the EU. However, with the fall out from the war continuing to affect relations with France in particular, the EU now seems more divided than ever before. And the resulting political and media attacks on the French and German governments could only complicate the already complex task of winning a 'yes' vote in any referendum on the euro.

Despite the fact that Blair seemed to change the justification for the war in Iraq on a number of occasions in the period immediately before the invasion, there are ways that it can be justified in terms of a New Labour vision of foreign policy. First, it is clear that Blair believed that he has taken a moral, rather that a *real politik*, line. His argument was that not only was the Iraqi dictatorship brutal and undemocratic but it was a threat to the stability of the region and the rights of many people in the Middle East and further afield. Therefore, there was a moral imperative behind the invasion, not a concern with state interests. Second, the war was an undermining of the Westphalian notion of sovereignty and the traditional view that it is wrong to depose undesirable regimes. It was a further development of the post-Cold War 'humanitarian internationalism' that Blair had invoked in defence of Britain's military engagements in Serbia and Sierra Leone. Third, Blair believes that his relationship with Bush has constrained the Americans in terms of the conduct of the war, the threat of further attacks on other countries and ensuring a UN role in the rebuilding process. Finally, Blair sees the split with France as opening up new alliances within the EU and ensuring that Britain has greater influence on its direction in the future. It also seems that Blair does want to rebuild relations with France and Germany and aims to join the Euro sooner rather than later (Rawnsley, 2003) (although with Brown declaring the euro tests only partially met, this may prove impossible). While Iraq has caused Blair problems in his party, the consequences in terms of his position in government and the country may be that he is stronger than ever before, if the post-war polling results are any indication.

Policy towards the EU in Labour's second term initially saw a renewal of the sort of 'activism' displayed during the first administration. As evidence, one could cite the approach of the Blair Government to the Constitutional Convention set up after the Laeken European Council in December 2001 to suggest ways of making the EU both more effective and more democratic. British negotiators have been quick to respond to this challenge with reform initiatives. They have produced proposals to replace the six-month presidency of the Council of Ministers with a system whereby individual councils covering different subjects choose their own chairperson for a two-and-a-half-year term. These chairs would then go on to form a steering group to drive through any agenda agreed by heads of government at the European Council (Straw, 2002). More recently, Whitehall has floated the idea of appointing a permanent president of the Council, although Peter Hain has had to deny suggestions that Blair might be offered the job as a retirement sweetener (*Financial Times*, 12/13 October 2002). Ministers have also stressed continually the importance of closing the 'delivery gap' between what Brussels legislates for, and what member states implement (Hain, 2002a, 2002b). According to this view, electorates are interested in practical results which benefit their everyday lives, and any improvement on this front would be the best way to increase the EU's legitimacy. In a significant development, Blair and Gerhard Schroder sent a joint letter to Jose Marie Azanar ahead of the Seville European Council, arguing the case for some of these proposals (*Financial Times*, 25 February 2002; see also Grabbe and Munchau, 2002).

Despite recent claims to be leading the debate in the Convention, the progress of this diplomatic offensive has been decidedly mixed to date. Under pressure from the prevailing current of opinion, the British delegation has been forced to accept the principle of a written constitution for the EU, despite opposition to this policy before the 2001 election (*Sunday Times*, 28 January 2001; Straw, 2002; *Financial Times*, 18 February 2002). Moreover, a draft of the first sixteen articles produced by the Convention has proved to be 'unacceptable' to Whitehall, which described them as too 'federalist'. A proposal recommending that the EU should have responsibility for co-ordinating the economic policy of member states raised fears that Britain would be forced to accept some types of tax harmonisation. Alternatively, a suggestion that the Union should have the competence to develop progressively a common defence policy has raised questions about Europe's future commitment to NATO (European Convention, 2002; European Convention, 2003). It is true that Labour's plan for rejuvenating the Council of Ministers has been received more positively in some quarters. But this has been joined by a Franco-German submission calling for the president of the Commission to be elected by the European

Parliament (*European Voice*, 16–22 January 2003). Besides, London's proposals reveal the rather limited approach that Labour has adopted towards the question of the EU's 'democratic deficit'. This preoccupation with strengthening the EU's executive capabilities underlines a typical British conception of top-down representative democracy. Any suggestion for widening the participation of EU citizens in the policy process is much less evident. Interestingly, the Blair Government has rejected a proposal for developing EU-wide political parties as a method of generating a genuine European demos: an idea that Giddens has taken up recently (Giddens, 2000; *Financial Times*, 1 December 2001).

It is certainly true that a 'democratic deficit' continues to exist when it comes to Labour's policy towards the euro. Despite initial optimism that the election victory would signal the beginning of a national debate and a referendum, ministers moved quickly to dampen down expectations of a campaign. To date, there is little sign of a change in this 'prepare and decide' strategy, with the Treasury continuing to guard jealously its jurisdiction over the five economic tests. Indeed, it has been argued in some quarters that Brown is trying to delay a decision until after the next election, when it is expected that he will succeed Blair and be the prime minister who takes Britain into the euro (Stephens, 2001). To the extent that Labour has a policy at all on this issue, it adds up to what the media are now calling 'eurocreep' (*Observer*, 25 October 2001). The argument here is that, the more the holidaying public becomes familiar with the single currency abroad, the less sceptical it will be about its introduction at home. At the same time, pro-European politicians are quick to point out that two-thirds of the electorate expect to be using the euro by 2010 (*Financial Times*, 9 October 2000; see also comments by Lord Marshall, *Financial Times*, 16 September 2000). However, recent reports suggest that there is still conflict over this strategy (Radice, 2003; *Financial Times*, 24 January 2003). As we saw above, while Blair sees the euro as a means of rejuvenating relations with France and Germany, Brown continues to be cautious.

Second Term Statecraft

What conclusions can we draw about the Blair Government's foreign policy since 1997? If we begin by taking into account the external structural context facing the Labour leadership, two observations appear to be in order. First, the 'fluidity' of the present environment differs somewhat from the more stable picture of bipolarity that faced Whitehall from approximately 1945 to 1990. It is important not to overstate this novelty. The existence of ethnic conflicts in Eastern Europe and elsewhere would have been familiar to British statesmen in the nineteenth and twentieth centuries. Similarly, the problem of managing an unpredictable American ally would have been common to all prime ministers from Churchill to Major. Second, while this more open and uncertain international system since 1990 contains new constraints, it is not without its opportunities for British diplomats, especially in the European sphere. Enlargement is currently disturbing the institutional terrain of the EU in a way that has dislocated the Franco-German axis, although the recent agreement between Paris and Bonn over the future of agriculture subsidies (not to mention Iraq and proposals for the Constitutional Convention) highlights the fact that this disruption may only be temporary (Peel, 2002). That said, British policy-makers may have their best chance in years to influence the future development of this regional organisation.

The second point to note is the continuity of Whitehall's response to this altered external context. We have already described Labour's ongoing desire to play a leadership role at the heart of Europe. At the same time, there is nothing especially new in this commitment to internationalism, even moral interventionism: these themes have been a key feature of Labour foreign policy throughout the twentieth century. But this is not to deny some notable achievements. The Blair Government has gone beyond its rhetoric to push for the international promotion of human rights. One could also include the progress made, until her resignation over Iraq, by Claire Short in the development portfolio. However, the key question is to what extent the twin objectives of influence and internationalism are complementary in the longer term. In the past, Labour leaders have certainly played down the latter in favour of the former, as evinced by their preference for siding with the USA during the Cold War (Jones, 1977). Moreover, since 1997, internationalism *in practice* has often added up to little more than blanket support for America: even in the face of opposition from many of Britain's allies. The war in Iraq appears to have linked Britain even more closely with the USA. It may also be a critical juncture for domestic politics. At present, it seems reasonable to conclude that Blair's foreign policy has been successful from a domestic point of view. However, war in Iraq may have long-term consequences for British foreign policy.

13

Conclusion: Defining New Labour

MARTIN J. SMITH

The New Labour project, whose origins can be traced variously to any of the decades of the post-war period (see Fielding, 2003), has been in existence at least since the Kinnock policy review of 1989, and has developed in its Blairite form since Tony Blair's election as leader in 1994. Is it too soon, as Zhou Enlai might have said, to determine its impact, or do two terms of a Labour administration mean that a clear shape to New Labour can be discerned?

The problem is that, while a New Labour agenda may now be defined – and to an extent implemented – there is little agreement even within the upper echelons of the Party about what New Labour means. How radical is New Labour? Is it Thatcherite or social democratic? Is it a third way? Is it a new way? As I have previously argued, in order to understand New Labour it is important to understand the constraints and dilemmas the Labour Government faces, and how it has drawn on a range of ideas and traditions, old and new, in order to develop responses (Ludlam and Smith, 2001). These responses have at times pulled Labour off into new directions, while at others they have seen Labour recycle ideas from the Conservative and social democratic canon (Kenny and Smith, 2001). This conclusion will examine how, after its longest consecutive period in government, Labour has responded to the dilemmas and constraints, and whether it has established a distinct New Labour project that will have a significant impact on the nature of Britain in the twenty-first century.

Tradition and Economics

According to Mick Hume (*New Statesman*, 2 December 2002), Leon Trotsky believed that 'Labour could never hope to change the world while it

211

lacked the guts to deny the Prince of Wales his pocket money.' Peter Mandelson (2002, xix), on the other hand, suggests that:

> the essence of New Labour is that it is a modernising project. But there are many aspects of Britain – the monarchy, the countryside and even Parliamentary procedures that are fixed parts of the 'British' way of life and do not conflict with the economic and social goals of a social democratic government.

These perspectives highlight the key dilemma of the Labour Party – that Labour is of the British political tradition – its outlook, its organisation, its goals and its conceptions of what is radical, exists within the parliamentary state and as, Flinders demonstrated in Chapter 8, within the Westminster model. Unlike left-of-centre parties in continental Europe, Labour did not develop out of a Communist party, or intense social conflict, but within the parliamentary system and a from liberal rather than a revolutionary tradition. As Clift emphasised in Chapter 3, Labour continues to take a different path from its sister parties on the Continent. Labour has never been a radical party in the sense of aiming to overthrow existing political and economic structures (as a host of critics have pointed out). The goals it has attempted to achieve in terms of greater welfare, equality and social justice have been set within the existing institutional, constitutional and economic context.

Despite the famous Clause 4 committing Labour to the public ownership of the economy, Labour has never made any fundamental challenge to the notion of private ownership within a market economy. Rather, it has attempted a range of mechanisms to improve the efficiency of capitalism – from nationalising key elements to introducing a range of planning mechanisms. But even when Labour was committed to extending public ownership in the 1940s, and to planning in the 1960s, the aim of the policies was to improve capitalism, not to replace it. No Labour Government (it could be argued that this was not true of Labour's programme in 1982) has ever sought to undermine capitalism, or to abolish private ownership. Despite Labour's long-term acceptance of the private, market economy, many commentators have argued that New Labour is Labour's adaptation to the free market capitalism of the post-Thatcher era.

Labour and the Thatcherite Agenda

It has almost become a cliché in certain circles that New Labour is a centre-left adaptation of the Thatcherite agenda (see Hay, 1999; Heffernan, 2001). Heffernan sees Blair and the New Labour leadership consolidating the dominant Thatcherite agenda through its 'accommodation to a new neo-liberal centre' (Heffernan, 2001, 170). Journalists and academics point to

Labour's adoption of privatisation, the acceptance of key elements of Conservative economic policy such as stable money and low inflation, the uncontested acceptance of the need to adapt to the requirements of private capital, cuts in benefits such as the disability and lone parent benefits, and the willingness to support the military goals of the USA, as elements of Labour submitting to the Thatcher agenda. It is difficult to deny that there have been continuities in terms of policy between the Labour Government and the Thatcher and Major Administrations. For example, there is a clear lineage between the education policies introduced by the Conservatives and those developed by New Labour in terms of greater central control, increased private funding, and the use of performance indicators and league tables (McCaig, 2001). It is also true that cuts in social security benefits, commitments to stable money and support for the USA have all been policies adopted by previous Labour Governments.

Nevertheless, continuities and even policy convergence are not the same as consensus, and indeed there are a number of reasons for similarities in policy areas between Labour and Conservative:

- Labour has been confronted by the success and popularity of Conservative policies in certain areas. For example, it is difficult to argue that there could be any benefit – political, economic or social – for the return of telecommunications or services such as gas or electricity to the public sector. The whole nature of the telecommunications industry has changed fundamentally since privatisation, and so the renationalisation of British Telecom would be a futile exercise. Indeed, through the selling-off of mobile phone licences, the government has done extremely well as a consequence of market competition. Mandelson (2002, xxv) suggests that Blair:

  openly, and rightly supported some of the economic reforms she had carried out – trade unions brought within a proper legal framework; industrial restructuring including some necessary privatisation; incentives and reward for success – while making clear his disagreement with her failures on economic stability, public sector investment, social division and, latterly, isolationism.

- It is extremely difficult for governments to change policies rapidly (see Richards and Smith, 2002). The Conservative Administration did not break fundamentally with the post-war trend of policies in welfare until relatively late in the third term. It takes considerable time to change policy direction, and Labour had little choice but to continue with a whole raft of Conservative policies in its first term. Considering the commitments Labour had made in the 1997 election and the administrative, financial and political difficulties of change, Labour could not immediately and rapidly undo eighteen years of Conservative inheritance.

Blair and Brown have always seen New Labour's project as a long-term strategy. As Mandelson (2002, xv) points out, it was seen to be necessary to achieve economic stability before investments in public services could be made.

- Both New Labour and Thatcherism have faced similar external constraints. Whatever view is taken of globalisation, there is little doubt that the external world had changed. New Labour took over government when many of the institutional arrangement and political certainties of the post-war world had been undermined. During the post-war era there were a particular set of policy arrangements and ideas that derived from the pre-war, Second World War and immediate post-war era. It was believed that the government could affect the organisation of society and the economy for the greater good. From these beliefs a range of policy prescriptions developed, based around Keynesian economic management and the welfare state, and placed within the framework of US economic and political hegemony and Britain's adaptation to the end of empire. Thatcherism was in some ways an attempt to deal with the unravelling of the post-war settlement, stagflation, economic decline, rising unemployment, uncontrollable public expenditure rises and growing dissatisfaction with welfare policies (which, of course, occurred in the context of the collapse of Bretton Woods, the deregulation of financial markets and the end of the Cold War). This was an adaptation that all governments have had to make in some form, and in most cases it has meant a shift towards policies associated with neo-liberalism rather than social democracy. Thatcherism found an economic alternative to Keynesianism but was never able to reconstitute key elements of the welfare state. As Driver and Martell (2002) remind us, any government that continues to spend over 40 per cent of GDP can hardly be described as laissez-faire. Nor was the Thatcher government able to come to terms with Britain's status post-empire – the Conservative have fought aggressively about the nature of Britain's position in the post-post-war world. However, through economic change, the initiation of the reform of welfare and the creation of a foreign policy vacuum, Conservatives had responded to the new global economic and political conditions that arose out of the disintegration of the post-war settlement. It was in this terrain that New Labour established its first government – a terrain which, of course, it did not create (although the previous Labour Government of 1974–9 was an important element in its construction) and to which it only had a limited ability to adapt. Consequently, what the Blair Government had to do was to create a Labour response to a new domestic, international economic and political structure. In some ways they did this by accepting elements of Thatcherism (such as the free market – but which party in government in the world rejects the market, North Korea?) but also by developing some significant differences.⌐

Non-Thatcherite Labourism

Developments within Labour have not occurred in a vacuum. Labour has adapted in relation to external changes, changing social relations and electoral disasters. Moreover, within the British party system, parties exist in relation to each other and therefore the changes that have occurred within Labour are related to those that have occurred within the Conservative Party. Labour did to some extent, as Hay (1998) and Heffernan (2001) argue, follow the model of party competition and shift towards the median voter. As a party that wanted to gain office they had little choice. Nevertheless, there are some central elements within New Labour that distinguish it very clearly from the Conservative Party, and especially the Thatcherite version of Conservatism. Indeed, these elements arc in fact fundamental beliefs, rather than elements of policy, that reflect an alternative world view. This is an important point. Labour and Conservatives may share policies while in fact seeing the world in different ways and having different ends for their policies.⌐

The Private Sphere

One of the areas where Labour is seen to share elements of the Thatcherite agenda is over its faith in the private sector through the extension of privatisation, and through the use of private finance in the public sector. However, it is important to think carefully about the meaning of 'private' in New Right and New Labour thought. The New Right position is essentially individualist – people are rational actors who are concerned with their own interests (and those of their immediate family). The famous, but not apocryphal, quote of Thatcher's is that there is 'No such thing as society but only individuals and their families'. While she may have regretted the quote – and Iain Duncan Smith has distanced himself explicitly from this view with his foreword to a book of Conservative essays called *There Is Such a Thing as Society* (Streeter, 2002) – it does speak to the core of new right thinking. The goal of Conservative policy was to free individuals from the state, the dependency culture and from taxation, to enable them to make their own choices and create their own opportunities. The goal of the New Right is to extend the private sphere so that people have responsibility for their own health, education and security. Consequently, the state does not have responsibility for ensuring the welfare of citizens or ameliorating the impact of the economy. This leads, in the words of J.K. Galbraith, to private affluence and public squalor as people find private solutions to public goods, and income is retained by individuals rather than the state. Moreover, as the well-off withdraw they want to pay less tax because they do not see why they should pay for collective goods from which they do not benefit, and so the public sector crumbles.

New Labour has rejected explicitly this notion of the individual and the private sphere. Labour does not see the relationship between the individual and the state as one of conflict, but rather one of interdependence. Two notions are important in New Labour's thought: one is the importance of the community and the need for individuals to belong to communities – and to make sacrifices for the community; and the second is the related notions of rights and responsibilities. Central to New Labour's thought is the belief that, if the state provides rights, citizens have responsibilities, so creating an implicit contract between the state and the individual. Within New Labour there is a commitment to public services, building communities and improving the communications between the state and the community. Thus Labour's position on law and order need not necessarily be seen as a continuation of the agenda set up by Michael Howard, but rather as an attempt to secure communities and to ensure that responsibilities are widely accepted. In this sense, New Labour has a more holistic approach to crime (see Chapter 11) which does see crime as being linked to issues of education, poverty and community.

Labour has stated explicitly its desire to end the private affluence/public squalor dichotomy. It has announced a relatively minor, but in many ways ideologically significant, policy to end the running-down of public spaces that was so evident in the Thatcher years. This government initiative is intended to clean up public spaces through the reduction of litter, vandalism and petty crime. Experiments have been undertaken, such as giving tenants in public housing much greater control over investment and organisation in their estates. This comes on top of more significant policy in terms of local regeneration through the local regeneration initiatives and EU funding, which is seeing many northern industrial towns flourishing after almost thirty years of decline.

The State

The New Labour conception of the relationship between the individual and the community underpins a very different notion of the role of the state. For the New Right, the state is fundamentally a force for bad because it is coercive, it undermines the freedom of the individual and it distorts markets. Thatcherism, however, did not develop a coherently New Right vision of the state (Gamble, 1988). Much of the Thatcherite notion of the state was based on traditional Conservative beliefs such as the need for hierarchy, authority and order, which run counter to the liberal conception of state activity (see Smith, 1995; Hay, 1996).

Labour continues to be a statist party. Labour sees the state as having a significant role in a whole range of activities, from public money for directing the railways to the provision of welfare services, to the provision of blood plasma (in December 2002, the Labour Government created a nationalised blood plasma company by buying a private company) and even subsidies for the deep-mine coal industry. Prabhakar illustrated in Chapter 10 the extent of New Labour's commitment to the welfare state, and Annesley and Gamble, in Chapter 9, highlighted the extent of economic innovation. As Richards and Smith demonstrated in Chapter 7, New Labour's state is concerned with creating instruments for intervening in society. Labour has developed a hybrid state that moves away from the top-down hierarchical elements of the Keynesian welfare state (KWS) and the anti-statism of the Thatcherite years. Labour has combined the devolution of power with a strong element of central control. Through the use of league tables and selective funding it has ensured that public-sector, and in some cases private-sector, actors have changed their behaviour in order to meet the government's goals. One of the clearest examples of the way in which Labour has intervened is in the issue of childhood poverty. A significant amount of money has been spent on targeting child poverty – it is seen as being a responsibility of the state as well as of parents. More interesting is the notion of Child Trust Funds, whereby children are to be given endowments to ensure all have some basic assets and to create the habit of saving. Such policies demonstrate the way in which New Labour has drawn on different sources. The notion that an individual should have responsibility for the use of assets, and that their decisions on those assets will affect their life chances is influence by the New Right. However, the notion that the state has a responsibility to provide those assets and seeing how they are used is an idea influenced much more by social democratic thinking (see Prabhakar, 2003).

The Constitution

Changes in the nature and the organisation of the state have, of course, been related to changes in the constitution. As Flinders points out in Chapter 8, many of New Labour's constitutional reforms may lack any radical substance, constrained as they are by the Westminster model. The prime example of how the weight of tradition has tied the process of reform is the way in which Blair supported an appointed rather than an elected second chamber. Democracy is not the first principle in the British political system. The code of the political elite is that they are accountable, but not necessarily responsive to, the electorate. Nevertheless, there is still a sharp division between Thatcherite and new Labour notions of the constitution (and in fact these division are greater now than they were throughout the twentieth century, when both parties more or less accepted the constitutional settlement). The Conservatives under Thatcher and Major were generally opposed to constitutional reform (though Major did introduce much greater freedom of information). Despite the loss of support for Conservative governments in Scotland and Wales, they were not prepared to consider devolution. The Conservatives were also strongly opposed to proportional representation and to any reform of the House of Lords. Any measure that violated parliamentary sovereignty was seen as an unacceptable challenge to the British tradition. Indeed, what Thatcher wanted to do was to reinforce parliamentary sovereignty and to strengthen the link between individual voters and the government. She was strongly opposed to any institution that diluted the ability of the parliamentary arena to make decisions. Hence Thatcher's strong opposition to the EU.

New Labour has *de facto*, if not *de jure*, had a significant impact on the notion of parliamentary sovereignty. The introduction of devolution has diminished the ability of Westminster to control all that goes on within the territory of the United Kingdom. Devolution may have much wider ramifications in the future, when there are different parties in charge in Westminster and in Scotland. However, devolution to the nations of the UK is only one element. There are a number of examples where power has shifted outside of Westminster, whether through the establishment of foundation hospitals, the incorporation of the European Convention on Human Rights, the development of regional mechanisms of governance, the use of citizens' juries and people's panels. While the effects of these changes may not be dramatic, they do signify a rethinking of the relationship between the citizen and the state, and could have a longer impact on the nature of decision-making in Britain.

The International Arena

Parliamentary sovereignty contains internal and external elements. Internally, it is concerned with control over policy within the territorial boundaries of the UK, while externally the focus is on relations with other countries. Developing in the nineteenth century when Britain was at the height of its imperial power, it is based on the idea that Britain is an independent nation which cannot have decisions imposed by external actors. Thatcher was very much committed to the nineteenth-century notion of sovereignty. For her, Britain's sovereignty was inviolate and she was therefore opposed to any institution that threatened to undermine it. Further EU integration is a threat to the very nature of the British state and constitution. For Blair, sovereignty is very different: he considers that Britain's position in the world is strengthened, not diminished, through international partnership and EU integration. Blair does draw on a strong tradition within Labour that is an attempt to reconcile Britain's position in the world with the loss of empire and a belief in international co-operation. However, Labour in government has always found it difficult to break from realpolitik, to drop the imperialistic perspective that still influences the British state, or to move out of the USA's sphere of influence as Chapter 12 demonstrates in relation to the war in Iraq.

Labour, as in other areas, is faced with a strategic dilemma. On the one hand is Blair's development of the internationalist strand within social democracy: that the world is interdependent; that Labour is now fully committed to the EU; that nineteenth-century notions of sovereignty are no longer applicable; and that Labour has a moral duty to help the poor in developing countries. As Buller demonstrated in Chapter 12, we have seen New Labour take substantive steps towards greater EU integration and, through Brown's policies on debt relief, help the Third World. On the other hand is the continuing sense that Britain has a world role, that the alliance with the USA is fundamental, and that ultimately the key driving force behind foreign policy is national self-interest (rather than interdependence). The impact of this dilemma is a continuing ambiguity in relation to the EU, with a seemingly growing reluctance to join the euro and difficult relations with both France and Germany over a range of issues (there is, however, some evidence that within the EU Britain is becoming leader of an alliance opposed to Franco-German hegemony within the EU). The pull of the Atlantic Alliance remains strong, with a preparedness to be isolated from EU allies in order to support US strategy on Iraq. Like much else in New Labour, foreign policy both resembles Conservative policy and is the opposite of it, containing elements that are similar and elements that are far removed from Conservative ideology.

Defining New Labour?

In the second term, Labour does have a vision. The government aims to modernise the economy, to maintain the welfare state, to improve the delivery of public services, to reduce levels of poverty (without necessarily reducing inequality), to integrate Britain into Europe, and to reform the constitution. As a package this is a relatively ambitious programme, but it is also a programme that is ideologically complex, that draws on many traditions, and that is not always consistent. Labour wants an enterprise economy and social justice, but the Gordian knot remains that enterprise and social justice may not go together. Labour is trying to reconcile them by ensuring that tax benefits allow the continuation of a low-wage economy, and that it is the middle-income earners rather than the rich who pay the main cost of Labour's social programme. Many of these conflicts and contradictions are not even sorted out within new Labour, with Brown and Blair often having different opinions on the direction the government should take.

However, it is the contradictions in New Labour that account for the different readings of Labour policy. As we have seen, Labour has faced a whole set of dilemmas that has resulted in them drawing on different traditions and thus developing policy that crosses ideological boundaries from the New Right through to traditional Labour beliefs; indeed, it seems that Blair and Brown draw on different traditions. One factor fundamental to the amorphous nature of New Labour is the electoral imperative. Two landslide victories have not erased the memory of eighteen years in opposition, and a third victory is seen as being essential to the implementation of the New Labour programme. Therefore Labour has been concerned, as Pattie illustrated in Chapter 2, to recreate its electoral coalition and to cement a link with the middle class, broadly defined, through a statecraft based on governing competence. It is this desire to convince the electorate of its competence that has resulted in Labour's concern with presentation (see Chapter 6). As Franklin illustrated, one of the problems is that the means – communication and presentation – have become the end. Perhaps more significantly, the need to keep on board this new electoral coalition has resulted in strange policy contradictions. These are demonstrated most strongly, perhaps, in the Home Office, where the Party traditions of liberalism on issues such as homosexual rights are combined with increasingly right-wing and populist stances on issues such as crime and immigration. The need to speak out directly to the electorate has had a significant impact on the leadership's relationship with its traditional supporters in the Party and the unions. As Ludlam pointed out in Chapter 5 while the Labour Party still depends heavily on the unions for support in elections, relations between the leadership and the unions have become fraught during the second term. Similarly, in Chapter 4, Shaw highlighted how, despite new mechanisms of consultation, the leadership is concerned with keeping a firm control on the party. However, it is important to remember that conflicts between membership and leadership have been an ever-present element in Labour's history: what has changed is the sometimes unquestioning support of the union hierarchy for the party leadership.

Within these contradictions, conflicts and competing tensions is there something that is distinctively New Labour? Below is an indication of some of the key elements that define the New Labour project, and two areas where Labour seems to have carved a distinct niche is in the nature of the state and the nature of welfare.

Towards a Plural State

While it is difficult to deny the continuing imprint of the Westminster model and executive sovereignty, the British state has changed. First, through the acceptance of the governance agenda, New Labour is prepared to adapt its method of intervention to suit the problem. Rhetorically, at least, the focus is on outcomes and therefore the means are of less importance. For example, in education, as Prabhakar demonstrated (Chapter 10), the government is prepared to use a combination of central control through targets, audit and testing, private finance and the adoption of new approaches, such as education action zones (EAZs), in order to achieve its goals. There is no longer the belief that there is one type of solution to the problem of providing public goods.

Second, the government has changed levels of decision-making. Clearly, with devolution important new levels of government have been established in Scotland, Wales and, at times, in Northern Ireland. However the changing level of state activity is much more complex than the shift to devolution. The Labour Government has attempted to diversify the mechanism for local control. Some of this has been through relatively traditional mechanisms such as regional government and enhancing the power of local government. However, interestingly, initiatives have been developed with the establishment of Health Action Zones and foundation hospitals (see Chapter 10). Like much of New Labour policy and ideology, its position on the state is replete with both contradictions and attempts to reconcile a range of constraints. Nevertheless, even if much of it is unintended, the state is changing – partly as a response to the failure of KWS, the impact of Thatcherism and an attempt to deal with problems in different ways. As Richards and Smith suggested in Chapter 7, it is a hybrid state, and one that has created an array of mechanisms for state actors. Of course, these changes create a whole set of questions that the government has failed to answer concerning lines of accountability when decisions and implementation are made across the public/private boundary.

Welfare State

The development of New Labour's policy in relation to the welfare state perhaps highlights most directly the changing (or not) direction of the Party. Welfare policy has always been central to Labour's policy. Because of reconciliation with the private market economy, it has not been able to tackle the root cause of inequality – capitalism. Labour's social democracy has been based on an amelioration of inequality through a welfare state. The welfare state has always been at the heart of the Labour project and all Labour politicians, both left and right have appealed frequently to the Atlee inheritance of the establishment welfare state. However, while the NHS is seen as being one of Labour's greatest goals, it has also caused the greatest headaches. On one side it has frequently been criticised for not achieving its goals of reducing poverty or inequality, but on the other, governments since the 1960s have been grappling with the issue of rising costs.

As Gamble and Annesley demonstrated in Chapter 9, the New Labour Government has attempted to tackle this in a number of ways. New Labour has drawn on a range of traditions in attempting to resolve the inherent contradictions between capitalism and welfare. First, interestingly, underpinning the whole of Labour's welfare strategy is the revisionist principle that it is necessary to sort out the economy in order to provide the economic growth for welfare policy. Brown has consistently stated that the economy has to be placed on a stable footing to enable Labour to meet its spending commitments on welfare. Of course, this creates a terrible tension within policy – the goal of a stable economy may undermine attempts to expand welfare. So, for example, it is striking that, while Labour has increased spending on welfare, at least in its first term, the extra spending was often less than the increase that had occurred under the previous administration. Moreover, Labour's spending remained much lower than much of continental Europe. As Hall (2003) reminds us, even Labour's spending plans up to 2005–06 will only take public spending up to 41.8 per cent of GDP, which is lower than the 44 per cent that was level during the Conservative Governments from 1979 to 1997. So, while Anthony Crosland's revisionism saw welfare spending being linked intimately to economic growth, that growth was to be generated through Keynesian economic policies. For New Labour, economic growth is to be achieved through a policy heavily influenced by fiscal conservatism: low inflation, reducing borrowing and controlling public expenditure (see Chapter 9).

Second, Labour has also drawn on social democratic tradition through its commitment to full employment, seeing, as Annesley and Gamble, pointed out (Chapter 9), a job as being the best route out of poverty. But even this apparent incontestably social democratic concept has been contaminated by the Thatcherite era. Labour, in principle, has a commitment to full employment, but the Party does not seem to accept the Marshallian concept that every one has the *right* to a job. Employment is based on conditions. On one side it depends the price of labour, and the government does not intend to ensure jobs for those it sees as pricing themselves out of the market. Labour has tried hard to maintain the flexible labour market that resulted from Thatcher's employment policy, and has resisted efforts at the EU level to strengthen employment rights. Toynbee (2003) demonstrates the ways in which the conditions and wages of the poorest workers have become much worse since the 1960s, despite the minimum wage. On the other hand, employment is tied to the responsibilities of the unemployed to undertake training to meet needs within the labour market. Underlying all this is a New Right principle that there is a need to break welfare dependency by tackling long-term unemployment.

Third, a crucial shift in New Labour's welfare is the shift from universal to targeted welfare. The debate surrounding this issue is vast and complex. It relates back again to the Marshellian notion of citizenship, which sees all citizens as having equal rights to the social benefits of society. Of course, the desire of the critics of New Labour for a return to univeralism is based on both a romanticism of the past and a utopianism about the future. It assumes that the social democratic welfare state was universalistic. While this was, in principle, true for access to services such as education and health, the reality was that there were great inequalities of access, with the middle class benefiting disproportionately from these services. In a utopian vein, it assumes that it is both possible and desirable to extend state benefits to all (should Tony and Cherie Blair get the same child benefit as the poorest?) and that this is the best way to distribute welfare. What has been central to Labour's policy, both in terms of specific welfare changes and tax changes, has been the targeting of benefits to groups such as pensioners and children. Indeed, these policies have had some redistributive effect, with the poorest increasing their income by between 3 per cent and 7 per cent and the richest 10 per cent seeing their income decline by nearly 4 per cent (Hall, 2003).

Finally, Labour has been prepared to use private intervention in the welfare sector. This is a considerable break with social democratic tradition, although even Aneurin Bevan had to reconcile the NHS with private practice. For New Labour, the role of the private sector is not to replace the welfare state but to augment the public mechanism for the delivery of welfare services. The most obvious example is in the provision of PFI, which is seen as a route for increasing investment in the public sector without increasing public borrowing. However, the involvement of the private sector is wider than that, and does build on the reforms introduced by the

Conservatives. In some cases it involves the contracting of private organisations to provide public services; examples include the use of private agencies to deal with the fostering of children. But it also involves the use of the private sector to fill in gaps and to rectify problems within public bodies – for example, the taking over by private companies of failing schools, or the use of private hospitals to treat NHS patients who are having to wait too long for treatment. Such policies contain elements of New Right thought in the belief that private provision can be more efficient than public. Nevertheless, a key difference exists in that the role of the private sector is to supplement and in a way improve, the provision of public goods rather than to replace them. Labour's approach is pluralistic – they believe that there are many services which are best provided by the public sector, and are prepared to use public ownership, for example, in certain aspects of the rail industry and for the provision of blood plasma.

Conclusion: The Many Heads of New Labour

New Labour is hydra-headed. The project is difficult to define, because it is full of contradictions and it presents a 'head' to suit the occasion. Because of electoral concerns it can present the same policy in a range of ways according to the audience. For example, taxation policy is at the same time about redistributing wealth, being prudent, and freeing the shackles on business. These contradictions mean that Labour defies the traditional left–right spectrum. Labour is not Thatcherite, because it has a strong faith in an interventionist state. Yet it also questions some of the traditional social democratic canons. It does not have a particular commitment to the labour movement or to intervention in the economy. It is also difficult to see New Labour as providing a third way, because it does not really have a coherent ideology that provides the principles behind a whole tract of policies. New Labour is an attempt to be a competent government while retaining electoral support, at the same time as tackling some of the fundamental problems that have haunted Britain since the collapse of the Keynesian welfare state. While drawing on a range of traditions may appear to be the best way to deal with these problems, it can create a new set. The greatest threat to New Labour may be the contradictions it is creating; the fact that the mix of policies may undermine one other. By trying to encourage enterprise and create social justice, Labour has reduced taxes for the rich and also created more support for the poor. The problem is that it is middle-income earners who are paying for this redistribution, but of course it is the middle-income earners that Labour has tried so hard to woo, and who are essential to electoral victory.

In the Conclusion of the predecessor to this book (Ludlam and Smith, 2001), I suggested that New Labour contained both radical and conservative potential, and argued that we may see a considerable modernisation of Britain, 'If Labour was to accept proportional representation for Westminster elections, restructure the welfare state, create a highly skilled workforce within the context of increasing levels of employment, join the single currency whilst continuing and extending the process of redistribution' (Smith, 2001, 267). Labour has reformed the welfare state and redistributed to certain sections of society. It has also increased levels of employment and has a programme of extending education and skills training. However, proportional representation and membership of the euro appear to have been pushed beyond the horizon of a future general election and may fall off the end of the Earth. In addition, Blair's position on the reform of the House of Lords and the Iraq situation highlight the pull of the British political tradition on the government and the essentially conservative nature of the New Labour project.

Nevertheless, the Cabinet reshuffle and organisational changes of June 2003 demonstrated the multi-faceted nature of New Labour and its potential for reformist surprises. The reforms abolished the territorial departments in Scotland and Wales, created a new Department for Constitutional Affairs, and signalled that a supreme court will replace the law lords. These reforms could mark a significant change in the constitution. Abolishing the Office of the Lord Chancellor, and reforming the judicial appointments commission to give it executive and not just monitoring powers, should finally separate judicial and legislative power in Britain. Abolishing the territorial departments showed that devolution had become embedded, and implied that relations between devolved areas and the centre might become direct rather than mediated by Westminster. Finally the establishment of the Department for Constitutional Affairs suggests that constitutional reform is central to New Labour and a further redistribution of power is possible. It is also possible that these reforms may produce little new, and are a further indication of the piecemeal nature of constitutional change in Britain. The reforms may be diluted by the embrace of Whitehall and the British tradition. However, New Labour can continue to spring surprises, even if they are rhetorical rather than substantial, and a third term may produce even further change in the nature of the British state and society.

Guide to Further Reading

2 Re-electing New Labour

As in previous elections, the Nuffield study edited by Butler and Kavanagh (2001) provides a good overview of the 2001 election contest. Some recent analyses of electoral behaviour in Britain can be found in Norris (2001) and King (2002). Heath *et al.* (2001) provide a comprehensive, book-length study of the electoral politics underlying the emergence of New Labour. Classic accounts of British electoral behaviour can be found in Butler and Stokes (1974), Sarlvik and Crewe (1983), Heath *et al.* (1985), and Evans and Norris (1999). The operation of bias in the British electoral system is analysed in detail in Johnston *et al.* (2001).

3 New Labour's Second Term and European Social Democracy

For extensive surveys of the parties of the European left, not least of the dilemmas and transformations of the 1980s and 1990s, see Padgett and Paterson (1991), Scharpf (1991), Anderson and Camiller (1994), and Callaghan (2000). Sassoon (1996) adds a grand, historical sweep. In terms of the dilemmas facing social democracy in the twenty-first century, Gamble and Wright's thought-provoking collection remains a key reference (1999) and Chris Pierson provides a pithy, concise and readable overview (2001). Clift (2003) provides an in-depth analysis of the French case. Glyn's edited collection (2001b) is a fine synopsis of the changing political economy of contemporary social democracy. Two important books edited by Cuperus *et al.* (1998 and 2001) group together the analysis of party elites and think tanks. Invaluable empirical evidence is collected and presented by Garrett (1998) and Swank (2002), and Volume 2 of Scharpf and Schmidt's collection (2000) provides excellent analyses of the social and economic policies pursued by social democratic governments in Europe. Finally, Paul Pierson's edited collection (2001) explores welfare policy dilemmas that are particularly pertinent to the study of contemporary social democracy.

4 The Control Freaks? New Labour and the Party

The origins of New Labour's centralising drive are analysed in Shaw (1994) and defended in Gould (1998). Shaw further discusses issues of both the internal democracy (2002) and of one highly controversial policy area (2003). The constitutional changes in the Party and their implications are discussed in Seyd (2001), and Seyd and Whiteley (2002). These two offer much relevant argument and data. A critical insider account is offered by a former Labour National Executive Committee member (Davies, 2000), and a journalist's observations are available in Jones (2002b).

5 New Labour, 'Vested Interests' and the Union Link

The classic text on the Labour–trade union links remains Lewis Minkin's extensive *Contentious Alliance* (1992). Its analytical framework, as well as other perspectives on the link, are discussed in Fielding *et al.* (2003), and was applied to recent relations in Ludlam (2001). Crouch (2001) and Dorey (2002) discuss the character of New Labour's outlook on industrial relations and social partnership, respectively, and TUC (2002) sets out the unions' second-term aspirations. Ewing (2002) provides an account of one key issue – union funding of the Party. Osler (2002) provides a highly critical and detailed account of New Labour's links with business. The websites of the TUC and the major unions are a major resource for anyone studying in this area.

6 A Damascene Conversion? New Labour and Media Relations

The changing character of political communication in Britain, along with the implications for democratic political procedures, are analysed and discussed in Franklin (1994, 1998, and 2003); a dissenting account is offered in McNair (2000). The impact of these political communication changes on the conduct of political journalism is assessed by Barnett and Gaber (2001). Columnist Nick Cohen (2002) and political journalists Nicholas Jones (2002b) and Peter Oborne (1999 and 2002) offer intriguing insider accounts of journalists' experiences of the lobby and their relationships with Alastair Campbell. Critics' arguments about recent contentious developments in the working of the Government Information and Communication Service (GICS) are the subject of three official reports: Mountfield (1997), and two reports by the Select Committee on Public Administration (1998 and 2001). The agenda-setting function of the Central Office of Information (COI) is explored by Garner and Short (1998) and Franklin (1999). Government strategies for news management, as well as the role of special advisers, is analysed in (Franklin, 1999 and 2003) and Oborne (1999 and 2002), and Campbell (2002). Details of government advertising expenditure, and concerns that such expenditure may constitute propaganda rather than the provision of information, are discussed in Franklin (1999), COI (2002) and, interestingly, by Tony Blair (1989) in his earlier post as opposition spokesperson for the Department of Trade and Industry.

7 The 'Hybrid State': Labour's Response to the Challenge of Governance

The overall agenda concerning Labour and the reform of the state is set out in the Modernising Government White Paper, Cmnd. 4310, 1999. The third way vision of the state is explained by Giddens (1998). Notions of governance and their relationship with the state are developed in Richards and Smith (2002), and Labour and governance is addressed in Newman (2001). The theory of joined-up government is laid out in Perri 6 *et al.* (2002) and the practice is discussed in Ling (2002). For insights into the workings of the centre over time, see Smith (1999) and Kavanagh and Seldon (2000), and under New Labour see Rawnsley (2001).

8   New Labour and the Constitution

New Labour's approach to the constitution is surveyed in Morrison (2001) and Forman (2002). Foley's (1999) book is strongly recommended, especially in relation to his analyses of 'constitutional fuels'. For a theoretical discussion of why constitutions matter, see Vernon (1996) and Berggren (2002). The annual reviews published by the Constitution Unit (Hazell, 1999; Hazell, 2000; Trench, 2001) are an invaluable guide to the evolution of specific reforms. King (2001) attempts to locate the reforms within a broader theoretical framework, and Alexander (1997) provides a lucid and insightful description of the history and background of reforms. For a detailed and sophisticated account of the enduring centrality of Parliament and the importance of the Westminster model, see Judge (1993). Blackburn and Plant (1999) and Brazier (1999) provide a detailed account of the constitutional agenda, whereas Sutherland (2000) provides an array of provocative and at times polemical essays written by a diverse range of observers.

9   Economic and Welfare Policy

A general assessment of the changes in New Labour's welfare state can be found in Powell, M. (ed.) (1999) *New Labour, New Welfare State? The 'Third Way' in British Social Policy* (Bristol: Policy Press). Critical accounts of the influence of the USA on New Labour's welfare strategy since 1997 can be found in Deacon (2000); Heron (2001); King and Wickham-Jones (1999); Peck and Theodore (2001). For a general assessment of the development of contemporary welfare states, see Esping-Andersen (1999). The Treasury website (*www.hm-treasury.gov.uk*) offers plenty of material on New Labour's economic strategy, which is also elaborated in Balls and O'Donnell (2002) The dilemmas and purposes of 'tax and spend' can be studied in the Commission on Tax and Citizenship (2000) *Paying for Progress: A New Politics of Tax* (Fabian Society).

10   New Labour and the Reform of Public Services

For more on the third way, Colin Leys (2001) outlines a critical account of New Labour's use of market mechanisms. Leys sets out the case for public services being funded and delivered solely by public institutions, especially the state. For a defence of the use of markets (which uses education as an illustrative case study) see James Tooley (1998). Rajiv Prabhakar (2003) explores some of the underlying principles that underpin New Labour's conception of the third way, looking particularly at the role played by stakeholding. For policy, government websites at the Department for Education and Skills, and the Department of Health both contain up-to-date information about policy measures. They also contain helpful links to related sites. The Treasury website (see notes on Ch. 9 above) is valuable for finding data on pre-Budget reports, Budgets and spending reviews. Newspapers such as the *Guardian* provide a forum for debate about the latest controversies. On the academic front, journals such as *Policy and Politics* and *The Political Quarterly* often contain articles relating to health and education.

11 Three Faces of New Labour: Principle, Pragmatism and Populism in New Labour's Home Office

The Home Office's responsibilities are generally neglected areas in the literature on the Labour Party. Taylor (1981) probably still provides the best account of the law and order policies of 'old' Labour. Charman and Savage (1999) and Morris (2001) offer reviews of New Labour's law and order policies since 1997. Useful insights into 'old' Labour's approach towards issues of race and immigration can be gleaned from Knowles (1992) and Carter and Joshi (1984). Post-1997 developments in this policy area are reviewed in Saggar (2001).

12 Foreign and European Policy

General academic surveys of British foreign policy are rare these days, and the interested student is probably better off consulting different sources for different aspects of the topic. On the 'special relationship', Smith (1990) provides a useful review of the subject, while Jones (1997) deals specifically with the Labour Party's perspective on Anglo-American relations. Students interested in Labour's ethical foreign policy should begin with Little and Wickham-Jones (2000). On Britain's relations with the EU, George (1998), H. Young (1998) and J. Young (2000) all represent excellent introductions to the subject, though see Buller (2000) for an alternative interpretation. Holden (2002) provides an in-depth survey of New Labour's European policy, while Beetham (2001) and Rosenbaum (2001) contain essays by most of the key public figures involved in the debate about Britain's future role in Europe.

References

Alexander, L. (1998) *Constitutionalism: Philosophical Foundations* (Cambridge University Press).

Alexander, Lord (2001) 'The Constitution We Deserve?', Denning Society Lecture, 3 October (London: The Denning Society).

Allender, P. (2001) *What's Wrong With Labour?* (London: Merlin).

Anderson, B. (2002) 'Mr Blair's Foreign Adventures Could Prove His Undoing', *The Independent*, 14 January 2002.

Anderson, P. and Camiller, P. (eds) (1994) *Mapping the West European Left* (London: Verso).

Anderson, P. and Mann, N. (1997) *Safety First: The Making of New Labour* (London: Verso).

Annesley, C. (2001) 'New Labour and Welfare', in S. Ludlam and M. J. Smith (eds), *New Labour in Government* (Basingstoke: Palgrave).

Annesley, C. (2003) 'UK Social Policy Since 1997: Between Europeanisation and Americanisation', *British Journal of Politics and International Relations*, Vol. 5, No. 2.

Arestis, P. and Sawyer, M. (2001) 'The Economic Analysis Underpinning the "Third Way"', *New Political Economy*, Vol. 6, No. 2.

Ashley, J. (2002) 'Puttnam is Right to Want Broadcasting to Stay British', *Guardian*, 31 July.

Ashley, J. (2003) 'The Knives Are Out but This Master of Spin Will Survive', *Guardian*, 16 January.

Aust, A. (2003) 'From "Eurokeynesianism" to the "Third Way": The Party of European Socialists (PES) and European Employment Policies', in G. Bonoli and M. Powell (eds), *Social Democratic Party Policies in Europe* (London: Routledge).

Baker, D., Gamble, A., Ludlam, S. and Seawright, D. (1996) 'Labour and Europe: A Survey of MPs and MEPs', *Political Quarterly*, Vol. 67, No. 4.

Baker, G. (2002) 'Upstairs, Downstairs in the Oval Office', *Financial Times*, 14 November.

Balls, E. (1998) 'Open Macroeconomics in an Open Economy', *Scottish Journal of Political Economy*, Vol. 45, No. 2.

Balls, E. and O'Donnell, G. (2002) (eds) *Reforming Britain's Economic and Financial Policy* (Basingstoke: Palgrave).

Barber, L. (1997) 'Life on the Outside', *Financial Times*, 3 December.

Barber, L. (2000) 'Late Nights in Nice', *Financial Times*, 9/10 December.

Barberis, P. (2000) 'Prime Minister and Cabinet', in R. Pyper and L. Robins (eds), *United Kingdom Governance* (Basingstoke: Palgrave).

Barker, T., Byrne, I. and Veall, A. (2000) *Ruling by Task Force* (London: Politicos/Democratic Audit).

Barnett, A. (1997) *This Time: Our Constitutional Revolution* (London: Vintage).

Barnett, S. and Gaber, I. (2001) *Westminster Tales: The 21st Century Crisis in Political Journalism* (London: Continuum).

Bartlett, W. (2000) 'Simply the Right Thing to Do: Labour Goes to War', in R. Little and M. Wickham-Jones (eds), *New Labour's Foreign Policy: A New Moral Crusade?* (Manchester: Manchester University Press).

Bassett, P. (1987) *Strike Free: New Industrial Relations in Britain* (London: Macmillan).

Bassett, P. (1991) 'Unions and Labour in the 1980s and 1990s', in B. Pimlott and C. Cook (eds), *Trade Unions and the Labour Party: The First 250 Years* (London: Longman).

BBC (2002) 'Tony in Adland', *Panorama*, 26 May.

Beetham, D., Ngan, P. and Weir, S. (2002) 'Democratic Audit: An Inauspicious Year for Democracy', *Parliamentary Affairs*, Vol. 55, No. 2.

Beetham, R. (ed.) (2001) *The Euro Debate: Persuading the People* (London: Kogan Page/Federal Trust).

Benn, T. (1981) *Arguments for Democracy* (London: Jonathan Cape).

Benn, T. (1998) 'Serbia Will not Be Bombed into Submission', *Observer*, 11 October.

Benn, T. (2002) *Free at Last!: Diaries 1990–2000* (London: Hutchinson).

Berggren, N. (2002) *Why Constitutions Matter* (New Brunswick, New Jersey: Transaction Press).

Bingham, Lord (2002) 'The Evolving Constitution', *European Human Rights Law Review*, Vol. 1.

Blackburn, R. and Plant, R. (1999) *Constitutional Reform* (London: Longman).

Blair, T. (1989) *Privatisation Advertising: The Selling of Water and Electricity* (London: The Labour Party).

Blair, T. (1996) *New Britain: My Vision of a Young Country* (London: Fourth Estate).

Blair, T. (1997) 'Europe Working For People', Speech at the launch of the UK Presidency of the European Union, Waterloo Station, London, 5 December (*www.fco.gov.uk/speeches*).

Blair, T. (1998a) *The Third Way: New Politics for a New Century* (London: Fabian Society).

Blair, T. (1998b) 'A Modern Britain in a Modern Europe', speech to the Annual Friends of Nieuwspoort Dinner, the Ridderzall, the Hague, Netherlands, 20 January 1998 (*www.fco.gov.uk/speeches*).

Blair, T. (1998c) 'The Third Way', speech to the French National Assembly, 24 March (*www.fco.gov.uk/speeches*).

Blair, T. (1999) Speech to the Economic Club of Chicago, 22 April (*www.fco.gov.uk/speeches*).

Blair, T. (2000a) 'Values and the Power of Community. Prime Minister's Speech to the Global Ethics Foundation, Tübingen University, Germany' (*www.pm.gov.uk/output/page906.asp*).

Blair, T. (2000b) 'Britishness and the Government's Agenda of Constitutional Reform', (*www.britishembassy.at/speeches/0003pm_britishness.rtf*).

Blair, T. (2001a) 'Prime Minister Tony Blair outside Number 10 after 2001 General Election Victory', (*www.pm.gov.uk/output/page3000.asp*).

Blair, T. (2001b) 'Third Way, Phase Two', *Prospect*, March.

Blair, T. (2001c) 'Prime Minister's Speech on Public Service Reform', 16 October (London: Downing Street Press Office).

Blair, T. (2002a) 'The Next Steps for New Labour', Speech delivered at the London School of Economics, 12 March (London: The Labour Party).

Blair, T. (2002b) 'At Our Best When at Our Boldest', Speech delivered at the Labour
Party Annual Conference, Blackpool, 1 October (London: The Labour Party).

Blair, T. (2002c) Statement to the Commons on the EU's Barcelona Summit,
18 March, *(www.parliament.thestationeryoffice.co.uk/pa/cm200102/cmhansrd/
vo020318/debtext/20318–06.htm#20318–06_spmin2)*.

Blair, T. (2002d) Evidence to the Liaison Committee of the House of
Commons, 16 July, *(www.parliament.the-stationary-office.co.uk/pa/cm/cmselect/
cmliaisn/10)*.

Blair, T. (2002e) 'Making the Right Choices at a Time of Destiny', Speech at the
Bush Presidential Library, Texas, 7 April *(www.fco.gov.uk/speeches)*.

Blair, T. (2003a) 'We Must Not Waste this Precious Period of Power', Speech delivered at the South Camden Community College, London, 23 January (London:
The Labour Party).

Blair, T. (2003b) 'We Have to Redefine Centre-Left Politics to Cope with a more
Insecure World', *Guardian*, 10 February.

Blumler, J. (1990) 'Elections, the Media and the Modern Publicity Process', in
M. Ferguson (ed.), *Public Communication: The New Imperatives* (London: Sage).

Blunkett, D. (2002) 'Integration with Diversity: Globalisation and the Renewal of
Democracy and Civil Society', in P. Griffith and M. Leonard (eds), *Reclaiming
Britishness* (London: The Foreign Policy Centre).

Bonoli, G. (2003) 'Conclusion: Towards a European Third Way?', in G. Bonoli and
M. Powell (eds), *Social Democratic Party Policies in Europe* (London:
Routledge).

Bonoli, G. and Powell, M. (eds) (2003) *Social Democratic Party Policies in Europe*
(London: Routledge).

Bottoms, A. E. (1995) 'The Philosophy and Politics of Punishment and Sentencing',
in C. Clarkson and R. Morgan (eds), *The Politics of Sentencing Reform* (Oxford
University Press).

Brazier, R. (1999) *Constitutional Practice* (Oxford: Oxford University Press).

Bromley, C., Curtice, J. and Seyd, B. (2001) 'Political Engagement, Trust and
Constitutional Reform', in A. Park, J. Curtice, K. Thompson, L. Jarvis,
and L. Bromley *et al.* (eds), *British Social Attitudes – The 18th Report*
(London: Sage).

Brown, C. (1998) 'Mutual Respect? Ethical Foreign Policy in a Multicultural
World', Paper presented to the International Studies Association, 17–21 March.

Brown, G. (1997) 'No Quick Fix on Jobs', *Financial Times*, 17 November.

Brown, G. (1999) 'Mais Lecture, 19 October 1999' (London: HM Treasury).

Brown, G. (2002) 'Speech to the Labour Party Conference, 30 September 2002'
(London: The Labour Party).

Brown, G. (2003) 'A Modern Agenda for Prosperity and Social Reform', Speech
delivered to the Social Market Foundation at the Cass Business School, London,
3 February (London: HM Treasury).

Buller, J. (2000) *National Statecraft and European Integration: The Conservative
Government and the European Union, 1979–97* (London: Pinter).

Bulmer, S. (2000) 'European Policy: Fresh Start or False Dawn?', in D. Coates and
P. Lawler (eds), *New Labour in Power* (Manchester: Manchester University
Press).

Bulpitt, J. (1988) 'Rational Politicians and Conservative Statecraft in the Open
Polity', in P. Byrd (ed.), *British Foreign Policy Under Thatcher* (Deddington:
Oxfordshire Philip Allan).

Burell, I. (2002) 'Blunkett Rejects "Zero Tolerance" Policy on Crime', *Independent*, 25 January.

Burney, E. (2002) 'Talking Tough, Acting Coy: What Happened to the Anti-Social Behaviour Order?', *Howard Journal of Criminal Justice*, Vol. 41, No. 5.

Burnham, P. (2001) 'New Labour and the Politics of Depoliticisation', *British Journal of Politics and International Relations*, Vol. 3, No. 2.

Butler, D. and Kavanagh, D. (2001) *The British General Election of 2001* (Basingstoke: Palgrave).

Butler, D. and Kavanagh, D. (2002) *The British General Election of 2001* (Basingstoke: Palgrave).

Butler, D. and Stokes, D. (1974) *Political Change in Britain: The Evolution of Electoral Choice* (London: Macmillan).

Cabinet Office (1997) *Guidance on the Working of the Government Information Service* (London: The Stationery Office).

Cabinet Office (2000) *Wiring It Up – Whitehall's Management of Cross-Cutting Policies and Services* (London: The Stationery Office).

Cabinet Office (2002) 'Organising to Deliver' *(www.cabinet-office.gov.uk/innovation/2000/delivery/organisingtodeliver/content.htm)*.

Cain, M. and Taylor, M. (2002) *Keeping it Clean: The Way Forward for State Funding of Political Parties* (London: IPPR).

Callaghan, J. (1983) 'Cumber and Variableness', in Royal Institute of Public Administration, *The Home Office: Perspectives on Policy and Administration* (London: Royal Institute of Public Administration).

Callaghan, J. (2000) *The Retreat of Social Democracy* (Manchester: Manchester University Press).

Callinicos, A. (2001) *Against the Third Way* (Cambridge: Polity Press).

Campbell, A. (2002) 'Time to Bury Spin', *British Journalism Review*, Vol. 13, No. 4.

Carlson, I. and Ramphal, S. (1999) 'Might Is Not Right', *Guardian*, 2 April.

Carter, B. and Joshi, S. (1984) 'The Role of Labour in the Creation of a Racist Britain', *Race and Class*, Vol. 25, No. 3.

Channel 5 TV (2002) *Control Freaks*, 28 September.

Charman, S. and Savage, S. P. (1999) 'The New Politics of Law and Order: Labour, Crime and Justice', in M. Powell (ed), *New Labour – New Welfare State?* (London: Polity Press).

Clark, F. (1970) *The Central Office of Information* (London: Allen & Unwin).

Clarke, H. D., Mishler, W. and Whiteley, P. (1990) 'Recapturing the Falklands: Models of Conservative Popularity, 1979–83', *British Journal of Political Science*, Vol. 20.

Clarke, H. D., Stewart, M. C. and Whiteley, P. (1998) 'New Models for New Labour: The Political Economy of Labour Party Support, January 1992–April 1997', *American Political Science Review*, Vol. 9.

Clarke, M. (2000) 'French and British Security: Mirror Images in a Globalised World', *International Affairs*, Vol. 76, No. 4.

Clift, B. (2001) 'Social Democracy in the 21st Century: *Still* a Class Act? The Place of Class in Jospinism and Blairism', *Journal of European Area Studies*, Vol. 8, No. 2.

Clift, B. (2002) 'Social Democracy and Globalization: The Cases of France and the UK', *Government and Opposition*, Vol. 37, No. 4.

Clift, B. (2003) *French Socialism in a Global Era: The Political Economy of the New Social Democracy in France* (London: Continuum).

234   *References*

Cm 4183 (1999) *Modernising Parliament: Reforming the House of Lords* (London: The Stationery Office).

Cm 4310 (1999) *Modernising Government* (London: The Stationery Office).

Cm 4534 (2000) *A House for the Future* (London: The Stationery Office).

Cm 4737 (2000) *The Government's Response to the First Report from the Liaison Committee on 'Shifting the Balance'* (London: The Stationery Office).

Cm 5090 (2001) *European Communities No. 1: Treaty of Nice Amending the Treaty on European Union, the Treaties Establishing the European Communities and Certain Related Acts* (London: The Stationery Office).

Cm 5291 (2001) *Completing the Reform* (London: The Stationery Office).

Cm 5511 (2002) *Your Region, Your Choice* (London: The Stationery Office).

Cm 5570 (2002) *Opportunity and Security for All: Investing in an Enterprising, Fairer Britain* (London: The Stationery Office).

CMPS (2002) 'Better Policy Making', *(www.policyhub.cmps.gov.uk/servlet/Menu?id=691)*.

Coates, D. (2001) 'Capitalist Models and Social Democracy: The Case of New Labour', *British Journal of Politics and International Studies*, Vol. 3, No. 3.

Coates, D. (2002) 'Strategic Choices in the Study of New Labour: A Response to Replies from Hay and Wickham-Jones', *British Journal of Politics and International Studies*, Vol. 4, No. 3.

Coates, D. and Hay, C. (2001) 'The Internal and External Face of New Labour's Political Economy', *Government and Opposition*, Vol. 36, No. 4.

Cohen, N. (1999) *Cruel Britannia: Reports on the Sinister and the Preposterous* (London: Verso).

COI (Central Office of Information) (1998) *Annual Report and Accounts 1997–1998* (London: The Stationery Office).

COI (Central Office of Information) (2002) *Annual Report and Accounts 2000–2001* (London: The Stationery Office).

Commission on Public–Private Partnerships (2001) *Building Better Partnerships: The Final Report of the Commission on Public–Private Partnership* (London: Institute for Public Policy Research).

Commission on Social Justice (1994) *Social Justice, Strategies for National Renewal* (London: Vintage).

Commission on the NHS (2000) *New Life for the NHS* (London: Vintage).

Cook, R. (1997a) 'Opening Statement by the Foreign Secretary, Mr Robin Cook, at a Press Conference on the FCO Mission Statement', 12 May *(www.fco.gov.uk/speeches)*.

Cook, R. (1997b) 'Human Rights into a New Century', Speech by the Foreign Secretary, 17 July *(www.fco.gov.uk/speeches)*.

Cook, R. (1997c) 'A Programme for Britain', Speech to the Overseas Club and Senate, Hamburg, 9 September *(www.fco.gov.uk/speeches)*.

Cook, R. (1997d) 'A United Nations for the Twenty-First Century', Speech to the UN General Assembly, 23 September *(www.fco.gov.uk/speeches)*.

Cook, R. (1997e) 'Britain's New Approach to the World', Speech to the Labour Party Conference, 2 October *(www.fco.gov.uk/speeches)*.

Cook, R. (1997f) 'The British Presidency: Giving Europe Back to the People', Speech to the Institute for European Affairs, Dublin, Ireland, 3 November *(www.fco.gov.uk/speeches)*.

Cook, R. (1998) 'Human Rights: Making the Difference', Speech to the Amnesty International Human Rights Festival, 16 October *(www.fco.gov.uk/speeches)*.

Cook, R. (1999) 'Pre-Helsinki Council debate', Speech to the House of Commons, London, 1 December (*www.fco.gov.uk/speeches*).

Cook, R. (2001a) Speech to the Hansard Society, 12 July.

Cook, R. (2001b) 'Making the Party's Policy Process Work', *Progress*, September/October.

Cook, R. (2001c) 'A Modern Parliament in a Modern Democracy', Annual State of the Union Lecture, Constitution Unit, UCL, 12 December.

Cook, R. (2002) Speech to the Hansard Society, 22 May.

Corry, D. and Holtham, G. (1995) *Growth with Stability: Progressive Macro-economic Policy*. (London: IPPR).

Costo-lobo, M. and Magalhaes, P. (2003) 'The Portuguese Socialists and the Third Way', in G. Bonoli and M. Powell (eds), *Social Democratic Party Policies in Europe* (London: Routledge).

Cowley, P. and Quayle, S. (2002) 'The Conservatives: Running on the Spot', in A. P. Geddes and J. Tonge (eds), *Labour's Second Landslide: The British General Election 2001* (Manchester: Manchester University Press).

Crewe, I. (2001) 'Elections and Public Opinion', in A. Seldon (ed.), *The Blair Effect: The Blair Government 1997–2001* (London: Little, Brown).

Crewe, I. and Särlvik, B. (1983) *Decade of Dealignment? The Conservative Victory of 1989 and Electoral Trends* (Cambridge University Press).

Crossman, R. (1975) *Diaries of a Cabinet Minister, Vol. 1* (London: Hamilton and Cape).

Crouch, C. (2001) 'A Third Way in Industrial Relations', in S. White (ed.), *New Labour: The Progressive Future?* (Basingstoke: Palgrave).

Cuperus, R. and Kandel, J. (eds) (1998) *European Social Democracy: Transformation in Progress* (Amsterdam/Berlin: Friedrich-Ebert-Stiftung/Wiardi Beckmann Stichting).

Cuperus, K., Duffek, K. and Kandel, J. (eds) (2001) *Multiple Third Ways. European Social Democracy Facing the Twin Revolution of Globalisation and the Knowledge Society* (Amsterdam/Berlin/Vienna: Friedrich-Ebert-Stiftung/Wiardi Beckmann Stichting/Renner-Institut).

Curtice, J. and Steed, M. (2002) 'The Results Analysed', in D. Butler and D. Kavanagh (eds), *The British General Election of 2001* (Basingstoke: Palgrave).

Dahrendorf, R. (1988) *The Modern Social Conflict* (Berkeley, California: University of California Press).

Dalton, R. J. (1996) *Citizen Politics: Public Opinion and Political Parties in Advanced Western Democracies*, 2nd edn (Chatham, NJ: Chatham House).

Davis, G. (2000) 'Policy Capacity and the Future of Governance', in G. Davis and M. Keating (eds), *The Future of Governance* (St. Leonards, New South Wales: Allen & Unwin).

Davies, L. (2000) *Through the Looking Glass* (London: Verso).

Deacon, A. (2000) 'Learning from the US? The Influence of American Ideas upon "New Labour" Thinking on Welfare Reform', *Policy and Politics*, Vol. 28, No. 1.

Deakin, S. and Reed, H. (2001) 'River Crossing or Cold Bath? Deregulation and Employment in Britain in the 1980s and 1990s', in G. Esping-Andersen and M. Regini (eds), *Why Deregulate Labour Markets?* (Oxford University Press).

Deighton, A. (2001) 'European Union Policy', in A. Seldon (ed.), *The Blair Effect* (London: Little, Brown).

Dempsey, J. and White, D. (2001) 'Not Rapid Enough', *Financial Times*, 17/18 November.

Denman, R. (1997) *Missed Chances* (London: Indigo).

Denver, D. and Hands, G. (1997) *Modern Constitutency Campaigning: Local Campaigning in the 1992 General Election* (London: Frank Cass).

Denver, D., Hands, G. and Henig, S. (1998) 'Triumph of Targeting? Campaigning in the 1997 Election', in D. Denver, J. Fisher, P. Cowley and C. Pattie (eds), *British Elections and Parties Review, Vol. 8: The 1997 General Election* (London: Frank Cass).

Department for Education and Employment (1997) *Excellence in Schools* (London: The Stationery Office).

Department for Education and Employment (2001) *Schools (Raising Standards, Promoting Diversity, Achieving Results): Building on Success* (London: The Stationery Office).

Department for Education and Skills (2001) *Achieving School Success* (London: The Stationery Office).

Department of Health (1997) *The New NHS: Modern, Dependable* (London: The Stationery Office).

Department of Health (2000) *The NHS Plan: A Plan for Investment, A Plan for Reform* (London: The Stationery Office).

Department of Health (2002a) *Delivering the NHS Plan, Next Steps on Investment, Next Steps on Reform* (London: The Stationery Office).

Department of Health (2002b) *For the Benefits of Patients: A Concordat with the Private and Voluntary Health Care Provider Sector* (London: Department of Health).

Department of Health (2002c) *The Government's Response to the House of Commons Health Committee's First Report on the Role of the Private Sector in the NHS* (London: The Stationery Office).

Department of Trade and Industry (1999) *Our Competitive Future* (London: Department of Trade and Industry).

Department of Trade and Industry (2002) *Modernising Company Law* (London: Department of Trade and Industry).

Dobson, F. (2002) 'Unhealthy Rivalry', *Guardian*, 4 June.

Dorey, P. (2002) 'Britain in the 1990s: The Absence of Policy Concertation', in S. Berger and H. Compston (eds), *Policy Concertation and Social Partnership in Western Europe* (Oxford: Berghahn).

Downes, D. and Morgan, R. (1997) 'Dumping the "Hostages to Fortune"? The Politics of Law and Order in Post-War Britain', in M. Maguire, R. Morgan and R. Reiner (eds), *The Oxford Handbook of Criminology* (2nd edn) (Oxford: Clarendon Press).

Downing Street Press Notice (2002) 'Greater Freedom Conceals Investing in Services', Downing Street Newsroom, 11 October 2002.

Downs, A. (1957) *An Economic Theory of Democracy* (New York: HarperCollins).

Driver, S. and Martell, L. (1998) *New Labour: Politics After Thatcherism* (Cambridge: Polity Press).

Driver, S. and Martell, L. (2002) *Blair's Britain* (Cambridge: Polity Press).

Dryzek, J. (1994) *Discursive Democracy* (Cambridge University Press).

Dunleavy, P. (1979) 'The Urban Basis of Political Alignment: Social Class, Domestic Property Ownership and State Intervention in Consumption Processes', *British Journal of Political Science*, Vol. 9.

Dunleavy, P. and Husbands, C. (1985) *Democracy at the Crossroads: Voting and Party Competition in the 1980s* (London: George Allen & Unwin).

Dunleavy, P., Margetts, H., Smith, T. and Weir, S. (2001) 'Constitutional Reform, New Labour in Power and Public Trust in Government', *Parliamentary Affairs*, Vol. 54, No. 3.

Dyson, K. (1999) 'Benign or Malevolent Leviathan? Social Democratic Governments in a Neo-Liberal Euro Area', *Political Quarterly*, Vol. 70, No. 2, pp. 195–209.

Easton, D. (1965) *A Systems Analysis of Political Life* (New York: John Wiley).

Electoral Commission (2001) *Election 2001: The Official Results* (London: Politico's).

Esping-Andersen, G. (1999) *The Social Foundations of Postindustrial Economies* (Oxford University Press).

European Convention (2002) *Treaty Establishing a Constitution for Europe (Conv 369/02)* (Brussels: The European Convention).

European Convention (2003) *Draft of Articles 1 to 16 of the Constitutional Treaty: Conv 528/03* (Brussels: The European Convention).

Evans, G. (1998) 'Euroscepticism and Conservative Electoral Support: How an Asset Became a Liability', *British Journal of Political Science*, Vol. 28.

Evans, G. (2001) 'The Conservatives and Europe: Waving or Drowning?', in A. Park, J. Curtice, K. Thompson, L. Jarvis and L. Bromley, (eds), *British Social Attitudes: 18th Report* (London: Sage).

Evans, G. and Norris, P. (eds) (1999) *Critical Elections: British Parties and Elections in Long-Term Perspective* (London: Sage).

Evans, G., Heath, A. and Payne, C. (1999) 'Class: Labour as a Catch-all Party?', in G. Evans and P. Norris (eds), *Critical Elections: British Parties and Voters in Long-Term Perspective* (London: Sage).

Evans, M. (2001) 'Studying the New Constitutionalism', *British Journal of Politics and International Relations*, Vol. 3, No. 3.

Evans, R. (2002) 'Twilight for the Zones', *Guardian*, 3 December.

Ewing, K. D. (2002) *Trade Unions, the Labour Party and Political Funding* (London: Catalyst).

Fairclough, N. (2000) *New Labour, New Language* (London: Routledge).

Fawcett, L. (2001) Political Communication and Devolution in Northern Ireland, a Report to the Economic and Social Research Council, award number L327253040.

Fielding, S. (2003) *The Labour Party: Continuity and Change in the Making of 'New' Labour* (Basingstoke: Palgrave Macmillan).

Fielding, S., Callaghan, J. and Ludlam, S. (2003) *Interpreting Labour: Approaches to Labour Politics and History* (Manchester: Manchester University Press).

Finlayson, A. (1999) 'Third Way Theory', *Political Quarterly*, Vol. 70, No. 3.

Fiorina, M. (1981) *Retrospective Voting in American National Elections* (New Haven, Conn.: Yale University Press).

Flinders, M. (2000a) 'The Politics of Accountability: A Case Study of Freedom of Information Legislation in the United Kingdom', *Political Quarterly*, Vol. 71, No. 4.

Flinders, M. (2000b) 'The Enduring Centrality of Individual Ministerial Responsibility Within the British Constitution' *Journal of Legislative Studies*, Vol. 6, No. 3.

Flinders, M. (2001a) *The Politics of Accountability in the British State* (London: Ashgate).

Flinders, M. (2001b) 'Mechanisms of Judicial Accountability in British Central Government', *Parliamentary Affairs*, Vol. 54, No. 1.

Flinders, M. (2002a) 'Governance in Whitehall', *Public Administration*, Vol. 80, No. 1.

Flinders, M. (2002b) 'Shifting the Balance? Parliament, the Executive and the British Constitution', *Political Studies*, Vol. 50, No. 2.

Flinders, M. and Smith M. (eds) (1999) *Quangos, Accountability and Reform: The Politics of Quasi-Government* (London: Macmillan).

Foley, M. (1999) *The Politics of the British Constitution* (Manchester: Manchester University Press).

Forman, F. (2002) *Constitutional Change in the United Kingdom* (London: Routledge).

Foster, C. D. (2001) 'The Civil Service under Stress: The Fall in Civil Service Power and Authority', *Public Administration*, Vol. 79, No. 4.

Franklin, B. (1994) *Packaging Politics: Political Communication in Britain's Media Democracy* (London: Arnold).

Franklin, B. (1998) *Tough on Soundbites, Tough on the Causes of Soundbites: New Labour and News Management* (London: Catalyst).

Franklin, B. (ed.) (1999) *Social Policy, The Media and Misrepresentation* (London: Routledge).

Franklin, B. (2003) 'A Good Day to Bury Bad News: Journalists, Sources and the Packaging of Politics', in S. Cottle (ed.), *News, Power and Public Relations* (London: Sage).

Franklin, M. N. (1985) *The Decline of Class Voting in Britain: Changes in the Basis of Electoral Choice 1964–1983* (Oxford University Press).

Freeden, M. (1999) 'The Ideology of New Labour', *Political Quarterly*, Vol. 70, No. 1.

Freeland, J. (2001) 'A Conference Not a Party', *Guardian*, 3 October.

Friis, L. and Murphy, A. (1999) 'The European Union and Central and Eastern Europe: Governance and Boundaries', *Journal of Common Studies*, Vol. 37, No. 2.

Frum, D. (2002) 'Myth IV: America Couldn't Care Less What the Rest of the World Thinks', *Daily Telegraph*, 24 October.

Gaber, I. (1998) 'A World of Dogs and Lamp-posts', *New Statesman*, 19 June.

Galbraith, J. K. (1992) *The Culture of Contentment* (London: Penguin).

Gamble, A. (1988) *Free Economy and Strong State* (London: Macmillan).

Gamble, A. (2002) 'Policy Agendas in a Multi-Level Polity', in P. Dunleavy, A. Gamble, R. Heffernan, I. Holliday and G. Peele, *Developments in British Politics, Vol. 6 (rev edn)* (Basingstoke: Palgrave).

Gamble, A. and Kelly, G. (2002) 'Britain and EMU', in K. Dyson (ed.), *European States and the Euro* (Oxford University Press).

Gamble, A. and Wright, T. (2000) 'Modernising Government?', *Political Quarterly*, Vol. 71, No. 3.

Gamble, A. and Wright, T. (1999) 'Introduction: The New Social Democracy' in A. Gamble and T. Wright, *The New Social Democracy* (Oxford: Basil Blackwell).

Gardner, C. (1986) 'How They Buy the Bulletins', *Guardian*, 17 September.

Garner, B. and Short, J. (1998) 'Hungry Media Need Fast Food: The Role of the Central Office of Information', in B. Franklin and D. Murphy (eds), *Making the Local News: Local Journalism in Context* (London: Routledge).

Garrett, G. (1994) 'Popular Capitalism: The Electoral Legacy of Thatcherism', in A. Heath, R. Jowell and J. Curtice (eds), *Labour's Last Chance? The 1992 Election and Beyond* (Aldershot: Dartmouth).

Garrett, G. (1998) *Partisan Politics in the Global Economy* (Cambridge University Press).
George, S. (1998) *An Awkward Partner*, 3rd edn (Oxford University Press).
Giddens, A. (1994) *Beyond Left and Right* (Cambridge: Polity Press).
Giddens, A. (1998) *The Third Way: The Renewal of Social Democracy* (Cambridge: Polity Press).
Giddens, A. (2000) *The Third Way and Its Critics* (Cambridge: Polity Press).
Glennerster, H. (1999) 'A Third Way?', *Social Policy Review*, Vol. 11.
Glennerster, H. (2001) 'Social Policy', in A. Seldon (ed.), *The Blair Effect: The Blair Government 1997–2001* (London: Little, Brown).
Glyn, A. (2001a) 'Aspirations, Constraints, and Outcomes', in A. Glyn (ed.), *Social Democracy in Neoliberal Times* (Oxford University Press).
Glyn, A. (ed.) (2001b) *Social Democracy in Neoliberal Times* (Oxford University Press).
Glyn, A. and Wood, S. (2001a) 'Economic Policy under New Labour: How Social Democratic is the Blair Government?', *Political Quarterly*, Vol. 72, No. 1.
Glyn, A. and Wood, S. (2001b) 'New Labour's Economic Policy', in A. Glyn (ed.), *Social Democracy in Neoliberal Times* (Oxford University Press).
Goldthorpe, J. H., Lockwood, D., Bechhofer, F. and Platt, J. (1968) *The Affluent Worker: Political Attitudes and Behaviour* (Cambridge University Press).
Goodman, A. (2001) 'Income Inequality', *New Economy*, Vol. 8, No. 2, pp. 92–7.
Gould, P. (1998) *The Unfinished Revolution: How the Modernisers Saved the Labour Party* (London: Little, Brown).
Grabbe, H. and Munchau, W. (2002) 'Europe's New Partnership', *Financial Times*, 13 February.
Graham, R. and Groom, B. (2000) 'A New Dynamic at Nice', *Financial Times*, 12 December.
Gray, J. (1998) *False Dawn* (London: Granta).
Gray, J. and Willets, D. (eds) (1997) *Is Conservatism Dead?* (London: Profile Books).
Green-Pedersen, C., van Kersbergen, K. and Hemerijck, A. (2001) 'Neo-liberalism, the "Third Way" or What? Recent Social Democratic Welfare Policies in Denmark and the Netherlands', *Journal of European Public Policy*, Vol. 8, No. 2, pp. 307–25.
Greenwood, J., Pyper, R. and Wilson, D. (2002) *New Public Administration in Britain* (London: Routledge).
Grieve Smith, J. (2001) *There Is a Better Way: A New Economic Agenda* (London: Anthem).
Hague, W. (1998) 'Thinking Creatively About the Constitution', Centre for Policy Studies, 24 February.
Hain, P. (2002a) 'The Future of Europe: Time for a New Vision', 29 January (*www.fco.gov.uk/speeches*).
Hain, P. (2002b) 'A New Constitutional Order for Europe', Speech to the European Union Convention, Brussels, 21 March (*www.fco.gov.uk/speeches*).
Hall, I. (2003) 'Labour's Taxation Policy', mimeo, University of Sheffield.
Hames, T. (1999) 'Foreign Policy', in P. S. Herrnson and D. S. Hill (eds), *The Clinton Presidency* (London: Macmillan).
Hamnett, C. (1999) *Winners and Losers: Home Ownership in Modern Britain* (London: UCL Press).
Hansard Society (2001) *Parliament: Making Government Accountable* (London: Hansard Society).

Harris, R. (1990) *Good and Faithful Servant* (London: Faber & Faber).

Haveman, R. (1997) 'Equity with Employment', *Renewal*, Vol. 5, Nos. 3 and 4.

Hay, C. (1996) *Restating Social and Political Change* (Buckingham: Open University Press).

Hay, C. (1999) *The Political Economy of New Labour: Labouring under False Pretences?* (Manchester: Manchester University Press).

Hay, C. (2002a) 'Common Trajectories, Variable Paces, Divergent Outcomes? Models of European Capitalism under Conditions of Complex Economic Interdependence', Paper presented at the Conference on the Convergence of Capitalist Economics: Competing Perspectives on the Organisation of Advanced Capitalism in the New Century, Wake Forest University, USA, 27–9 September.

Hay, C. (2002b) 'Globalisation, "EU-isation" and the Space for Social Democratic Alternatives: a Reply to Coates', *British Journal of Politics and International Studies*, Vol. 4, No. 3.

Hay, C. and Watson, M. (1999) 'Labour's Economic Policy: Studiously Courting Competence', in G. Taylor (ed.), *The Impact of New Labour* (London: Macmillan).

Hazell, R. (1999) *Constitutional Futures* (Oxford University Press).

Hazell, R. (2000) *The State and the Nations* (Exeter: Imprint).

Hazell, R. (2001a) *Unfinished Business: Implementing Labour's Constitutional Reform Agenda for the Second Term* (London: UCL Press).

Hazell, R. (2001b) 'Reforming the Constitution', *Political Quarterly*, Vol. 72, No. 1.

HC 300 (2000) *Shifting the Balance: Select Committees and the Executive*, First Report of the Liaison Committee, Session 1999–2000 (London: The Stationery Office).

HC 748 (2000) *Independence or Control?*, Second Report of the Liaison Committee, Session 1999–2000 (London: The Stationery Office).

HC 321 (2001) *Shifting the Balance: Unfinished Business*, First Report of the Liaison Committee, Session 2000–2001 (London: The Stationery Office).

HC 224 (2002) *Select Committees*, First Report of the Modernisation Committee, Session 2001–2002 (London: The Stationery Office).

HC 692 (2002) *Select Committees: Modernisation Proposals*, Second Report of the Liaison Committee, Session 2001–2002 (London: The Stationery Office).

HC 984 (2002) *Evidence from the Prime Minister*, First Special Report of the Liaison Committee, Session 2001–2002 (London: The Stationery Office).

HC 1168 (2002) *Modernisation of the House of Commons: A Reform Proposal*, Second Report of the Modernisation Committee, Session 2001–2002 (London: The Stationery Office).

HC 494 (2002) *The Second Chamber: Continuing the Reform*, Report of the Public Administration Committee Session 2001–2002 (London: The Stationery Office).

Heath, A. F., Jowell, R. M. and Curtice, J. K. (1985) *How Britain Votes* (Oxford: Pergamon Press).

Heath, A. F., Jowell, R. M. and Curtice, J. K. (eds.) (1994) *Labour's Last Chance? The 1992 Election and Beyond* (Aldershot: Dartmouth).

Heath, A. F., Jowell, R. M. and Curtice, J. K. (2001) *The Rise of New Labour: Party Policies and Voter Choices* (Oxford University Press).

Heffernan, R. (2001) *New Labour and Thatcherism: Political Change in Britain* (Basingstoke: Palgrave Macmillan).

Held, D. (1995) *Democracy and the Global Order* (Stanford, Calif.: Stanford University Press).

Held, D. and McGrew, A. (2000) 'The Great Globalization Debate: An Introduction', in D. Held and A. McGrew (eds), *The Global Transformations Reader* (Cambridge: Polity Press).

Held, D., McGrew, A., Goldblatt, D. and Perraton, J. (1999) *Global Transformations* (Cambridge: Polity Press).

Henderson, R. (1997) 'Britain and the EU: A Fresh Start', Speech to the EU IGC Working Group, 5 May (*www.fco.gov.uk/speeches*).

Heron, E. (2001) 'Etzioni's Spirit of Communitarianism: Community Values and Welfare Realities in Blair's Britain', *Social Policy Review*, Vol. 13.

Hill, C. (2001) 'Foreign Policy', in A. Seldon (ed.), *The Blair Effect* (London: Little, Brown).

Hirschman, A. O. (1970) *Exit, Voice and Loyalty: Responses to Decline in Firms, Organizations and States* (Cambridge, Mass.: Harvard University Press).

Hirschman, A. O. (1985) *Shifting Involvements: Private Interest and Public Action* (Oxford: Basil Blackwell).

Hirst, P. (1994) *Associative Democracy* (London: Polity Press).

Hirst, P. (1999) 'Globalisation and Social Democracy' in A. Gamble and A. Wright (eds), *The New Social Democracy* (Oxford: Basil Blackwell).

Hirst, P. and Thompson, G. (1996) *Globalisation in Question* (Cambridge: Polity Press).

HL 17 (2002) *House of Lords Reform*, First Report of the Joint Committee on House of Lords Reform, Session 2002–2003 (London: The Stationery Office).

HM Treasury (1998) *Modern Public Services for Britain: Investing in Reform: Comprehensive Spending Review: New Spending Plans 1999–2002* (London: The Stationery Office).

HM Treasury (2000a) *Prudent for a Purpose: Building Opportunity and Security for All: 2000 Spending Review: New Public Spending Plans 2001–2004* (London: The Stationery Office).

HM Treasury (2000b) *Prudent for a Purpose: Working for a Stronger and Fairer Britain* (London: The Stationery Office).

HM Treasury (2001a) *Investing for the Long-Term: Building Opportunity and Prosperity for All* (London: The Stationery Office).

HM Treasury (2001b) *Productivity in the UK: Enterprise and the Productivity Challenge* (London: HM Treasury).

HM Treasury (2002a) *Opportunity and Security for All: Investing in an Enterprising, Fairer Britain: New Public Spending Plan 2003–2006* (London: The Stationery Office).

HM Treasury (2002b) *The Strength to Make Long-Term Decisions: Investing in an Enterprising, Fairer Britain* (London: The Stationery Office).

HM Treasury (2002c) *Steering a Steady Course: Delivering Stability, Enterprise and Fairness in an Uncertain World* (London: The Stationery Office).

HM Treasury and Department of Work and Pensions (2001) *The Changing Welfare State: Employment and Opportunity for All* (London: The Stationery Office).

Holden, R. (2002) *The Making of New Labour's European Policy* (Basingstoke: Palgrave).

Holmes, M. (1985) *The Labour Government 1974–79: Political Aims and Economic Reality* (Basingstoke: Macmillan).

Hombach, B. (2000) *The Politics of the New Centre* (Cambridge: Polity Press).

Home Office (2000) *Probation Statistics, England and Wales 2000* (London: Home Office).

Home Office (2001) *Community Cohesion. A Report of the Independent Review Team* (London: Home Office).

Home Office (2002a) Changes to Citizenship Rules Will Right Historic Wrong (London: Home Office).

Home Office (2002b) *Control of Immigration: Statistics United Kingdom, 2001* (London: Home Office).

Home Office (2002c) *Home Office Annual Report. The Government's Expenditure Plans 2002–03 and Main Estimates 2002–03 for the Home Office* (London: Home Office).

Home Office (2002d) *Justice for All* (London: Home Office).

Hoop, R. (2003) 'Social Policy in Belgium and the Netherlands: Third Way or Not?', in G. Bonoli and M. Powell (eds), *Social Democratic Party Policies in Europe* (London: Routledge).

Howe, G. (2001) 'The Facts of Life on Europe', *Financial Times*, 29 May.

Huber, E. and Stephens, J. (2001) 'The Social Democratic Welfare State' in A. Glyn (ed.), *Social Democracy in Neoliberal Times* (Oxford University Press).

Hughes, C. and Wintour, P. (1990) *Labour Rebuilt: The New Model Party* (London: Fourth Estate).

Hutton, W. (1995) *The State We're In* (London: Cape).

Hutton, W. (1997) 'X Marks the Spot for the Start of the Euro Race', *Observer*, 7 December.

IPPR (2001) *Building Better Partnerships* (London: IPPR).

Irvine, Lord (1998) Lecture to the Constitution Unit, 8 December.

Iversen, T. (2001) 'The Choices for Scandinavian Social Democracy in Comparative Perspective' in A. Glyn (ed.), *Social Democracy in Neoliberal Times* (Oxford University Press).

Jacobs, M. (2000) *Paying for Progress: A New Politics of Tax for Public Spending* (London: Fabian Society).

James, A. and Raine, J. (1998) *The New Politics of Criminal Justice* (Harlow: Addison Wesley Longman).

Jessop, B. (2002a) 'Multi-Level Governance and Meta-Governance', in I. Bache and M. Flinders (eds), *Multi-Level Governance: Interdisciplinary Perspectives* (Oxford University Press).

Jessop, B. (2002b) *The Future of the Capitalist State* (Oxford: Polity Press).

Johnson, N. (2001) 'Taking Stock of the Constitution', *Government and Opposition*, Vol. 36, No. 3.

Johnston, R. J., Pattie, C. J. and Allsopp, J. G. (1988) *A Nation Dividing? The Electoral Map of Great Britain 1979–1987* (London: Longman).

Johnston, R. J., Pattie, C. J., Dorling, D. F. L. and Rossiter, D. J. (2001) *From Votes to Seats: The Operation of the UK Electoral System Since 1945* (Manchester: Manchester University Press).

Johnston, R. J., Pattie, C. J., Dorling, D. F. L., Rossiter, D. J., Tunstall, H. and MacAllister, I. (1998) 'New Labour Landslide – Same Old Electoral Geography', in D. Denver, J. Fisher, P. Cowley and C. Pattie (eds), *British Elections and Parties Review, Vol. 8: The 1997 General Election* (Frank Cass: London).

Johnston, R. J., Rossiter, D. J., Pattie, C. J. and Dorling, D. F. L. (2002) 'Distortion Magnified: New Labour and the British Electoral System, 1950–2001', in L. Bennie, C. Rallings, J. Tonge and P. Webb (eds), *British Elections and Parties Review, Vol. 12: The 2001 General Election* (London: Frank Cass).

Jones, B. (1977) *The Russia Complex: The British Labour Party and the Soviet Union* (Manchester: Manchester University Press).

Jones, N. (1999) *Sultans of Spin* (London: Gollancz).
Jones, N. (2001) *The Control Freaks. How New Labour Gets Its Own Way* (London: Politico's).
Jones, N. (2002a) 'Spin City' *The Politico*, Vol. 1, No. 1.
Jones, N. (2002b) *The Control Freaks: How New Labour Gets Its Own Way*, 2nd edn (London: Politico's).
Jones, P. M. (1997) *America and the British Labour Party: The Special Relationship at Work* (London: I. B. Tauris).
Jospin, L. (1999) *Modern Socialism* (London: Fabian Society).
Jospin, L. (2002a) *My Vision of Europe and Globalization* (London: Policy Nertwork/Polity Press).
Jospin, L. (2002b) *Je M'Engage: Présider Autrement* (Paris: l'Atelier de Campagne).
Judge, D. (1993) *The Parliamentary State* (London: Sage).
Kaldor, M., Smith, D. and Vines, S. (1979) *Democratic Socialism and the Cost of Defence* (London: Croom Helm).
Katz, R. S. and Mair, P. (1995) 'Changing Models of Party Organization and Party Democracy: The Emergence of the Cartel Party', *Party Politics*, Vol. 1.
Kaufman, G. (1997) *How to Be a Minister* (London: Faber & Faber).
Kavanagh, D. and Richards, D. (2001) 'Departmentalism and Joined-Up Government: Back to the Future?', *Parliamentary Affairs*, Vol. 54, No. 1.
Kavanagh, D. and Seldon, A. (2000) *The Powers Behind the Prime Minister* (London: HarperCollins).
Kavanagh, T. (2002) 'Don't Be Fooled by this Death', *British Journalism Review*, Vol. 13, No. 2.
Kelly, G. and Lissauer, R. (2000) *Ownership for All* (London: IPPR).
Kelly, G., Kelly, D. and Gamble, A. (1997) *Stakeholder Capitalism* (London: Macmillan).
Kenny, M. and Smith, M. J. (2001) 'Interpreting New Labour: Constraints, Dilemmas and Political Agency', in S. Ludlam and M. J. Smith (eds), *New Labour in Government* (Basingstoke: Palgrave).
King, A. (1993) 'The Implications of One Party Government', in A. King (ed.), *Britain at the Polls 1992* (Chatham, NJ: Chatham House).
King, A. (2001) *Does the UK Still Have a Constitution?* (London: Sweet and Maxwell).
King, A. (ed.) (2002) *Britain at the Polls, 2001* (Chatham, NJ: Chatham House).
King, D. and Wickham-Jones, M. (1999) 'Bridging the Atlantic: The Democratic (Party) Origins of Welfare to Work', in M. Powell (ed.), *New Labour, New Welfare State? The Third Way in British Social Policy* (Bristol: Policy Press).
Knowles, C. (1992) *Race, Discourse and Labourism* (London: Routledge).
Krepon, M. (2001) 'Lost in Space: The Misguided Drive Toward Anti-Satellite Weapons', *Foreign Affairs*, Vol. 80, No. 3.
Labour Party (1964) *Crime – A Challenge to Us All* (London: The Labour Party).
Labour Party (1997) *New Labour: Because Britain Deserves Better* (London: The Labour Party).
Labour Party (1999) *Verbatim Report of the 98th Conference of the Labour Party Held in the BIC, Bournemouth Sunday 26 September–1 October* (London: The Labour Party).
Labour Party (2001) *Ambitions for Britain* (London: The Labour Party).

Labour Party NEC (National Executive Committee) (1997) *Partnership in Power* (London: The Labour Party).

Lafontaine, O. (1998) 'The Future of German Social Democracy', *New Left Review*, No. 227.

Lamy, P. and Pisani-Ferry, J. (2002) 'The Europe We Want', in L. Jospin (ed.), *My Vision of Europe and Globalization* (London: Policy Network/Polity Press).

Le Grand, J. (1997) 'Knights, Knaves or Pawns? Human Behaviour and Social Policy', *Journal of Social Policy*, Vol. 26.

Leonard, M. (ed.) (2002) *Re-ordering the World: The Long Term Implications of September 11* (London: Foreign Policy Centre).

Lewis, J. (2001) 'The Decline of the Male Breadwinner Model: Implications for Work and Care', *Social Politics*, Summer.

Lewis-Beck, M. (1990) *Economics and Elections: The Major Western Democracies* (Ann Arbor, Michigan: University of Michigan Press).

Leys, C. (2001) *Market-Driven Politics: Neoliberal Democracy and the Public Interest* (London: Verso).

Liaison Committee (2002) 'Minutes of Evidence', *(www.publications. parliament...cmselect/cmliason/1065/106501.htm)*, 16 July.

Ling, T. (2002) 'Delivering Joined-up Government in the UK: Dimensions, Issues and Problems', *Public Administration*, Vol. 80, No. 4.

Lipsey, D. (1999) 'Revisionists Revise', in D. Leonard (ed.), *Crosland and New Labour* (London: Macmillan).

Little, R. and Wickham-Jones, M. (2000) *New Labour's Foreign Policy: A New Moral Crusade?* (Manchester: Manchester University Press).

Louis, W. M. R. and Bull, H. (eds) (1986) *The Special Relationship: Anglo-American Relations since 1945* (Oxford: Clarendon Press).

Ludlam, S. (2000) 'New Labour: What Counts Is What's Published', *British Journal of Politics and International Studies*, Vol. 2, No. 2.

Ludlam, S. (2001) 'New Labour and the Unions: The End of the Contentious Alliance?', in S. Ludlam and M. J. Smith, *New Labour in Government* (Basingstoke: Palgrave).

Ludlam, S. and Smith, M. J. (2001) *New Labour in Government* (Basingstoke: Palgrave).

Ludlam, S., Bodah, M. and Coates, D. (2002) 'Trajectories of Solidarity: Changing Union-Party Linkages in the UK and the USA', *British Journal of Politics and International Relations*, Vol. 4, No. 2.

Ludlam, S., Taylor, A. J. and Allender, P. (2002) 'The Impact of the Political Parties, Elections and Referendums Act (2000) on Trade Union Election Campaigning in 2001', *Representation*, Vol. 38, No. 4.

Mair, P. (2000) 'Partyless Democracy – Solving the Paradox of New Labour?', *New Left Review*, No. 2.

Mancini, P. (1999) 'New Frontiers in Political Professionalism', *Political Communication*, Vol. 16, No. 3.

Mandelson, P. (2002) *The Blair Revolution Revisited* (London: Politico's).

Mandelson, P. and Liddle, R. (1996) *The Blair Revolution: Can New Labour Deliver?* (London: Faber & Faber).

Marquand, D. (1988) *The Unprincipled Society: New Demands and Old Politics* (London: Jonathan Cape).

Marquand, D. (1998) 'The Blair Paradox', *Prospect*, May.

Marquand, D. (1999) 'Populism or Pluralism? New Labour and the Constitution', Mishcon Lecture, University College London, May.

Marsh, D. and Rhodes, R. A. W. (eds) (1992) *Implementing Thatcherite Policies: Audit of an Era* (Buckingham: Open University Press).
Marsh, D., Richards, D. and Smith, M. J. (2001) *Changing Patterns of Governance: Reinventing Whitehall* (Basingstoke: Palgrave).
McCaig, C. (2001) 'New Labour and Education, Education, Education', in S. Ludlam, and M. J. Smith (eds), *New Labour in Government* (Basingstoke: Palgrave).
MccGwire, S. (1997) 'Dance to the Music of Spin', *New Statesman*, 17 October.
McNair, B. (2000) *Journalism and Democracy: An Evaluation of the Public Sphere* (London: Routledge).
Millar, J. (2000) 'Lone Parents and the New Deal', *Policy Studies*, Vol. 21, No. 4.
Miller, W. L. and Mackie, M. (1973) 'The Electoral Cycle and the Asymmetry of Government and Opposition Popularity', *Political Studies*, Vol. 21.
Milne, S. and McGuire, K. (2001) 'Hack Watch', *Guardian*, 22 January.
Ministère de L'Economie, des Finances, et du Budget (2001) 'Projet de Loi de Finances pour 2002', *Les Notes Bleues*, Hors-série, September.
Minkin, L. (1978) *The Labour Party Conference* (Manchester: Manchester University Press).
Minkin, L. (1992) *The Contentious Alliance: The Trade Unions and the Labour Party* (Edinburgh: Edinburgh University Press).
Morris, A. (2000) 'Something Old, Something Borrowed, Something Blue, but Something New? A Comment on the Prospects for Restorative Justice under the Crime and Disorder Act 1998', *Criminal Law Review*, January 2000.
Morris, T. (1989) *Crime and Criminal Justice Since 1945* (Oxford: Basil Blackwell).
Morris, T. (2001) 'Crime and Penal Policy', in Seldon, A. (ed.), *The Blair Effect* (London: Little, Brown).
Morrison, J. (1998) 'The Case Against Constitutional Reform', *Journal of Law and Society*, Vol. 25, pp. 510–35.
Morrison, J. (2001) *Reforming Britain* (London: Reuters).
Mortimore, R. (1995) 'Politics and Public Perceptions', in Ridley, F. F. and Doig, A. (eds), *Sleaze: Politicians Private Interests and Public Reaction* (Oxford University Press).
Mountfield, Lord (1997) *Report of the Working Group on the Government Information Service* (London: The Stationery Office).
Muet, P.-A. (2000) 'Achieving Full Employment', in Policy Network, *Achieving Full Employment* (London: Policy Network).
Mulgan, G. (2001) 'Joined up Government: Past, Present and Future', paper presented at the British Academy Conference on Joined up Government, 30 October.
Mullard, M. (2001) 'New Labour, New Public Expenditure: The Case of Cake Tomorrow', *Political Quarterly*, Vol. 72, No. 3.
Muncie, J. (1999) 'Institutionalized Intolerance: Youth Justice and the 1998 Crime and Disorder Act', *Critical Social Policy*, Vol. 19, No. 2.
Muncie, J. (2002) 'A New Deal for Youth? Early Intervention and Correctionalism', in G. Hughes, E. McLaughlin and J. Muncie (eds), *Crime Prevention and Community Safety. New Directions* (London: Sage).
Newhouse, J. (2001) 'The Missile Defence Debate', *Foreign Affairs*, Vol. 80, No. 4.
Newman, J. (2001) *Modernising Governance: New Labour, Policy and Society* (London: Sage).
Nickell, S., Nunziata, L., Ochel, W. and Quintini, G. (2001) *The Beveridge Curve, Unemployment and Wages in the OECD from the 1960s to the 1990s – Preliminary Version* (London: Centre for Economic Performance, London School of Economics).

Nicoll, A. (1998) 'Arms Exports May Face Stricter Scrutiny by MPs', *Financial Times*, 2 July.

Nicoll, A. (1999) 'Seeking a Level Battlefield', *Financial Times*, 3 June.

Nissan, D. and Le Grand, J. (2000) *A Capital Idea: Start-up Grants for Young People* (London: Fabian Society).

Norris, P. (2001) 'Apathetic Landslide: The 2001 British General Election', in Norris, P. (ed.), *Britain Votes 2001* (Oxford University Press).

Norton, P. (2000) *Strengthening Parliament: The Report of the Commission to Strengthen Parliament* (London: The Conservative Party).

Oborne, P. (1999) *Alastair Campbell, New Labour and the Rise of the Media Class* (London: Aurum Press).

Oborne, P. (2002) 'A Flea in the Government's Ear', *British Journalism Review*, Vol. 13, No. 4.

Osler, D. (2002) *Labour Party PLC: New Labour as a Party of Business* (London: Mainstream).

Padgett, S. and Paterson, W. (1991) *A History of Social Democracy in Post War Europe* (London: Longman).

Panebianco, A. (1988) *Political Parties: Organization and Power* (Cambridge University Press).

Parekh, B. (2000) *The Future of Multi-Ethnic Britain* (London: Profile).

Parekh, P. (2000) 'Defining British National Identity', *Political Quarterly*, Vol. 71, No. 1.

Pattie, C. (2001) 'New Labour and the Electorate', in S. Ludlam and M. J. Smith (eds), *New Labour on Government* (Basingstoke: Palgrave).

Pattie, C. J., Dorling, D. and Johnston, R. J. (1997) 'The Electoral Politics of Recession: Local Economic Conditions, Public Perceptions and the Economic Vote in the 1992 British General Election', *Transactions, Institute of British Geographers*, Vol. 22.

Pattie, C. J., Dorling, D. F. L. and Johnston, R. J. (1995) 'A Debt-owing Democracy: The Political Impact of Housing Market Recession at the British General Election of 1992', *Urban Studies*, Vol. 32.

Peck, J. and Theodore, N. (2001) 'Exporting Workfare/Importing Welfare-to-Work: Exploring the Politics of Third Way Policy Transfer', *Political Geography*, Vol. 20, No. 3.

Peel, Q. (2002) 'A Breach in the Entente Cordiale', *Financial Times*, 30 October.

Performance and Innovation Unit (2002) 'Adding it Up', *(www.addingitup.gov.uk/epc/epc_overview1.cfm)*.

Perri 6, Leat, D., Seltzer, K. and Stoker, G. (2002) *Towards Holistic Governance: The New Reform Agenda* (Basingstoke: Palgrave).

Persson, G. (2001) *2001 Congress Opening Speech*, November (Stockholm: SAP).

PES (Party of European Socialists) (1993) *The European Employment Initiative ('Larsson Report')* (Brussels: PES).

PES (Party of European Socialists) (1999) *A European Employment Pact: For a New European Way* (Brussels: PES).

Pierson, C. (2001) *Hard Choices: Social Democracy in the Twenty-First Century* (Cambridge: Polity Press).

Pierson, C. and Castles, F. G. (2002) 'Australian Antecedents of the Third Way', *Political Studies*, Vol. 50, No. 4.

Pierson, P. (ed.) (2001) *The New Politics of the Welfare State* (Oxford University Press).

Pisani-Ferry, J. (2000a) 'Les Chemins du Plein Emploi', in Pisani-Ferry, J. (ed.), *Plein emploi*. (Paris: Conseil d'Analyse Economique/La Documentation Française), pp. 13–198.

Pisani-Ferry, J. (2000b) 'Full Employment: France', in *Achieving Full Employment* (London: Policy Network), pp. 13–34.

Pitts, J. (2001) *The New Politics of Youth Crime. Discipline or Solidarity?* (Basingstoke: Palgrave).

Plant, R. (1999) 'Crosland, Equality and New Labour', in D. Leonard (ed.), *Crosland and New Labour* (Basingstoke: Macmillan).

Powell, M. (ed.) (1999) *New Labour, New Welfare State? The 'Third Way' in British Social Policy* (Bristol: Policy Press).

Prabhakar, R. (2003) *Stakeholding and New Labour* (Basingstoke: Palgrave).

Putnam, R. (2000) *Bowling Alone: The Collapse and Revival of American Community* (New York: Simon & Schuster).

Pym, H. and Kochan, N. (1998) *Gordon Brown: The First Year in Power* (London: Bloomsbury).

Radice, G. (2003) *How to Join the Euro* (London: Foreign Policy Centre).

Rawnsley, A. (2003) 'Now for the Home Front', *The Observer*, 20 April.

Rawnsley, A. (2001) *Servants of the People* (Harmondsworth: Penguin).

Rentoul, J. (1995) *Tony Blair* (London: Little, Brown).

Richards, D. (197) *The Civil Service under Thatcher* (Brighton: Sussex Academic Press).

Richards, D. and Smith, M. J. (2001) 'New Labour, the State and the Constitution', in S. Ludlam and M. J. Smith (eds), *New Labour in Government* (Basingstoke: Palgrave).

Richards, D. and Smith, M. J. (2002) *Governance and Public Policy in the UK* (Oxford University Press).

Rosenbaum, M. (ed.) (2001) *Britain and Europe: The Choices We Face* (Oxford University Press).

Rossiter, D. J., Johnston, R. J. and Pattie, C. J. (1999) *The Boundary Commissions: Redrawing the UK's Map of Parliamentary Constituencies* (Manchester: Manchester University Press).

Routledge, P. (1998) *Gordon Brown: The Biography* (London: Simon & Schuster).

Routledge, P. (2001) 'It May Pay but Journalism It Ain't', *British Journalism Review*, Vol. 12, No. 4.

Ryner, M. (2000) 'Swedish Employment Policy after EU Membership', *Osterreichische Zeischrift für Politikwissenschaft*, Vol. 29, No. 3.

Saggar, S. (2001) 'The Race Card, Again', *Parliamentary Affairs*, Vol. 54, No. 4.

Sanders, D. (1996) 'Economic Performance, Management Competence and the Outcome of the Next General Election', *Political Studies*, Vol. 44.

Sanders, D., Ward, H. and Marsh, D. (1987) 'Government Popularity and the Falklands War: A Reassessment', *British Journal of Political Science*, Vol. 17.

Sarlvik, B. and Crewe, I. (1983) *Decade of Dealignment: The Conservative Victory of 1979 and Electoral Trends in the 1970s* (Oxford University Press).

Sassoon, D. (1996) *100 Years of Socialism* (London. I B Tauris).

Sassoon, D. (1998) 'Fin-de-Siècle Socialism: The United, Modest Left', *New Left Review*, No. 227.

Scammell, M. (1991) 'The Impact of Marketing and Public Relations on Modern British Politics', Unpublished Ph.D. thesis, University of London.

248   *References*

Scharpf, F. (1991) *Crisis and Choice in European Social Democracy* (Ithaca, NY: Cornell University Press).
Scharpf, F. and Schmidt, V. (eds) (2000) *Welfare and Work in the Open Economy: Vol. 2* (Oxford University Press).
Schwenninger, S. R. (1999) 'World Order Lost: American Foreign Policy in the Post-Cold War World', *World Policy Journal*, Vol. 16, No. 2.
Select Committee on Liaison (2002) *Minutes of Evidence, Rt. Hon. Tony Blair, Questions 1–19, Tuesday 16 July 2002* (London: The Stationery Office).
Select Committee on Public Administration (1998) *The Government Information and Communications Service: Report and Proceedings of the Select Committee together with Minutes of Evidence and Appendices, HC770* (London: The Stationery Office).
Select Committee on Public Administration (2001) *Special Advisers: Boon or Bane? Fourth Report together with the proceedings of the Committee and Appendices, HC293* (London: The Stationery Office).
Seltzer, I. (2001) 'Why Blair Has Got George W. So Wrong', *The Times*, 4 January.
Seyd, P. (2001) 'Labour Government/Party Relationships: Maturity or Marginalisation?', in A. King (ed.), *Britain at the Polls* (Chatham, NJ: Chatham House).
Seyd, P. and Whiteley, P. (2002) *New Labour's Grassroots: The Transformation of the Labour Party Membership* (Basingstoke: Palgrave/Macmillan).
Seymour-Ure, C. (1968) *The Press, Politics and the Public* (London: Methuen).
Seymour-Ure, C. (2000) 'Prime Ministers and Presidents' News Operations: What Effects on the Job?', in H. Tumber (ed.), *Media Power, Professionals and Policy* (London: Routledge).
Shaefer, S. (2000) 'Campaign to Make Young "Think Twice" before Sex', *Daily Telegraph*, 10 October.
Shaw, E. (1994) *The Labour Party Since 1979: Crisis and Transformation* (London: Routledge).
Shaw, E. (2002) 'New Labour – New Democratic Centralism?', *West European Politics*, Vol. 25, No. 3.
Shaw, E. (2003) 'What Matters Is What Works: The Third Way and the Case of the Private Finance Initiative', in W. Leggett, S. Hale and L. Martell (eds), *The Third Way and Beyond: Criticisms, Futures and Alternatives* (Manchester: Manchester University Press).
Sheldrick, B. (2002) 'New Labour and the Third Way: Democracy, Accountability and Social Democratic Politics', *Studies in Political Economy*, Vol. 67, No. 1.
Sherman, J. (2002) 'Whitehall Chief Tells Blair to Curb Advisers' Powers', *The Times*, 27 March.
Smith, D. and Lorenz, A. (2000) 'Push Comes to Shove', *Sunday Times*, 9 July.
Smith, M. J. (1995) 'Reforming the State', in S. Ludlam and M. J. Smith (eds), *Contemporary British Conservatism* (London: Macmillan).
Smith, M. J. (1999) *The Core Executive in Britain* (London: Macmillan).
Smith, M. J. (2001) 'The Complexity of New Labour' in S. Ludlam and M.J. Smith (eds), *New Labour in Government* (London: Palgrave).
Smith, S. (1990) 'The Special Relationship', *Political Studies*, Vol. 38.
Soskice, D. (1997) 'Stakeholding Yes; the German Model No', in G. Kelly, D. Kelly and A. Gamble (1997) *Stakeholder Capitalism* (London: Macmillan).
Sozialdemokratische Partei Deutschlands (2002) 'Legislative Programme 2002–2006' passed at the Berlin Party Congress, 2 June (Berlin: SPD).

Spear, J. (2000) 'Foreign and Defence Policy', in P. Dunleavy, A. Gamble, I. Holliday and G. Peele, *Developments in British Politics*, 6 (revd edn) (Basingstoke: Palgrave).

Statham, P. (2002) 'The United Kingdom', in J. ter Wal (ed.), *Racism and Cultural Diversity in the Mass Media* (Vienna: European Research Centre on Migration and Ethnic Relations).

Stephens, P. (1997) 'A Foot in the Club', *Financial Times*, 15 December.

Stephens, P. (1998) 'The Blame Game', *Financial Times*, 18 May.

Stephens, P. (2000) 'A Dangerous Lack of Direction', *Financial Times*, 21 January.

Stephens, P. (2001) 'Britain's Euro Policy Gets Fixed', *Financial Times*, 22 June.

Stephens, P. (2002) 'A Sheriff in Need of Deputies', *Financial Times*, 5 April.

Straw, J. (2002a) Speech by the Foreign Secretary at the Hague, 21 February 2002 (*www.fco.gov.uk/speeches*).

Straw, J. (2002) 'Strength in Europe Begins at Home', speech, Edinburgh, 27 August.

Streeter, G. (ed.) (2002) *There Is Such a Thing as Society* (London: Politico's).

Sutherland, K. (2000) *The Rape of the Constitution* (Exeter: Imprint).

Socialdemokratiska Arbetarepartiet (2001) *Party Program of the Social Democrats Adopted by the Party Congress in Västerås*, 6 November (Stockholm: SAP).

Socialdemokratiska Arbetarepartiet (2002) *Working Together for Security and Development: The Election Manifesto of the Swedish Social Democrats 2002–2006* (Stockholm: SAP).

Swank, D. (2002) *Global Capital, Political Institutions, and Policy Change in Developed Welfare States* (Cambridge University Press).

Symons, Baroness (1997) 'New Government, New Foreign Policy', speech to the Canadian Foreign Service, 10 October 1997, (*www.fco.gov.uk/ speeches*).

Talani, L. (2000) 'Who Wins and Who Loses in the City of London from the Establishment of European Monetary Union', in C. Crouch (ed.), *After the Euro* (Oxford University Press).

Tawney, R. H. (1961) *The Acquisitive Society* (London: Fontana).

Taylor, A. (1996) 'New Politics, New Parliament', Speech to Charter 88, 14 May.

Taylor, I. (1981) *Law and Order – Arguments for Socialism* (London: Macmillan).

Taylor, I, (1983) *Crime, Capitalism and Community* (Toronto: Butterworth).

Taylor, M. (2001) 'Too Early to Say? New Labour's First Term', *Political Quarterly*, Vol. 72, No. 1.

Thompson, N. (2002) *Left in the Wilderness: The Political Economy of British Social Democratic Socialism since 1979* (Chesham: Acumen).

Timmins, N. (1997) 'Blair Aide Calls on Whitehall to Raise its PR Game', *Financial Times*, 9 October.

Tomaney, Y. and Ward, N. (2001) *A Region in Transition* (Aldershot: Ashgate).

Tooley, J. (1998) *Education Without The State* (London: Institute of Economic Affairs).

Toynbee, P. (2003) *Hard Work: Life in Low Pay Britain* (London: Bloomsbury).

Toynbee, P. and Walker, D. (2001) *Did Things Get Better? An Audit of Labour's Successes and Failures* (Harmondsworth: Penguin).

Trades Union Congress (2002) *Modern Rights for Modern Workplaces* (London: Trades Union Congress).

Trench, A. (2001) *The State of the Nations 2001* (Exeter: Imprint).

Unison (2000) *What's the Labour Government Ever Done for Us?* (London: Unison).

Vandenbroucke, F. (1998) *Globalization, Inequality, and Social Democracy* (London: IPPR).

Vartiainen, J. (1998) 'Understanding Swedish Social Democracy: Victims of Success?', *Oxford Review of Economic Policy*, Vol. 14, No. 1.

Vernon, J. (1996) *Re-reading the Constitution* (Cambridge University Press).

Vickers, R. (2000) 'Labour's Search for a Third Way in Foreign Policy', in R. Little and M. Wickham-Jones (eds), *New Labour's Foreign Policy: A New Moral Crusade?* (Manchester: Manchester University Press).

Waldfogel, J., Danziger, S. K., Danziger, S. and Seefeldt, K. (2001) *Welfare Reform and Lone Mothers' Employment in the US*, CASE paper 47 (London: LSE).

Walker, D. (2002) 'Hold the Centre', *Guardian*, 21 November.

Walker, D. (2003) *In Praise of Centralism: A Critique of the New Localism* (London: Catalyst).

Wanless, D. (2002) *Securing Our Future Health: Taking a Long-Term View* (London: The Stationery Office).

Watt, N. (1999) 'Blair Berates Old Labour Snobs', *Guardian*, 7 July.

Watt, R. (2001) 'Blair in Row as Whitehall Adverts Soar by 157%', *Guardian*, 26 April.

Weir, S. and Wright, A. (1996) *Power to the Back Benches?* (London: Scarman Trust).

Westergaard, J. (1999) 'Where Does the Third Way Lead?', *New Political Economy*, Vol. 4, No. 3.

White, M. (2002) 'Labour "Broke the Rules" On Pre-Election Advert Spending', *Guardian*, 25 May.

White, S. (1998) 'Interpreting the Third Way: Not One Route but Many', *Renewal*, Vol. 6, No. 2.

White, S. (ed.) (2001) *New Labour: The Progressive Future?* (Basingstoke: Palgrave).

Wickham-Jones, M. (2000) 'New Labour in the Global Economy: Partisan Politics and the Social Democratic Model', *British Journal of Politics and International Studies*, Vol. 2, No. 1.

Wickham-Jones, M. (2002) 'British Labour, European Social Democracy and the Reformist Trajectory: A Reply to Coates', *British Journal of Politics and International Studies*, Vol. 4, No. 3.

Williams, H. (2001) 'Haunted by the Ghosts of Suez', *Guardian*, 18 September.

Williams, M. (1999) *Crisis and Consensus in British Politics* (London: Palgrave)

Williams, M. (2000) 'The Impact of Mountfield: A Detailed Analysis in the Department for Education and Employment', Unpublished M.A. thesis, Trinity and All Saints University College.

Wilson, R. (1999) 'The Civil Service in the New Millenium', Speech.

Wintour, P. (1998) 'New Blow for Cook in Ethics Battle', *Observer*, 11 October.

Woods, M. (2002) 'Was There a Rural Rebellion? Labour and the Countryside Vote in the 2001 General Election', in L. Bennie, C. Rallings, J. Tonge and P. Webb (eds), *British Elections and Parties Review, Vol. 12: The 2001 General Election* (London: Frank Cass).

Woolf, M. (1998) 'Brown's Blunders', *Financial Times*, 3 July.

Woolf, M. (2000) 'Much Ado about the UK's Inward Investment', *Financial Times*, 10 June.

Young, H. (1983) 'The Department of Civil Liberties', in Royal Institute of Public Administration, *The Home Office: Perspectives on Policy and Administration* (London: Royal Institute of Public Administration).

Young, H. (1997a) 'Not a Promised Land', *Guardian*, 1 May.

Young, H. (1997b) 'Euro-X Marks the Spot of Incredulity', *Guardian*, 11 December.

Young, H. (1998) *This Blessed Plot* (London: Macmillan).

Young, H. (2000) 'Blair Can no longer Afford to be Vague about the Euro', *Guardian*, 24 February.

Young, H. (2002) 'This Good Cop, Bad Cop Routine is Working – So Far', *Guardian*, 22 October.

Young, J. (2000) *Britain and European Unity*, 2nd edn (Basingstoke: Palgrave).

Young, M. (1958) *The Rise of the Meritocracy, 1987–2033* (London: Thames & Hudson).

Index

Voluntary Assisted Returns
   Programme, 190

Wakeham Commission, 130
Wakeham, Lord J., 30
Wales, 63, 73, 75, 78, 143, 221
Walker, D., 174, 176
War on terrorism, 187
Washington, 196
Welfare consensus, 157; policy, 151,
   158; state, 174, 222; systems, 157
Welfare-to-work, 6, 113, 145, 149
Welsh Assembly, 53, 63, 68, 85;
   election (1999), 12, 25; leadership
   election, 14, 63
Westergaard, J., 42
Western Europe, 199
Westminster model, 108, 114, 117,
   123–4, 126, 142–3, 218, 221
Westphalian notion, 207
*What's the Labour Government Ever
   Done for Us?*, 74
Whelan, C., 90, 96, 103

White, M., 67
White, S., 37
Whitehall, 106, 108, 111, 115–19,
   121–2, 194–5, 200, 203, 205, 208,
   210
Wickham-Jones, M., 3
Wilson, H., 32, 33
Wilson, Sir R., 97, 114, 120, 122
Windfall tax, 113
Working class, 86, 174
Working Families Tax Credit (WFTC)
   44, 153–4
Works Council Directive, 199
World War Two, 194

Yelland, D., 103
Yorkshire and Humberside, 136
Young Communist League (YCL), 5
Young, H., 178
Young, M., 7,
Young offenders, 182–3
Youth Justice and Criminal Evidence
   Act (1999), 181–2